believe
BIGGER

{ DISCOVER THE PATH
TO YOUR LIFE PURPOSE }

Marshawn Evans Daniels

HOWARD BOOKS
AN IMPRINT OF SIMON & SCHUSTER, INC.

New York   London   Toronto   Sydney   New Delhi

Howard Books
An Imprint of Simon & Schuster, Inc.
1230 Avenue of the Americas
New York, NY 10020

First Howard Books hardcover edition March 2018

HOWARD and colophon are trademarks of Simon & Schuster, Inc.

For information about special discounts for bulk purchases, please contact Simon & Schuster Special Sales at 1-866-506-1949 or business@simonandschuster.com.

The Simon & Schuster Speakers Bureau can bring authors to your live event. For more information or to book an event, contact the Simon & Schuster Speakers Bureau at 1-866-248-3049 or visit our website at www.simonspeakers.com.

Manufactured in the United States of America

Artwork provided by Constance Wilson

10 9 8 7 6 5 4 3 2 1

Library of Congress Cataloging-in-Publication Data has been applied for.

ISBN 978-1-5011-6567-2
ISBN 978-1-5011-6569-6 (ebook)

To the four chambers of my heart—
the women who taught me to believe bigger.

My grandmothers, Lendell Rogers Evans
and Pearline Young Veal.

My great aunt, Effie Jane Rogers.

My mother, my first home, Mary Veal Evans.

I pray I can birth the dreams you didn't
have a chance to live.

contents

Growth Zone

Glory Zone

PART THREE
Activate
Step into More

CONFESSIONS

I *don't know my purpose.*

Five words that most of us as women of faith are afraid, even embarrassed, to say aloud. We talk around purpose. We encourage others to enter it. But so many of us don't truly, confidently know it for ourselves.

That's okay. You're not alone. The majority of women on the planet—Believers included—don't know their purpose either. It's not popular for a Believer to confess that she loves God, and she trusts God, but she doesn't know why God sent her here, and she's not crystal clear as to what God wants her to do.

But purpose is not supposed to be an ever-seeking, never-finding, illusive, impossible-to-grasp type of thing.

God wants you to know what your purpose is.

When we look at our lives, we see chaos. When God looks at our lives, He sees a map. He sees your beginning and your end, and all of

Heaven (even right now) is constantly seeking to move you forward and closer to your divine destination.

God is a God of impeccable order, intention, and structure. Nothing that has occurred in your life is a coincidence. Everything you've encountered—even the things that seemed awful—has been part of your journey.

And while you might intrinsically know that you're on some kind of a journey, you may not know exactly where you are, where you're going, *and most importantly*, why you're ultimately here. We're going to explore that together. I'll help you see that your life makes more sense than you realize.

That your past or even present pain is not a penalty.

That there are hidden patterns embedded in your experiences containing God's direction and ultimate intention for your life.

Your purpose isn't lost. Purpose isn't even something you find. It's something you uncover. God already designed you for it and you're already being guided by it. It's what led you to this book. During our journey together, it is my prayer to help you embrace it and enter it. You are more important than you can possibly imagine and more gifted than your mind can conceive.

*To live the life God intends,
we must first put on God's lens.*

Truth is . . . you've created an outdated life and identity for yourself. It's probably focused on achieving success or comfort, or just avoiding conflict and failure. Your life, the way you know it right now, gives you a certain level of confidence, predictability, and let's be honest . . . control.

But deep within, you know there is an unlived life waiting for you. One with only your name on it. One God has destined you for all along.

You may not be able to fully see it, but you can sense it.

It calls to you.

You begin to thirst for it. A life of relevance. Substance. Confidence. Clarity. Impact. Beauty and elegance. A life soaked in divine significance.

The simple secret to awakening your purpose is to understand how purpose works. Your life, you see, is a map made up of five key life stages. God intends for you to advance through each stage in order to enter your true purpose and fulfill your life mission. However, many of us are stuck in one of the five stages and don't even know it. I didn't. Over time, I discovered not only how to advance through the stages, but what God had been calling me to all along. In this book, I am going to share what I learned about God's peculiar path of divine reinvention so you can find your God-given purpose, too.

I will help you understand your ultimate calling and show you the path (and beliefs necessary) to get there. But before you proceed further, be forewarned.

Entering your purpose will first require an exit.

To unleash the greater you, God will disrupt you and dismantle you.

He will humble you. He will use any means necessary to get your attention. He will even break you so He can rebuild you anew. To fulfill your true life mission, you will have to unlearn who you have been, and muster the courage to discover who you really are, what you possess, and how God designed you.

In the pages that follow, you'll see how purpose is often embedded in the middle of your mess. Frustration, betrayal, disappointment, health scares, sudden loss, career changes, and seasons of unexpected disruption and transition may be linked to the master mission God has you here to complete. I'm inviting you right now to look at purpose in a fresh new way.

My intention is that as you turn each page in this book, you'll gain the confidence and clarity needed to be who God has already called you to be, and do what He has already designed you to do.

PART ONE

Awaken

DISRUPTION

IS THE

INVITATION

chapter one

COUNTDOWN TO CHAOS

{ WHEN AMBITION MEETS INSECURITY }

I finally met someone who really saw me. He pursued me and wooed me. I'd never thought in a million years I'd *actually* find a man that was good-looking, successful, God-loving, and interested in me.

Most people saw me as confident, together, ambitious, and accomplished, and in many ways this was true. But as much as I hate to admit it, I was also insecure about being single. I just didn't want anyone to know it. So I pretended like being single and alone was a good thing. It was a God thing. I learned how to spin it—something most Believers and churchgoers know how to do oh-so well.

I was the good girl, fully committed to never embarrassing God or my family. I tried to do everything right. No drinking. No drugs. No wild partying. No sex. I got good grades, won lots of awards, had leadership roles and scholarships.

That does not get you asked out on a lot of dates. Sure, being a "good girl with strong values" will certainly make your dad proud. Your pastor will tout you in front of others as someone to emulate. But the truth is, I wanted a man to woo me.

People told me to stay strong. They said that the wait would be worth it. And, of course, I trusted 'em—all of them. My parents, singles ministry leaders, authors, relationship experts, couples married for a gazillion years, and God Himself. I was living in what often felt like a permanent state of *it's-not-your-time-yet-but-keep-waiting-he-is-eventually-going-to-come-and-sweep-you-off-your-feet-one-day-just-not-today* rejection.

But instead of wallowing and allowing anyone to see how much this hurt, I played dress-up. I covered my insecurity and loneliness with achievement, which, of course, was celebrated and rewarded. I'll tell you more about my spiral into success addiction later. Suffice it to say, I was good at it.

But then, I finally met someone.

He was everything I had prayed for and desperately wanted but was afraid to believe I would ever actually find. But here he was. He wasn't intimidated. He was actually attracted to my ambition, my love for God, and my quirky ways. This incredibly handsome (and successful) man who had an athletic build, a megawatt smile, and a magnetic "everything-will-be-okay" personality couldn't stop calling *me* beautiful. I'd been in pageants and onstage competitions most of my life, but I never got compliments like these from handsome men—not as a teenager, not in college, and not really as an adult.

He wore a cross around his neck and always had a Bible in his hand. He didn't mind courting me long-distance. I was in Atlanta and he was in Chicago. And I didn't mind that he was ten years older than I was, divorced with three kids, and had had a vasectomy. He was willing to get it reversed for me, he said, or we'd figure something out. Cloud nine had decided to stop by my doorstep and scoop me up. I was totally ready for the love-conquers-all journey ahead. We were in love, our chemistry was magical; we'd face life as a team, and I was in heaven.

Heaven was hearing three kiddos call me Mom, giving the baby girl nighttime baths, and taking the older boys to baseball and football practice. Heaven was searching for and finding a home for all of us to live in and call our own. Heaven was figuring out how to grocery shop for and somehow make breakfast for our soon-to-be family of five, while also miraculously finding a few seconds to brush my teeth and get myself together before 7 a.m.

I loved being a bonus mom. I loved being in love. I loved it so much that after we got engaged, I decided to give up the life I'd created (the one that so many people envied) and my dream business to be a mom and a wife. It wasn't even a hard decision. I was so sick and tired of people asking me—*for years*—if I even wanted children, or if I *ever* wanted to get married. Hearing that from other women of all ages hurt the most—especially those I admired and those who were Believers. Of course I wanted it. It was like people thought a driven, successful woman couldn't possibly *also* want to change diapers and have a wedding. They seemed to be saying there was no way God would have designed someone *like me* for both.

So when we got engaged, my heart knew right away that *this* was what I had been waiting for. I was twenty-nine, and *this* felt way more significant than all of the things I had done, and it felt far more rewarding than *any* award I'd ever received. So I began the process of closing down my über-successful and super-sexy sports agency and told my pro-athlete clients in the NFL and NBA (the ones that are virtually impossible to land to begin with) that I'd be finding them alternative representation. I released my staff. I closed down my physical office, a two-story loft-style space I had poured a crazy amount of money into decorating and building out. I ended my endorsement contracts with companies like Gatorade, Tiffany & Co., Nike, and Rolls-Royce. I also gave up producing an awards show I founded called *The Caring EDGE Awards* that honored celebrities and athletes for their charitable endeavors—an event near and dear to my heart, and one that was so close to inking a national television deal.

I started releasing, ending, and packing for a life shift from the South to the Windy City . . . all the while still planning an over-the-top wedding. I mean, that's what you do when it's worth the wait, right?! *This* wedding would symbolize God's faithfulness, goodness, and promise. Plus, my fiancé promised he would take care of me in the transition, and that I could finally take a break for a while from the grind-exhausting pace I was used to. Again, heaven. I felt blessed and like God was just smiling on me . . . maybe even rewarding me for all of those years of sacrifice and commitment. I was trying on dresses, flipping through bridal magazines, choosing colors (I went with blush pink, chocolate, and champagne by the way), taste-testing food for the reception, finishing marriage counseling with an amazing spiritual mentor, and purchasing not just his ring, but three necklaces to present to each of his children during the ceremony. I wanted them to know I was vowing to love them as my own, too. I kept pinching myself during the engagement photo shoot, wondering if this was really happening to someone like me.

❧ THAT MONDAY MORNING ☙

Six days before the wedding, I opened my eyes feeling giddy, like a girl on Christmas morning. My Prince Charming was on his way to take me into the life of my dreams. Today was the day he would be flying in from Chicago to Atlanta for "wedding week." He had an early morning flight, and I had set the alarm on my phone so that I wouldn't oversleep and miss picking him up from the airport.

We had talked the night before, confirming schedules, going over the $13,952 in final fees that needed to be taken care of within the next twenty-four hours, and ga-ga-goo-gooing over how excited we were to be getting married. Suddenly, our conversation was interrupted—not by him or me though. I'd felt this overwhelming sensation of God's presence. The spirit came in quickly, like swiftly rising rushing rapids that immediately submerged my soul. I'm not even sure I fully told my fiancé goodbye. I just knew that I needed to go. I told him I'd see him in the morning, and hung up the phone.

What happened next was an intense, supernatural encounter with God like I'd never experienced before. It was as if Heaven opened up and embraced me with warm, fiery arms. I started praising, crying, and praying in a tongue I'd never uttered. I didn't feel in control of my words, my emotions, or my body. But I also wasn't out of control. I was just present. It felt like I was at a private campfire, worshipping uninhibited and unaware of time or surroundings, surrendered to the magnitude of God's unexplainable, undeniable, and uncontainable presence. My arms were lifted, and I lost myself in the intimacy and intensity of spirit-driven communion. The word *worship* doesn't quite explain it. It was an all-consuming encounter.

Once it all subsided, my heartbeat slowed back down and I sat straight up on my burgundy sofa with my eyes still closed, taking deep, cautious breaths. I hadn't even felt the streams of tears falling down my face. I took one more breath and asked myself: *What just happened here?* I opened my eyes, blinking and allowing my vision to adjust. It was like I had just come out of a dark tunnel and into the light. I had no idea what had just happened. I still can't fully describe it, but I knew I had had a special encounter of immersion *in* God. At the time, I believed it was a sign, confirmation that I was indeed ready to walk down the aisle and that God was assuring me of His presence, removing any doubts or last-minute wedding jitters. That night, I went to sleep drained from the encounter, yet on a high. When Monday morning came around, I was ready.

I was so ready that I opened my eyes before the alarm even went off. I took a deep breath, and with a smile on my face, I thanked God for this day and the beauty of this season. Then I rolled over to my left and reached for my cell phone, which was charging on the nightstand. As expected, I had gotten my daily love note, a morning text message from my fiancé. He religiously sent a sweet text message in the morning, every morning, usually before I woke up. This one said how excited he was to see me in just a few hours and that he was at the airport about to board his flight. I replied with a simple "I love you too and I'll see you soon."

His flight wouldn't get in for another two hours, so I decided to check email from my phone before I jumped in the shower to get ready. There were two unopened emails at the top of my inbox. One was from the hotel that was housing guests for the wedding, confirming our 10:30 a.m. appointment for a final walk-through. We'd be heading straight to the hotel from the airport. I recognized the name of the sender of the other email as well. It was from my fiancé's ex-wife. We'd been in contact here and there over the months, and more recently to prepare the kids for their trip to Atlanta for the wedding. I figured she wanted to confirm some details. However, when I looked at the subject line it read: "Apology."

She really hadn't been very nice to me for the last several months—there were days when she wouldn't even acknowledge my presence, even when we were just a few feet away from each other. I figured she was finally apologizing for her dismissive attitude and negative energy. I opened the email. It was paragraphs long . . . like really long. My eyes were moving, reading each word line by line, but my mind didn't comprehend. I'll give you the general idea of the email and paraphrase it to spare you (and me) the godless details:

> I'm sorry to tell you that your fiancé is doing to you the very thing he did to me. I know because I've been sleeping with him through-out your relationship as recently as this month, and in your new house . . . the one you haven't even moved in to yet.

I don't think I was taking deep breaths. I'm not sure I was even breathing at all. This little phone with a small screen had delivered a big message. I sat up in the bed and reread the message again. It hadn't changed. Then, coincidently, I got a text message from him. He was boarding his flight.

I shook it off. *It's not true*, I told myself. After all, this woman didn't like me. She'd never liked me. She was jealous of the fact that we're getting married and was just trying to get under my skin. I mean, why wait until today? Why wait until he was boarding his flight. Why now?

I decided I just needed to call him. He was my best friend and we told each other everything. He'd be just as shocked and annoyed at these shenanigans as I was. My fiancé and I were a team. At least we would be in shock together, and move on unfazed . . . together.

I called, and my Prince Charming picked up right away after the second ring. I could hear the flight attendant in the background telling the passengers to take their seats.

I quickly shared the gist of the email: "Look, I got an email just now from your ex and she is saying that the two of you have been sleeping together." He said—and this I remember very well—"Oh my God! I knew she was going to do something like this. Sweetie. Don't believe her. I have to go now and turn off my phone. My flight is taking off now, but don't believe her. I'll see you shortly. I love you. Don't believe her. I love you."

Three times he said, *Don't believe her.*

Once the call ended, I sighed with relief. *Of course* I shouldn't believe her. She didn't like me.

But then my spirit got unusually quiet and calm. It said nothing and felt nothing. It was still. And it was anchored in this newfound place of deep serenity. It was like an ancient oak tree had planted itself in my soul. I wasn't scared. I wasn't panicking, worried, or even anxious. I didn't feel anything. I was present. I was clear-minded. And then the Holy Spirit simply said, "*Get dressed.*" So I did.

I hopped in the white luxury SUV my fiancé had bought for me. I was really, really hesitant about letting him do that. I'd never had a man offer to take care of and provide for me in that way. And, financially, I'd never *needed* it. I was a hard worker, and I was successful. I put my seatbelt on, and as I put the car in reverse to pull out of my garage, I reflected on the conversation I'd had with my father before I agreed to go to the car dealership with my fiancé ten months earlier. I'm a daddy's girl, and once my father assured me that part of blending your life with someone is learning to let them care and provide for you, I relented. It was time to relinquish my title as an independent woman. The car had always been a reminder to me to let my guard down, to trust, to receive, to surrender, to love, and to be loved.

Once I got on the highway, I decided to call her, the ex-wife, while I drove to the airport. She answered in a nonchalant tone, and I could tell right away that she'd been expecting my call. She'd been on my end of this type of conversation many times before. I didn't say much. I told her I had received her email and I wanted to understand what her purpose was. I listened, and she just talked and talked and talked about how horrible their relationship had been, about the he-said-she-said saga that had been going on since they were in junior high, and about how much she loved him but could no longer stay with him because he was a cheater. I just listened. Most of it felt like a conversation with a teenager in the middle of a high school love triangle. Only she was ten years my senior and this wasn't high school. Over the last year and a half, she'd had very little to say to me, mostly small talk, but now, six days before my wedding, she had so much to "open up" about.

It was like an out-of-body experience. As I listened, I felt like a lawyer handling a case for a client, listening to a story about someone else's life. My inner lawyer/investigator really did kick in for one moment. She claimed to have been in my bed with my fiancé in my house.

There was no way she had been inside. I was certain of that. My fiancé and I had talked about creating and safeguarding our sacred space. We had *long* conversations about boundaries and this being *our* home. I had spent months searching for a home, picking out furniture, and making sure the kids would have a place that they loved and where they felt loved. We had also decided to wait until we were married to have sex, and we had decided not to even sleep in the new bed I picked out for us until after we were married and I officially moved in as his wife. So I asked if she could describe the inside of my new home. Her voice beamed with pride: "*I most certainly can.*"

She went straight for the bathroom, describing not the guest bathroom on the main floor, but the one upstairs in my master bedroom. The master bedroom I had just finished decorating on my last trip. This woman, who had her *own* fiancé, detailed to me where the towels were, placed in an interesting, cramped little nook—an odd place you'd never look or be able to describe unless you'd been there and someone had told you where to get 'em. I had picked the location. I'd thought it would save space. And then she described a small wicker basket that I had for personal feminine care items, inside of a drawer.

I realized she had been there. Shock set in. This was her payback not to me, but to him. I was caught in the crossfire—a casualty in a war I didn't realize had been going on for more than half of my life. The oak tree expanded to fill up even more of the space in my soul. There was no apology and no remorse, only satisfaction. So, gracefully, I stopped her diatribe and I said: "Okay. Thank you for letting me know."

Now in retrospect, there were 101 things I could have said. Had the oak tree not been occupying the space held by my normal self, I would have had a few other choice words. But in the moment, peace replaced panic. I pulled into the airport parking garage. I don't remember exiting the highway or anything about the ride other than that sobering, stunning conversation. I went inside and decided to hide out and blend into the background around baggage claim. I wanted to see my fiancé before he saw me.

I fidgeted with the ring on my finger and watched him from afar. That's when I knew for sure. He was standing at the carousel waiting for his bags to arrive. The strong, charming, self-assured person that I had come to know wasn't there.

I believe we have our natural eyes, and then we have spiritual eyes that enable us to discern what others cannot see . . . but exactly what God is trying to show. With my spiritual eyes, I saw a different demeanor, a countenance of embarrassment and a cloak of shame. It was oozing from him. When I was ready to emerge from the crowd, I walked until he saw me. We had picked each other up from the airport a dozen times or more over the last year of our long-distance courtship. This time there were no smiles. There was no enthusiasm. There was no joy, and no running to meet each other with a kiss and warm embrace. There was only fear, its cousin nervousness, and, without a doubt, there was shame. He didn't have to say a thing. I knew.

❧ WHEN HEAVEN BECOMES A LIVING HELL ❧

We went and sat at a restaurant inside of the airport and talked. He said a bunch of words about how none of it was true, and I felt like I was listening to a little boy explain how he hadn't stolen cookies out of the cookie jar when he had crumbs all over his face. I just blinked. And stared.

I'm sure the fact that I was so calm completely freaked him out. Thank God we were in a public place that had lots of people from Homeland Security on the premises. And thank God Heaven had decided on this day to grow an oak tree inside of me. It took up every inch of space, making sure this encounter didn't go a different way.

He *eventually* admitted the allegations were true. He had been unfaithful. He had allowed her into the house that I gave up my life for and into the bed that I thought we were both waiting for. Much of the rest of the conversation is a blur. I do remember asking if he had *at least* used protection. When he said no, I almost lost it right there in the airport. I suddenly noticed the forks *and* knives on the table in front of me. I had held on to my virginity for thirty years. Thirty. Long. Years. I had guarded my heart. I had honored God with my body. I believed this man who had pledged adamantly before my father that he was "waiting until marriage" because he had found the one. Yeah. I was about to lose it then. That's when I realized I didn't know him.

We left the airport restaurant for the parking garage and sat in the car for probably another hour so we could talk more privately. I don't remember anything he said. All of his words sounded like the gibberish from Charlie Brown's teacher. I do remember taking my ring off. He wouldn't accept it, so I dropped it in the cup holder in the car. I *really* think he thought that since we'd made it to the car, we'd be on our way. After all, we had a morning meeting with the hotel. We were supposed to be doing a final on the cake tasting, and we were slated to review the seating chart with our wedding coordinators, all before 3 p.m. We had a full day and an even fuller week planned.

Nope. The oak tree and I were unmoved. I didn't care where *he* was going or what *he* was going to do, but *he* wasn't leaving that airport with me. No sir. I wanted him to be crystal clear about where we stood: "We are *not* getting married. You need to let your friends and family know."

There were no tears on my part . . . not at this point. I was resolute and didn't even think twice, not for single moment, about us moving forward toward matrimony. I didn't care what others would say or think. Those thoughts never entered my mind. I *was*, however, ready to leave the airport, tired of going in circles, tired of hearing *I'm sorry*, and tired of seeing his face. Arms crossed, I walked with him back into the airport. He apologized again . . . and again. I said I would contact the wedding planners and let them know the wedding was off. His brown skin had gone pale.

When he awkwardly hugged me goodbye, it was like embracing a stranger. He walked away, pulling his suitcase with one hand and balancing a large backpack over his shoulder with the other. He turned around, taking a last look, and for the first time *I finally saw him*. In a blink of a moment, God allowed me to see with clarity that he *was* ashamed. He was secretive, exposed, and embarrassed. He wasn't a bad person, but in that moment I knew shame and secrecy, unfortunately, were a part of the fabric of his life.

As my "Prince Charming" walked away, I remember asking God why I hadn't seen or discerned this essence before. Why now? Over time, I realized that I hadn't been ready until now.

We can't see what we're not ready to believe.

I wouldn't have listened. God had indeed tried to show me. Looking back, there had been signs. Nothing glaring. Nothing obvious. But I had a lack of peace. I hadn't paid attention to the reality that infidelity was a pattern and lifestyle in his family . . . for generations. I thought I was being open, forgiving, and nonjudgmental. On occasion, he would overreact to little things. Like me not eating the piece of a pork chop he cut up, and me instead picking the piece off his plate that I wanted. Or him not wanting me to "out dress" him when we were making plans for the wedding rehearsal dinner. Saying he didn't want to look like a bum standing next to a princess. Or him getting annoyed when my travel schedule was unclear. I later learned he was managing rendezvous with other women, and my lack of predictability wasn't helping. There were little skirmishes here and there over *nothing*. No major blowouts. Just moments that felt odd in my spirit and didn't make sense. I didn't want to overanalyze or read into something that wasn't there. I mean, shedding Ms. Independent meant letting him cut that pork chop and hand feed you what *he* wants you to have . . . right?

❴ IGNORING IGNORANCE ❵

In going through pre-marriage counseling, you learn so much about compromise and being selfless. I never wanted to be viewed as inflexible or incapable of "submission." I wanted to show that I could love. I could give. I could serve, be a caretaker, and homemaker.

Everyone around me seemed to see me as *"Marshawn.com"* so to speak. Even family and friends. The assumption was that *I* couldn't cook, clean, and conform to what it takes to a be real wife. At least that's how I felt. But, I never had a chance to show who I could be without actually being in a relationship.

Projections can often feel like ongoing rejection.

Even my fiancé used to say that he feared my work consuming me over our relationship. So I learned to sacrifice. That's what Christ did, right? He gave the ultimate sacrifice because he loved us that much. That's what a "loving" supportive woman is supposed to do. Right?

But, now I felt lost at being myself. I sacrificed so much of who I was to become a giver, a lover, a supporter, a *real* wife, and a mother. I changed my priorities even though my devotion and dedication were constantly questioned. *Did I really want this? Was I really ready? Could I accept the total package of the relationship . . . and all it's baggage?*

He often asked questions that I didn't understand. I was *already* sacrificing. Why wasn't that enough? What else needed to be proved?

A man will always be insecure about your commitment when he has commitment issues.

And vice versa, but those were not my issues. I had approached this relationship in a responsible, trusting, and loving manner. But, you can't recognize what you don't know to look for.

I even sacrificed my right to frustration and disappointment . . . putting my feelings and *emotional standards* on the back burner and believed it to be "loving submission." What do I mean? I allowed his ex-wife to be disrespectful toward me because I was following *his* lead. I assumed, because they had kids, that *baby-mama-drama* just came with the territory. I told him that her attitude and words were hurtful. He saw my tears. I did my very best to love their children like my own. He knew she was being mean-spirited and downright evil. Yet, he continued to treat her like a friend . . . well, really like a wife whose feelings came first. *I missed the obvious.* And, I (trying to be the bigger person . . . a loving Christian and supportive step-mother-to-be), just accepted the status quo and believed that it would somehow get better.

He just wasn't emotionally available. Believing otherwise was an illusion. He wasn't ready for a relationship at this level even though he wanted to be, which he later explained and apologized for. Looking back, he really hadn't even been divorced that long. All of this explained why he complained about very insignificant things.

There were signs.

I sacrificed my need (and my birthright) to be respected because a loving wife is supposed to sacrifice, right? *Well, whose job was it to protect me?* I guess I relinquished that to my fiancé, too. But a woman should always retain that duty. It's called intuition. We should never ignore it. It's sacred and it's how God guards us, guides us, and grooms us.

But I didn't realize I had surrendered my good sense little by little and lie by lie by turning a blind eye after blind eye. I thought I was trusting God to work everything out. But God's role is simply sounding an alarm from within . . . troubling your spirit with a recurring whisper. Others may not see it or sense it, but deep inside *you* know it. Plus, I was busy proving. The hustle 'n bustle of planning a wedding, putting "me" on hold, preparing to move my life, become a *real* wife, do laundry, and cook for a tribe consumed the space necessary to see what I couldn't see: This relationship *never* stood a chance. Not a healthy one. I was changing. I do believe he was trying, but he was still stuck . . . unprepared to walk with and love a woman living at higher frequency. *Sacrifice without sobriety is just silly.* Being drunk in love isn't sexy. When a man has been unable to face and fix his past, he brings his past into his present. We can't rewrite reality. We can only choose to wake up.

❧ HOW DID I END UP HERE? ☙

So, I left the airport, I got back in the car, and started to head home. From my car speaker phone, I called my mom and asked her to get my dad. I then asked the two of them to patch my brother in via three-way over the phone. I told them what had just happened, and they were in total shock. I still didn't cry. I calmly told them what I needed and assured them I was fine. I felt nothing. I just needed my mom to call the wedding planners and for them to help me stop the wedding train because I was getting off.

In my sports business, I often dealt with public relations nightmares and fixed "scandals" for my clients. We called it crisis management. I was in crisis-management mode, and it really felt as though I was handling a matter for a client; I was simply letting my team know what needed to be done. I don't remember how all of the meetings for that day or the next got canceled. My mom and the wedding planners figured it all out, I suppose. When I arrived home, I plopped down on my woolly, burgundy couch. The same one that had been an oasis of worship just the night before. And then my phone rang. It was a dear friend, Jamye, an amazing swimsuit designer who was making me a custom swimsuit for the honeymoon. She had called to confirm my mailing address.

That is when the floodgates opened. The oak tree turned into a weeping willow and the tears just flowed. I told her there would be no wedding. Somehow she heard me through the sniffles and panicked breathing. She said she loved me and that God would get me through this. I hung up and buried my head in the cushions. Worship had turned to wailing. Thankfully God had extended just the right amount of grace. I didn't have a meltdown while driving in the car. I wasn't at the airport being detained by Homeland Security for losing my cool; I didn't pick up any knives from the table when he admitted to sleeping with another woman. I was at home.

But, God, how did I end up here? Two of my close girlfriends from law school, Nicki and Cloteen, had been told the wedding was canceled, and they insisted on bringing me some food that evening, even though I told them I just wanted to be alone. Funny how someone else's shame drives you into seclusion, huh? I had nothing to be ashamed of, but I was. I was humiliated and heartbroken. Being I-got-your-back-no-matter-what kind of girlfriends, they showed up at my doorstep anyway. I hadn't eaten all day and they didn't know what to get me, so they got me a little bit of everything. Four huge entrées! That made me laugh and broke the ice. Their presence that night was everything. As I crawled into bed, weary from the longest day of my life, I managed to pull out my Bible and it opened up at Romans 13:11:

> *The hour has already come for you to wake up from your slumber, because our salvation is nearer now than when we first believed.*
>
> —*Romans 13:11 (NIV)*

Awaken from my slumber. Oh, I was awakened all right. I was baffled at how easy it had been to unconsciously sleepwalk through a relationship, to go through the motions without ever knowing it.

My heart was in pieces, yet it had only begun to break. Still, something inside of me was grateful that I hadn't been blindsided by this *after* I was married. In the days that followed, I realized that God interventions aren't sexy, but they are necessary. I didn't have words for an audible prayer that evening. I *did* know that God heard me anyway. Deep inside I knew God had a plan, and even in the midst of this pain, a purpose. My heart and soul were bleeding but listening. If this was an invitation, Heaven had my full attention.

{ BY ANY MEANS NECESSARY }

Now, hopefully I have your attention. Let me be up-front and say that this book isn't about infidelity or my life story. It's not about blame, forgiveness, or finding the right relationship. It's about awakening, entering, and fulfilling *your* purpose, your true calling. *If* you've ever prayed the prayer, "God, use me," God will use *any* means necessary to align you on the path of purpose. That includes pain from your past and present.

Chaos is often God's way of inviting us to step into our calling.

God uses disruption as a catalyst to get our attention and prepare us for our next season, even if the process is ugly. The mess I just shared with you, that was my call to wake up from a season of slumber I hadn't even known I was in. The mess was also a message.

Could it be that you are sleepwalking, too? Think about it. Has disruption—painful or unexpected events—intruded into your life . . .

dismantling your plans, putting a dent in your dreams, or piercing your hope and trust?

Every woman who will be used mightily by God will inevitably face betrayal and disappointment along the way. Betrayal is God's most consistent avenue for igniting and awakening his sleeping warrior princesses. Disappointment is God's tried-and-true catalyst for greater calling. Every woman will have her heart broken and her virgin hope defiled. I'm not alone. You're not alone and no woman is exempt. But . . .

+ *What if the hurt, disappointment, wounding, and betrayal are actually a shaking and an awakening?*

+ *What if all that you've been through didn't happen* to *you, but happened* for *you?*

+ *What if the drama has something to do with the very thing God sent you here to do?*

God is stubborn and steadfast when it comes to getting His daughters on *His path*, the divine path that takes us to our promised land and aligns us with destiny. I *thought* I was on it. But I was wrong. I was living a good life, but Heaven was calling me higher. To get there, I'd have to dig deeper.

My instinct was to ask *why* I ended up in this position; *why* God would allow this to happen to me. But those were the wrong questions. The better question was this: *God, where are you taking me?* I'll explain more, but remember that. *Where* is more important than *why*.

That's a question God stands ready to answer and a question we'll mull over and figure out together. Brace yourself. The answer itself is a God-guided adventure. If you've been through (or are going through) a corridor of pain, you're in good company. The pathway to purpose almost always travels through the door of pain first. You're not forgotten. You're not somehow unqualified because you've faced imperfection and made some mistakes. And you're not off God's radar.

In fact, the opposite is true. You're exactly who God wants and needs in this very moment and for such a time as this. You may not be a woman scorned like I was, wrestling to believe in your own beauty, worth, intelligence, and value. Or maybe you are. Your story and awakening might be different than mine, but I'm certain of this: *God loves us too much to leave us.*

In the pages that follow, I'm going to share sister-to-sister what I've learned about getting up after you've been knocked so far down a pit you can't even see the possibility of daylight above you. We're going to discover the steps to entering God's master purpose and plan for *your* life (no matter what you've been through), and how God mysteriously and lovingly is leading you *right now* into your true calling, a life soaked in His significance. That's what God did for me. He invited me to rise, align with, and awaken the real me—the woman He created me to be.

My heart tells me that you are anointed for more, too. If you're experiencing some kind of disruption . . . a life shaking, a soul stirring, *and* an unexplainable craving for your next level, one that glorifies God, then I'm here to tell you that your new season is waiting. God is vying for your attention.

Heaven is calling you higher and deeper, too.

chapter two

SPLIT-ROCK MOMENTS

All my fountains are in you.
—Psalm 87:7

{ DECISION UNMAKING }

Is this your correct new address? That was the question the insurance company emailed me the next morning. I was starting to despise morning emails on my phone at this point. My fiancé had added me to his life insurance policy and it was now ready to be processed and signed. Go figure. Right then I knew "wedding week" was going to be a long week. My parents came into town the next day as well. They weren't scheduled to arrive until later that week, but I suppose there is something about calling your wedding off six days prior that will inspire your parents to get in a car and travel eight hundred miles just to see if you're okay.

I didn't have time *not* to be okay. My phone rang off the hook with sweet souls checking on me. Then the caterer, the venue, the videographer and photographer all wanted to talk about how I planned to handle the unpaid balances. Plus, out of towners had already purchased their airplane tickets and paid for their hotel rooms in full and in advance. I had so many decisions to make . . . or unmake. Could our tickets for the honeymoon be refunded? What were we going to do with the thousands of dollars' worth of flowers that had already been ordered? And, what was I going to do now with my wedding dress? Actually, dresses . . . I had gotten more than one.

Unmaking decisions is way harder than making decisions!

The biggest question in my mind and on my heart was how the kids were doing. How were their young minds and tender hearts handling all of this? I was so ready to become their bonus mom. In my heart, I already was. At some point during the week, I spoke with them briefly and assured them that I'd love them for life; that would never change, and everything would be okay. Maybe I was secretly talking to myself.

Still, there was no time to dwell. The phone would ring again with yet another decision needing to be unmade. Since so many people had their airline tickets and couldn't get their money back, I made the best of the circumstances and turned the rehearsal dinner into a celebration dinner and gathering of friends. I was blown away by the outpouring of love and the number of people who said, wedding or no wedding, we will be there for you. We'll hug you. Pray with you. Cry with you. We're going to love on you.

And that's exactly what happened. Friends flew in and filled up every inch of my small townhouse. Dozens of others stayed at the host hotel once I ran out of room.

Saturday night rolled around and it was time for the rehearsal-turned-celebration dinner. I "suited up"—eyelashes on, full face of makeup, long wavy curls, and a strapless hot pink cocktail dress purchased for the occasion . . . well, sort of. I smiled. I gave away (and received) more hugs than I thought humanly possible. Somehow I mustered the strength to hop on a microphone and thank everyone for coming. Talk about amazing grace. The food was incredible. The restaurant owner, a good friend of mine, threw in lots of extra treats and bites. It was a beautiful night. I felt pretty good and certainly well loved. Maybe this wasn't going to be so difficult after all.

{ CURBSIDE CONVERSATIONS }

The next morning, the calendar alert on my mobile phone went off. It was time for me to get my hair and makeup done. Apparently, today was my wedding day. Someone had forgotten to tell my phone that I wasn't getting married. I spent the day with friends still in town. This would be their last day with me before returning to their homes. I had moments of sadness here and there, but thankfully everyone succeeded at keeping my mind busy and occupied with conversation and activity. My cousin Mary hosted a barbecue at her clubhouse, which felt like a family reunion, so it was actually a fun day.

That night, about ten of us went to dinner. The food was divine, and then it was time for dessert. Everyone got something different. I ordered turtle cheesecake with an Oreo cookie crust. Tonight was a night that called for as much chocolate as the chef could fit on one plate. As I picked up my fork to dive in, I couldn't help but notice that the dessert on the plate across from me looked like an angelic four-tiered slice of wedding cake. Then it really sunk in. This *was* my wedding day and there was no wedding. I wasn't engaged. I wasn't a bride. I wasn't at the altar, nor was I eating overpriced seared trout or cutting my rhinestone-encrusted almond-flavored wedding cake with buttercream icing at a reception dripping in crystals and covered with champagne and blush-pink flowers. There would be no need for my two wedding gowns, the silk-covered photo album handmade by my beautiful mother, or the custom-made veil. Reality didn't just sink in . . . it hit me like a ton of bricks.

I was *supposed* to be dancing right about now. My bridesmaids were *supposed* to be in gowns, not sitting with me at a crowded restaurant wearing jeans. No rice. No bubbles. No limousine. I'd been smiling all day, but I was *not* okay. I could feel the onslaught of tears welling up like raging rapids about to break loose, so I excused myself and made a beeline for the ladies' room. The tears just started flowing. I wish I could say I had a quiet meltdown, but that would not be true. I have no idea what the women in the other stalls were thinking. I knew I was going to need every single roll of toilet paper and all the paper towels I could get my hands on. Instead of dancing in a ballroom with my groom, I was shedding uncontrollable tears in the stall of a smelly bathroom. Definitely not what I'd had in mind.

I realized for the first time that I was absolutely, positively, and unequivocally not in control. I wasn't sure if I'd have what it would take to recover. I was in there less than two minutes before my maid of honor, one of my best friends from childhood, Tiffany, came a-looking for me. I didn't have to say a word before her arms were wrapped around me. I couldn't see her clearly, the tears weren't cooperating or stopping, but I could hear her voice. She reassured me that all was going to be okay. I kept hearing that.

❴ D-DAY ❵

The next day, it was time for all of my friends and family who had lovingly descended upon Atlanta to return to their homes. I pulled up in my car to the host hotel, where lots of friendly faces were already outside waiting to say their goodbyes. It looked like a mini block party! The valet was nice enough to let me park my car right in front. I stood on the curb with my back leaning against the SUV given to me by my fiancé and just observed. Everyone seemed so happy, playful, and vibrant. There was a post-church-happy-to-see-you-but-sad-to-see-you-go energy in the air.

I'd competed in pageants for years, so I was a professional smiler and mask-wearer. I looked like I was doing okay, but the real me was not smiling, she was crumbling. In that moment, time stood still and every-thing slowed down around me. Right there, right then, on one of the busiest streets in the city, I was going to have a heart-to-heart curbside chat with God. I had just one question: *God, why did this happen to me?*

Now, I know I said earlier that asking "why" is the wrong ques-tion, but at this point, I hadn't been in therapy yet! And I wasn't ask-ing from a woe-is-me standpoint. It was probably the purest, most raw moment I'd had in my life. The part of me secretly bleeding on the inside needed to hear from Heaven right at that moment. Everyone was about to leave, and the onset of stillness, loneliness, and the sobering reality of unwanted singleness was just hours away. I *needed* to know *why*. A God-what-are-you-doing, what's-going-on kind of "why?" Even when our words are off, God is perfectly able to hear our heart. A second after I silently asked *God, why did this happen to me?* Heaven swiftly and softly answered: *You're going to be able to change the lives of women like never before.* I didn't know what God meant, but I knew He meant it.

⟫ HEALING HURDLES ⟪

Once everyone left, that's when the real healing began. My inner tough girl had taken a blow. It forced her to sit down long enough for me, the *real me*, to take off my mask and realize that it was actually okay for my heart to break. Slowing down and sitting still was hard at first. As women, we're wired to work and drown ourselves in noise. I entered ten months of reflection, quiet time, and soul-searching. I read thirteen books, never missed a Sunday at church, and kept weekly appointments with a therapist. I'd never met with a therapist before, but I knew it was essential that I care for myself (also something I'd never really done before). Staying busy and taking care of others was my normal. I had no idea how I'd ended up in this mess, but I also knew there was something "God-made" for me on the other side. I didn't know what it was, but I made up my mind that I wasn't going to let myself go to waste.

When I reflected on that curbside chat with God, I was resentful and curious at the same time. Why did *I* have to go through hell just to be able to help other women? That didn't seem fair. *I don't even really get along with women*, I thought. I had a small circle of some amazing and close girlfriends, but professionally I hadn't had the best encounters working with women. In truth, I was mad, frustrated, and upset at God for *allowing* me—the good girl—to end up in this place.

As I gave myself permission to be raw, sometimes cranky, and honest with God about my frustrations, He responded with gentle care. Turns out, He can handle it. He let me get it *all* out. God never rushes us. He simply leads us. In time, I embraced that this really wasn't a punishment, it was God giving me a new vision.

Make no mistake about it. Soul-searching is hard work. No one likes it, not at first. It's ugly. It's dirty. And it's not quick. It's easier to abandon our part and just let God do all the work, but healing is an inside job that requires our participation.

> *In order for God to work through us, He must first do a new work in us.*

It requires our surrender, our attention, and our full participation. Here's the good news. I've come to learn that when we're wounded, weary, and wandering, curiosity, not clarity, is often all we need. Just like God met a curious Moses in the center of a burning bush, God will meet us in the middle of peculiar circumstances and lead us in peculiar ways, too. I gained a deeper appreciation for God's voice in this time. I filled up five journals full of revelations, ideas, and encouraging whispers from above. There were some hard days for sure, and some even harder questions. How was I going to pay my bills? That was a big one. I had closed down my sports agency for love and I was left holding the bill. I had a luxury SUV that I didn't buy and now couldn't afford. I had a mortgage and a laundry list of vendors from the wedding that still needed to be paid.

Thankfully, two things happened. First, my now ex-fiancé and I talked about how to handle the obligations. I couldn't run from this. I'd have to untie this intertwined relationship strand by strand. Most of our conversations were amicable. We didn't fight before and, even now, that hadn't changed. He wasn't mean or vindictive. I saw that he really wasn't a bad guy, he just had some really bad, deal-breaking and relationship-ending habits. He had a good heart, but it wasn't whole. It's impossible for a man to *properly* love a woman if his soul is still severely wounded.

Thankfully, he was adamant about making sure I didn't drown in debt caused by his infidelity. He also agreed to cover my car payments for the next year. Around this time I had a close girlfriend who was going through a really ugly divorce, so I knew that my situation could have been a lot worse. I was grateful—still hurt, but grateful.

Second, once I embraced the fact that I really was not okay, I realized I had to make time for myself so that I would have a chance to one day be okay. I didn't have the energy to market my business or develop a plan to make money. Depression will do that to you. I was operating on empty. I had released all of my clients, and I wasn't sure where my income was going to come from. But God's directive never changed. He told me to sit still, rest, and trust Him to provide. Bill collectors would still want checks, cash, or charge, but I took God at His word. As I surrendered, speaking engagements and television requests started to come in out of nowhere. Well-paying ones. I didn't seek them out, and the timing of *how* and *when* they appeared showed me that God would indeed provide. He was in control. He was with me and He was making space for my heart to heal and for my mind, body, and soul to rest. My bills were paid and I didn't have to worry about how I'd survive. I had some pretty dark days and now have an intimate appreciation for how difficult depression can be to overcome. You're literally fighting for your life and your inner light. There were days where I wouldn't have gotten out of bed but for a speaking engagement or a TV appearance.

My father and brother checked on me daily. My mother called me every single morning. My close girlfriends kept me lifted up. Some of the ones I thought would be there weren't, but some of the ones I never expected to care, did. God is funny like that. A major shift doesn't just clean up one area of your life—it can lead to a total life makeover. I just knew that I couldn't do this alone, which was both humbling and soul anchoring. And once I took off my mask and cape, I realized I didn't have to. Through it all, I learned a priceless lesson:

> *Your heart can break without it breaking you, and when the breaking begins, God stands ready to catch you.*

Nothing takes God by surprise. Nothing is too messy for God to use. In fact, that's what God does. God will allow your heart to break so He can build the type of heart Heaven needs. A breaking often happens just before a major breakthrough.

FROM WEB-SPINNING TO PRAYING AGENDA-LESS PRAYERS

For the first few months after the wedding, I still wrestled with whether or not to give up on the relationship completely, which is still a little embarrassing to admit. Walking away from someone or something you desire is never easy. It's easier to settle and stick with what you know. I was torn between forgiving and forgetting. Turned out that forgiving wasn't the hard part. When you're *in love*, love doesn't stop overnight. Forgetting was the hard part. I kept trying to make it make sense. I think it's what we often do as women. We try to find a silver lining and put broken pieces back together. We make do with what we have. I call it web-spinning—our tendency as women to *create* significance, make sense of nonsense, and assign our own meaning instead of allowing God to reveal it in His way and on His timeline. That innate inner fixer, living in every woman I know, is the part of us that self-assigns the task of making things better. But I soon discovered that I was totally ill-equipped to repair what only grace could glue together.

I now see that I was praying the wrong prayer! I was asking God to heal and fix the relationship, to give me *my* heart's desire, but that wasn't happening and there were no signs that it would. Eventually I shifted and dared to pray a *surrendered*, agenda-less prayer, opening myself fully to what God wanted to do (not just what I wanted God to repair). I got down on my knees, bowed my head, and quieted my spirit. The prayer was simple: *God, can this be healed? Will you restore this relationship? Do you want me to hold on?*

Once again, the answer was swift and clear! With my eyes closed and head still bowed, I saw two massive, bold black letters flash before me with an exclamation point at the end:

"NO!"

I don't usually see words when I pray, I hear them; but this time, I *saw* them. The visual of those two letters is etched in my mind forever. It wasn't the answer I wanted, but God was crystal clear. Though it was the answer that I needed, I wasn't sure I'd be strong enough to receive it and act on it. I kept working on myself, and my ex would send me updates on how his own soul-searching journey was progressing. He had asked me and my parents for forgiveness, and was trying to win me back. I remained hopeful that God would turn that "*NO!*" into a "*YES!*".

I spoke with my ex one evening and the conversation turned to the topic of trust. I had no idea how I'd ever be able to trust him again. He explained it was just something I'd have to do for us to move forward. When he said it would take faith, something in my spirit intervened and sat straight up. The oak tree was back, and we (me and my inner oak tree) both knew in the spirit that this time something was off. Even if he sincerely meant what he was saying, God was saying it wasn't true and that being able to trust would *never* happen here.

A lot of people said that it was courageous for me to call my wedding off. Most don't know I wrestled for months with whether or not to give it another shot. I believed God could use us as a future testimony. But one evening when my ex-fiancé informed me that it was taking me too long to forgive him and he was now done, I realized that God was ending what I didn't have the strength to end myself.

I stared, totally dumbfounded, at the phone, and I felt like a fool. How dare *he* tell me *I* was taking too long? After I'd cared for, and given up my whole [insert expletive!] life for, him and his children? No sir. I'm amazing. I'm generous and I don't deserve this. In that moment, I *knew* I was worth waiting for and that I certainly deserved the time and space to heal. That I knew for sure.

He spewed out apologizes: "I'm sorry I ruined your life." My flesh, the part of me that wanted to nail him to a cross and make him feel as low as humanly possible, wanted to say, *Yes you did.* My wounded heart wanted him to feel a lick of what I was feeling. Pain. Embarrassment. Full-blown anger and seething shame. But then as I was standing just ten steps away from the burgundy couch where God and I had had that supernatural encounter, the Holy Spirit quickly hijacked my flesh spiral and interrupted my response and said, *Do not receive that! That's not true.*

I had a choice. As much as I hated this conversation, I needed to put my God glasses on and *choose* my reaction. My response would either cancel or confirm his words, which were about to become a curse if I wasn't careful. In a grace-filled and God-guided moment of clarity, I calmly said, "You didn't ruin my life. You didn't give me my life and it's not yours to ruin." Peace returned back to me. I told him goodbye and got off the phone.

Remember, God loves us too much to leave us. He will use any means necessary to not only get our attention, but also free us from foolishness.

I knew, even then, that this conversation was one that I wouldn't have had the courage to initiate on my own. This call was actually a present gift-wrapped in thorns. After all, even Christ the Savior came riding in on a donkey! My rescue came via an unconventional delivery method as well. This was not rejection. This was protection, redirection, and God's way of being selective.

⟨ SPLIT-ROCK MOMENTS LACED WITH SWEET PROMISES ⟩

Once distractions are out of your life, you have space to focus on your future. Let me tell you, it's hard to move forward when you're still entertaining foolishness. Foolishness can be any kind of distraction—anything that is keeping you from the breakthrough and life God has for you. It has to go. My journaling, counseling, reading, and time with God went to deeper levels during this period. I could finally focus on me, no longer being pulled by the past and lured by a naïve illusion of a happy ending.

Not every ending is happy, but you'll never experience happiness while clinging to what God is ending.

As I immersed myself in stillness, I kept coming across scriptures about walking through deserts. That couldn't be a coincidence. I certainly felt like I was in a desert, in a season of seeking and searching. One verse in particular stood out and kept calling for my attention and exploration. I couldn't move on, so I parked myself at Isaiah 48:21 for a few days.

> *They did not thirst when he led them through the deserts;*
> *he made water flow for them from the rock;*
> *he split the rock*
> *and water gushed out.* (*NIV*)

As I meditated on that verse, I had a life-shifting epiphany, and I finally realized what I was going through. This wasn't just a breakup. So many other things in my life had imploded as well. My company closed down. I lost my staff and all of my blue-chip clients, and my money was mismanaged by my management company (another story for another time), sending all my hard work down the drain. I lost my identity. I lost my drive. And, I *also* lost my craving for striving and doing life the way I had always done it. I had lost the crutches that I was accustomed to clinging to. This wasn't a breakup, this was a God-orchestrated shake-up of my life from stem to stern; the type referenced in Hebrews but one I never really understood until now:

> *His voice that time shook the earth to its foundations; this time—he's told us this quite plainly—he'll also rock the heavens: "One last shaking, from top to bottom, stem to stern." The phrase "one last shaking" means a thorough housecleaning, getting rid of all the historical and religious junk so that the unshakable essentials stand clear and uncluttered.*
> *—Hebrews 12:26–27 (MSG)*

Now, Isaiah 48:21 made clear that I was experiencing a split-rock moment.

As I was journaling about this verse, the Holy Spirit took over my pen and I just got out of the way, writing everything Heaven was revealing. Initially, I'd felt abandoned and isolated with all of the desert references. But now I was seeing something different. God actually uses momentary suffering to create a "split-rock moment"—one that *intentionally* strips, strengthens, steers, and supplies us for greater purpose, if we will get out of God's way and let him have His way.

Let's dissect this verse together. It's refreshingly full of sweet promise—the kind that unearths resilience and invites courage. Hearing what God is affirming in you and for you is key to believing in something bigger than the obstacles and overwhelm that seem to be overpowering you.

> *They did not thirst when he led them through the deserts;*
> *he made water flow for them from the rock;*
> *he split the rock*
> *and water gushed out. (NIV)*

The first word is *They*. That means we're not alone. There are others with us and others who are and have been exactly where we are. I was drawn to the phrase *he led*. There's a promise here. If we can let God lead, we won't thirst. But the longer we try to do things our way, the longer we'll thirst with a thirst that can never be satisfied. We have to let go of being in control.

Ouch. I trusted God. I'd been walking with God for a long time. He had done amazing things in me, for me, and through me. But I liked being in control. Maybe you do, too. Actually, I'm sure you do. It's far easier to ask God to bless our chosen efforts than to let God take us into unknown places.

Now look at the phrase *he made* the water flow. In a "desert season" of life, the thirsty can never refresh themselves. Why not? We're in a desert. God allows us to enter desert seasons not to discourage us, but to detox us. He removes the *God substitutes*—all of the things and people we instinctively and habitually turn to to get filled up. Thing is . . . nothing, no matter how good, loving, or God-inspired, can ever fill the space only God can properly occupy. Substitutes are like artificial sweeteners, preservatives, and man-made toxic chemicals we were never designed to stomach. If we rely on them too much, those things pollute our heart and cripple our connection to God.

For me, that substitute was my company. I liked being busy. I liked feeling and looking important. Secretly, success and the illusion of appearing and feeling significant had taken the place of God in my life. But once the substitute goes away, God shows us it was never really there. It was always a mirage . . . a false sense of security, something we conjure up and connect to when we're feeling insecure and incomplete. Substitutes will never satisfy. *If it's not God, it's not real.*

The verse also states that God made the water flow *for them*. All of this didn't happen *to* you, but *for* you. That was hard to swallow. How could a painful season soaked in betrayal and sprinkled with traces of evil be *for* me?

But then God totally messed me up with the last part: water flowed *from the rock*. I've seen and touched a lot of rocks in my life. I even took geology in college, but I don't remember ever learning about massive reservoirs of water being *inside* rocks. Still, my pen kept a-writing. The message was becoming clear: *Water represents life. We can't survive without it. God keeps new life, streams of living water, hidden in hard places. Why? It's the last place the enemy would think to look.* How could this be?

He split the rock. This visual had me on the edge of my seat. Picture yourself wandering through a desert, fooled by mirage after mirage of oasis after oasis. Each turns out to be a deep pool of dirt. Just when you feel like your thirst is going to take your life, you come upon a huge rock or boulder. Unsure if it is real, you use your last bit of strength to climb to the top. Standing straight up, struggling to find your footing, you balance your fragile body with one hand on the rock and lift the other desperately in the air. You look to the Heavens and cry out: "God! I thought you were supposed to take care of me! I can't go any further. Can't you see me? Can't you see that I'm thirsting here . . . that I'm dying? Where are you?"

Instantly, the rock you're standing on inexplicably splits wide open. The flood doesn't engulf or overwhelm you. Instead, it sweetly washes over, invigorates, and lovingly carries you. The split makes room for a divine oasis. It's refreshing, amazing, perfect, and right on time. As you drink, you finally quench the deeper thirst you've been looking to satisfy but never knew existed. You no longer have to settle for substitutions. *This* is worth the wait. You'll never go back to drinking man-made bottled-up illusions again. No more artificial stimulants. Now the sacred center of your soul knows a truth discoverable only after trekking through a grueling desert:

If it isn't God, it isn't real.

Isaiah 48:21 is an explanation of God's *process* and a declaration of an irrevocable *promise*. Even in the midst of pain, there are life-giving, refreshing streams on the inside of us waiting to come forth. God is no longer going to give us the kind of artificial, man-made, self-assembled sources we're used to. God will unleash from *within us* a supernatural oasis—one overflowing with streams that will not only supply us, but also supply others that need us and are waiting for us. Remember, we're not alone in this desert. There are others thirsting, too.

This scripture was my burning bush. God had my attention. It seemed utterly impossible, but at the same time, it was clear to me.

God loves us too much to leave us or lose us, so instead he splits us so that true significance can flow from within us.

Sometimes God shakes up our lives and splits us open so something new can emerge. Without pain, we'd never experience the refreshing gift of healing. It is in the refreshing that we find what God wanted all along. Us. He just wants you—your heart, your affection, your trust, and your communion. *You* are the prize. Our daddy God wants to spend time with His daughters. You are who God is after.

This scripture manifested in my life right on time. I'd just discovered that my ex had gotten married . . . to someone else . . . mere months after all of this mess. But this time I didn't (completely) spiral downhill. I knew there was a bigger picture.

The end of my engagement wasn't just about the end of a romantic relationship; it was the end of an outdated relationship with myself . . . old beliefs about who I thought I was and needed to be. Perhaps rescripting is what God is doing in your life, too? Maybe it's time to split from some aspect of your life as you currently know it. Maybe you're like me: a striver, an achiever, a pleaser, a doer, a perfecter, a permission-asker, a figure-outer, a controller, and a fixer. Striving and self-leading aren't evil, but when we rely on them too much, they do block us from entering God's next level of anointing. Any stubborn attachment to a God substitute—be it your career or those you care for—will always block God's best.

We like to take refuge in the familiar, but God is calling us to see beyond our circumstances and to believe *bigger*. He intends for us to shift from our comfort zone into His glory zone. We don't have to know exactly what that looks like. Entering our ultimate anointing and true zone of significance requires curiosity, faith, and . . . oh, complete surrender. We can't split the rock on our own. Believe me, God will go to drastic lengths to get the attention of His darling daughters—and that most certainly includes you. You will no doubt experience drama and trauma that won't always make sense. The reason for heartbreak, betrayal, and loss may never be explained.

If we desire a God-led life, we must get comfortable with mystery. Instead of seeking answers, we must seek first the kingdom of

Heaven—thirsting for God's heart, not just His hands. God knows what He is doing and He doesn't owe us explanations.

He does, however, promise to lead us. When we've veered too deeply onto the wrong path, God will split us from ourselves and from whatever no longer serves the bigger life waiting to emerge. God uses disruption, a split-rock moment, as a catalyst to awaken us.

> *When God breaks what we've built, God is building something better and bigger.*

What do you sense God trying to break up in your life right now? What are you most afraid to let go of?

An ending must precede a new beginning. If we're brave enough to believe beyond what we feel and see, seasons of pain can uniquely prepare us for and propel us in an (E)ntirely (N)ew (D)irection.

I didn't have a first dance. That hurt. The whole thing hurt. Rest assured, God will always reserve a place to dance with His daughters. The floor, however, must be worthy of our footsteps. Six days before walking down the aisle, my world *seemed* to shatter, and life as I knew it came to an END. Little did I know that God had a greater mission in mind. He has one for you, too. Your new life and a greater mission, one soaked in significance, awaits you.

chapter three

STINKING, SHRINKING THINKING

For God has not given us a spirit of fear . . .
—2 Timothy 1:7

One evening, as a young preteen, I was sitting on the floor in our living room, peering through the brown metallic blinds that covered the windows. I had a great view of the neighborhood and front yard. I was bored, so I just stared out the window, waiting for something exciting to happen. I saw one of my neighbors walking briskly. I didn't know her name, but I knew she was married and had two kids—a boy and a girl. I had seen her husband cut the grass and her kids playing outside from time to time. I was curious as to why she was in such a ponytail-flinging, arm-swinging hurry. My little eleven-year-old-or-so self leaned in closer, widening the blinds so that I could get a better look. After all, I could see her; she couldn't see me. At least that's what I thought.

I started to question that theory when my neighbor abruptly stopped smack in front of our house, turned her body, and stared right in my direction. Still holding on to the last morsel of my "blind" faith,

I held my ground and stared back. Then she crossed the street, came up our walkway, and rang the doorbell.

It was getting a bit dark at this point, and I heard my dad shout from the back of the house that he would be getting the door. Now, I knew that staring was not polite, so I wondered if I was about to get in trouble. Still, curiosity lured me off the living room floor and to the front door. I tucked my little head under my dad's arm as he held the door open. It turned out that the neighbor had an emergency and needed a babysitter. She asked if I was available and willing to watch her kids for a few hours.

I looked up at my dad and he said it was up to me. I'd never been hired for something before, and I'd never watched any kids beside my little brother, Corey, who was just a year younger than me, but I was up for the challenge. I threw on some shoes, grabbed a jacket, and reported for duty!

As we scurried to her house, she gave me the run-down on the kids' names, their evening schedule, and what I needed to do to make sure her house didn't burn down and her kids didn't end up in the ER under my care. Then she was gone! When she got back a couple of hours later, the kids were in bed, the house was quiet, and I'd tried to minimize the aftermath of playtime by putting their toys away.

She thanked me for filling in on such short notice, explained that she hadn't been able to stop by the bank before returning home, and pulled out two bills—a $1 bill and a $5 bill.

With one in each hand, she put the bills in front of me and said, "Which do you want?"

Hmph. I wasn't expecting that question. I hadn't thought about what my compensation might be. Here I was again staring. I didn't know what to do. What I really wanted to say was, "I'll take both, please."

But I was too polite for that. I looked at the $5 bill. And, then back at the $1 bill. It was like a tug-of-war in my heart, each pulling at me.

Seeing that I was stuck, my neighbor tilted her head, looked at me over her glasses, and said, "It's your choice. It doesn't matter to me. Which one do you want?"

Right away I felt guilty and greedy for looking at the $5 bill. In retrospect, I know I had earned the $5 bill. I spent two hours watching two exhaustingly rambunctious kids (clearly blessed with energy and quick wit) on short notice and even cleaned up afterward. Let's not even mention the incredible feat of putting two kids (who don't know you) to bed for the first time. Heavens!

Yet still, I didn't feel it was right or polite to reach for more. So I settled for less.

"I'll take the dollar."

"Are you sure?" she said.

I paused and then said, "Yes. I'm sure."

"Okay. Here you go."

I went home proud that I had done something new. I was pretty darn proud of that $1 bill, too. Not because of the amount, but because of what it represented: *I had earned something on my own.* That was a beautiful lesson I learned early about responsibility and reliability. However, there were a few bitter thorns in that lesson, too.

lesson #1:
If you allow yourself to settle for less,
no one is obligated to stop you.

I wanted *my neighbor* to tell me that I had earned the $5. I wanted *her* to tell me that it was okay to want more, and for *her* to make it easy for me to choose more by removing less (the $1 bill) as an option. I wanted *her* to tell me I was good enough . . . that I was worthy of making more and receiving more. I wanted her to make the bigger, braver, bolder decision *for me.* But she didn't. Little did I know, she couldn't.

Truth is, *you* are the one responsible for believing in you and for embracing the fact that more is available to you. It's wonderful when someone is there to make life easier and to push you to believe bigger, but it doesn't often go down like that.

Lesson #2:
No matter how much you try to hide,
bigger will do what it takes to find you.

By "bigger," I mean the more that God has in store for you in any given moment. I was certain no one could see me behind those blinds. I thought I was safe. And really I thought my presence was insignificant. Who'd care that I was there anyway? I mean, at age eleven, people see you but they don't really *see* you. They talk *at* you. They teach you; they tell you what to do and what not to do.

But I was mistaken. When I least expected it, someone *did* see me. I didn't even realize I was hiding. I had gotten good at staying out of the way. I was never shy, but people made me nervous. What would they think? What would they say? Would I be the last to be picked or the first to be dismissed? Would I be enough? Or worse, maybe I would be too much. Rather than someone seeing me as weak and insecure, instead of me giving others the opportunity to reject me, I mastered the art of protecting myself from rejection, aka hiding. I know I'm not the only one.

Today, I realize that hiding is something we as women do very, very well. We hide from our higher purpose, thinking no one really sees us. We'll talk more in depth later about our shared habit of hiding. But, for now, think about how we hide behind our titles as moms, wives, ladder-climbers, givers, servers, and success-makers. We hide behind our career and under our stuff. We hide behind our mascara, perfect-picture-painting photos, our never-let-em-see-you-sweat mantras, our manicured toes, and our shoes. Yes, we certainly hide behind shoes. We even hide out in churches 'n pews. Just when you *think* no one is looking, even when it seems like your presence is insignificant, God sees things completely different.

You can hide from people, the uncomfortable, and from things you fear. But the good news is we can never tuck ourselves so far away that God can't find us. God can, and often will, send someone you don't even know to invite you to meet a bigger version of you.

Lesson #3:
You'll never boldly pursue what you don't feel you deserve. What you expect determines what you accept.

Why did I feel that reaching for the $1 bill was the right thing to do? I *accepted* less because I *expected* less. Expectations are what we *really* believe to be true about ourselves and what we're worthy of receiving.

I felt guilty and greedy when I looked at the $5 bill. Perhaps you can relate? How many times have you really wanted to go for something outside your comfort zone—like a promotion, an opportunity, or a chance to have your voice heard, but felt it was inappropriate? By inappropriate, I mean unladylike or unbecoming of a woman . . . especially a Godly woman. You want to speak up, you want to make the bolder decision, but instead you shrink, you silence yourself, you clam up, you keep letting someone else go before you, you stop . . . you settle. You don't want to be an inconvenience. You don't want to take up too much space.

To be honest, I felt unworthy. It wasn't that I thought I'd done a bad job. I just thought I *was* bad. Like, in general. I was a burden. I was a problem. I made too many mistakes, and said and did the wrong thing. I didn't want that, so I learned to make decisions that wouldn't make me look greedy, inappropriate, overbearing, unlikable, or needy. I still wrestle with this!

Later, I'll share more about my early childhood experiences growing up as a black girl in a predominantly white neighborhood and how that created some serious esteem and identity battles. It made me wonder where I belonged and where and who I deserved to be.

I didn't realize that I'd built my life on a shaky foundation, paved with unstable bricks held together by approval, disappointment, faulty thinking, shame, and wounded self-esteem. You see, expectations represent our core *self*-beliefs. Again, expectations are not just what we want, they are what we *really* believe to be true about *ourselves* . . . who we are and what we deserve. They shape our life experiences—what we choose, who we choose, and what we receive, do, and become.

lesson #4:
Bigger decisions birth a bigger life.

As young girls, we slowly but steadily internalize some faulty thinking and become wired to reach for what we think is *appropriate* (the right thing to do) or *attainable* (the best we can do).

When we are fed protocol instead of purpose, we settle for less. We reach for $1 bills instead of fives. It happens to all of us, and it becomes easy to miss the everyday, inconspicuous invitations to experience more. I can look back at how I was still making $1 decisions when I met and attracted my now ex-fiancé into my life. On the surface, he was amazing. He was a great father and talented in a number of ways. However, God had told me multiple times that this wasn't it. This wasn't the one. It was a gentle inner nudging—not a loud command. But I didn't pay attention. I assumed my doubts were just jitters. Everyone (and I mean everyone) loved him. I had no clue that he was sleeping with other women while I was keeping my cookies in the cookie jar.

But wounded esteem was certainly in play. Wounds misalign our wisdom. What we think is wisdom is really regret in the driver's seat. I had a great career and was successful. But one thing that eluded me was love. And the side comments about me being a "career" woman came laced with innuendo that I would never be a desirable wife or mom.

Well, as you know, my ex had three kids and a seemingly ready-made life that I could just walk into. Secretly, I wanted to prove I could make something in my *personal* life work. I wanted to be a wife and mom more than I wanted to be a public success story. A prover like me is always up for a challenge, and that was the problem. Because I have an underlying addiction to solving, achieving, and proving, I can end up reaching for unassigned obstacles as opposed to the ordained, and often veer in the direction opposite of my calling. Wounds are that powerful. As such, *the pressure to prove others wrong puts us on the wrong path.*

Each of us has a sneaky, subconscious inner setting that defaults us to playing it safe and settling for *something*. However, that $5 bill represents the bigger that is in store for each of us. It's a choice. God is always inviting us to see and seize the bigger, higher, and bolder.

> *Bigger is about going where God directs and aligning with what is most blessed.*

If we could only believe at our core that God has amazing things planned for us. *We can't wait to see it before we believe it, we must believe it to see it.* If we want to experience a bigger life, we must be intentional in mustering the faith necessary to make the *bigger* (often peculiar) decisions, whatever they look like . . . especially when they make us uncomfortable.

❧ THE ROAD TO BIGGER ❧

Disruption, if misunderstood, can put a dent in our confidence. I've come to learn that it's really divine timing at work. One of the primary purposes of disruption is to show us what is already within us. Obstacles are meant to reveal your anointing—your divine strength, not your weakness. God uses split-rock moments to unveil and realign us with His greater vision for us. Disruption delivers a message God needs us to pay attention to right now—one we'd otherwise ignore. The mess is meant to mature our outlook and upgrade our thinking and beliefs. That may sound easy and overly simplistic—or it may sound terrifying. What it requires, nonetheless, is that you give yourself permission.

+ *What if* you gave yourself permission to reach higher and have more and more $5 moments?

+ *What if* you stood tall versus shrank when insecurity, opinion, and anxiety visit you?

+ *What if* you really believed in your potential and power and not just your imperfections?

Now let that marinate for a moment. I've been taught and told by the saints, scholars, and powers that be that believing in yourself is taboo. We're supposed to believe in God.

Sure. But God made us who we are, and I believe He did so on purpose. The trouble is, most of us don't know how to believe in *ourselves*—especially in a world where believing unapologetically in yourself is considered unladylike or unholy. I believe this faulty teaching has created more depression among believers than anything out there "in the world."

This thinking stems from the pressure of cultural norms, false humility, and religious thinking, not from above. In Romans 12:3, the Bible says not to think more highly of yourself than you should, but it doesn't say not to think highly of yourself. In fact, it emphasizes that God has "apportioned to each a degree of faith [and a purpose designed for service]" (AMP). I believe the reason God wants us to have a strong, all-things-are-possible self-image, to believe bigger, is for the very purpose of us being *able* to fulfill *our* purpose.

And, I believe Heaven connected us so I could affirm for you two sweet, but necessary truths:

1. You matter.

2. You can do anything you think you can. Nothing is impossible when we believe.

Our trust in God is not somehow separate from our belief in ourselves. To the contrary, divine trust and self-belief are linked together by the umbilical cord of purpose. We cannot fulfill our destiny with just one or the other. We need both. We need a healthy and hearty self-image to even have the audacity to pursue all God has in store for us. Notice I didn't say we need a strong self-image to believe in God. I meet women every day who love God, but they don't really *like* themselves. Truth be told, most of us as women spend an inordinate amount of our time trying to fix our faults or find a way to simply "live with" ourselves. We believe more in our imperfections than our incredibleness. Well. I've discovered this:

If you don't learn to celebrate yourself, you'll settle for a life where you simply tolerate yourself.

Purposeful living is a celebration of your anointing . . . the good stuff God gave you! The road to bigger begins with bigger belief. It requires a greater sense of trust in God, a *certainty* that God is for you and not against, and that God is indeed *with* you. You're never alone. Bigger belief also requires a greater appreciation for yourself—who you are and how God purposefully built you. It is impossible to fulfill your purpose if you can't embrace the purposefulness of all that makes you you—the warts, the wonderful, and everything in between.

When we confidently anticipate more of God and from God (because we truly trust that God is indeed *for* us, and not out to get us or whip a lesson into us), we anticipate goodness. When we learn to believe bigger in *ourselves*, we give ourselves permission to accept that goodness. This is the essence of what it means to believe bigger: *to expect to experience more.*

Here is an example of what bigger belief looks like. During a vacation, I decided to try a new experience: I took a helicopter ride from the airport on the island of St. Lucia in the Caribbean to a landing pad close to the hotel where I was staying. Now, the most nerve-wracking part of the flight was certainly the liftoff. Being in a helicopter is nothing like being on an airplane. In a helicopter you feel every wind gust. It's a tighter, smaller space, and it's noisy. So noisy that you must wear headphones to protect your ears, and to hear from and communicate with the pilot. But the view is incredible. On the ground, the terrain of trees would simply seem like a relentless jungle, dangerous and difficult to navigate. But, from the air, you can see what's impossible to comprehend from the ground. Crystal-blue waters, glorious hillsides, and breathtaking shores. You have a fuller, more fantastic grasp of the bigger picture. You can see God's canvas when you step away from what you'd normally only see up close. Believing bigger is the equivalent of disciplining yourself to get on the chopper! Even if it's uncomfortable. Even if it stretches you. Even if you're afraid of heights . . . which, in some way, we all are.

Isaiah 55:8–9 speaks to this idea of elevating our thinking and, with it, our believing.

> *"My thoughts are nothing like your thoughts," says the Lord.*
> *"And my ways are far beyond anything you could imagine.*
> *For just as the heavens are higher than the earth,*
> *so my ways are higher than your ways*
> *and my thoughts higher than your thoughts." (NLT)*

This passage really illustrates how essential it is for us to gain what I call a *God's-eye view.* And it explains what God is after when disruption bulldozes its way into our plans . . . it's about learning *how* to think higher, see higher, and live at a higher frequency. He is inviting us into *His* mind and *His* view of our present, our past, and our future.

God seeks to elevate us into a state of unshakable confidence in who we are and boldness in seeing His plans. When we look at our circumstances and ourselves, we might see a mess, but God sees a masterpiece. Our gender is not a curse. It's part of our calling. Our insecurities do not define us. They are what actually reveals and attracts destiny to us. We're created in God's image. To reject ourselves is to reject God *and* the one-of-a-kind reflection that only we can showcase of Him.

When we believe bigger, we decide bigger. And decisions literally create our future. Disruption, then, gives us a sacred opportunity to strengthen our relationship with God as we're stretched to believe bigger, decide bigger, and live bolder. The Bible says in Ephesians 2:10 (one of my favorites!) that "we are God's workmanship, created in Christ Jesus to do good works, which God prepared *in advance* for us to do."

God has already given us permission. He actually precommissioned us, *in advance*, to live fearlessly and unapologetically. It's time we give ourselves permission, too. I truly believe this is the message Heaven wants our hearts to hear. Otherwise, we'll continue to decide ourselves *out* of the very life and miracles we've been praying for, and we'll miss the path of significance we were handmade for.

Insecurity will always make room for and attract insecure people.

I'm responsible for the beliefs, fantasies, insecurities, and decisions that attracted my ex into my life. His presence was the fruit of years of faulty thinking.

My babysitting reflection is ultimately about permission—about taking elevated responsibility for the present circumstances your beliefs have built. Believing bigger is a matter of giving yourself greater permission—permission to receive and act upon the gift of exponential belief from a limitless God. Remember, *disruption comes to detach us from the part of ourselves that is incapable of entering a bigger future.*

Think about this for a moment before you move on to the next section. *In what ways have your thoughts, insecurities, and limiting beliefs about yourself been* blocking *your next blessing?* We'll keep unpacking this together. But sit with this question for a moment. One of the most courageous things a woman can do is choose to call out, and then work on, her own flawed thinking.

{ NEW THINKING, NEW BEING }

You might be wondering *how* to create a new way of thinking and believing. That was certainly the most challenging, daunting part for me. Change is rarely easy and the mind is one stubborn thingamajigger! For me, the first key was committing to growth. I knew it was going to be a process. I knew I couldn't force my heart to heal. Healing is and always will be God's territory. The good news is healing is also His expertise—physical, mental, emotional, financial, and spiritual healing as well. So instead of focusing on growing my external accomplishments, I committed to focusing on self-care.

The second key was learning to be honest with God about my self-doubts *and* my doubts in God. I was mad at God. Mad at God for letting me end up in this situation. Mad at Him for not making the warning signs more glaring earlier. Mad at how he allowed me, his daughter, to be humiliated. He was supposed to protect me. But, mostly, I was mad at myself for not seeing the signs earlier. By allowing myself to recognize the rawness, I was able to move toward *reinvention.* Just as a doctor can't operate on an unidentified condition, we can't engage the healing process unless we identify what's broken.

And, finally, I put my pride aside. I had to ask for help. I needed to connect with others who had that God's-eye view. That. Was. So.

Hard. *I don't like transparency.* I don't like looking weak. And I don't really like asking for help. It always feels like an invitation for rejection and disappointment. But isolation can turn into a dungeon. We can't let disruption and disappointment disconnect us from those that can actually elevate us.

❧ THE PROMISED LAND ❧

God uses disruption to free us from our comfort zone and to get us where we're needed so we can do what we've been predesigned to do.

+ If you've been praying for God to intervene in your life or for God to use you at a higher level . . .

+ If you've been praying for God to show you your purpose, to have His way in your life, or to give you more clarity and courage to live your life on His terms . . .

Then what you are *really* asking is (1) for God to disrupt and recalibrate your faith and make you *capable* of believing bigger—embracing God's higher view of you. And (2) you're asking to enter the BIG—a faith place and purpose space (B)uilt (I)n (G)od. Bigger is *our* promised land, a place that aligns us with our divine assignment and activates the BIG abilities, blessings, and powers within us. It's our place of impact, our sweet spot, our zone. When I say bigger is calling you, it's the land of God's promises and provision I'm referring to.

Now, I didn't realize this while I was in the midst of rebuilding my life, confidence, and heart. But before we dive more into the process God took me through to uncover my true purpose (it's the process he's already taking you through now), I wanted to explain this *belief* thing. It's everything. So let's delve a bit deeper into it now.

{ THE BATTLE BEGINS }

The thief comes only to steal and kill and destroy.
—John 10:10 (part one) (NRSV)

So we know God has a bigger place for us. At least, I pray that's something you're beginning to believe. That bigger place is linked to who God made you—your uniqueness, your light, your God-authorized brilliance, beauty, and bravery. It's your inner incredibleness. God only births the incredible. *Incredible is* who *God is and it is* how *you were made.* Believing bigger is daring to believe in our incredibleness.

We also know God uses disruption to interrupt our belief patterns, upgrade our self-image, and to mature our outlook to elevate our thinking. Disruption ultimately triggers divine reinvention in our lives. *Reinvention is coming into alignment with what God originally intended.* Higher purpose exists solely in the center of God's *original* plan for our lives. Aligning us with it is how God puts us on *the path* to the bigger He chose well before we were born. God intentionally designed us to fulfill our life mission—meaning God has *already* authorized you to pursue it, pre-loading you with all the provisions you'll ever need, so you can arrive at your bigger space and have bigger impact.

So why is it so hard to get there? Where does the stinking, shrinking thinking come from?

Well, what you have to understand is that there is an enemy warring for our souls—a devil sent to steal, kill, and destroy; a ruler of darkness here to dim and extinguish our incredible light by any means necessary. The enemy can't stand the idea of BIG things happening in us, and can't handle the impact of the incredible manifesting through us. So the enemy focuses on delaying or destroying us, and like a thief in broad daylight, commits to stealing 'n sabotaging what's in store for us. The enemy is exceptionally clever and cunning at *hijacking*—getting us to turn our power of belief against us. There is a battle already in progress. Our life purpose, our light, and our incredibleness are at the heart of the fight. Since our beliefs determine what we birth, this battle begins with the battle for our belief first.

The battle is an ongoing, never-ending tug-of-war waged by two competing voices, each vying for the right to lead us and all that is within. Each pulls at us, and the winner gains the ability to influence, shape, and determine what we believe *about* ourselves, what we believe is *for* us. I call these two voices *little me* and *Future ME*. They battle for our self-image, perspective, and ultimately, our voice. Whichever belief is in the driver's seat, whichever voice we're listening to, that's the one leading us and creating our future for us. We'll start with the evil voice, the resident snake in the grass.

⁘ MEET *LITTLE ME* ⁘

Little me is the voice of fear, the devious little voice that pollutes our inner confidence by whispering doubt, worry, and hesitation. Think of *little me* as a bully who thrives on being our biggest inner-critic. *Little me* is a master at invading our heart and hijacking our mind with disbelief. *Little me*'s sole mission and objective is to keep us from becoming all that we are meant to become.

Little me is a straight-up hater, a voice that grows stronger and more persuasive each time we choose less instead of more. And *little me* needs and breathes fear like you and I need and breathe air. *Little me* is shrewd and slick, unapologetically brutal, and at times, disguises itself as logic and rationale. Oh, and *little me* loves to keep you busy and your mind swimming in the sea of self-sabotage and confusion. *Little me* will say whatever it takes to get us to shrink, settle, or waffle until we're eventually stagnant, self-conscious, stumbling, and stuck. *Little me* is intent on stopping you from getting on that helicopter by any means necessary. Why? *Little me* knows that divine, God-glorifying momentum in our lives happens when we allow Heaven to string together a series of bigger moments, moments where we believe bigger, decide bigger, and live bolder. Once you have that God's-eye view, you'll see how small and insignificant *little me* really is.

My friend. In order to elevate, to heal, and to enter the highest version of ourselves, we must identify when *little me* is running wild in the corridors of our mind and meddling with our beliefs.

❧ NOW MEET *FUTURE ME* ❧

I came that they may have life, and have it abundantly.
—John 10:10 (part two) (NRSV)

Future ME is the voice of faith, the courageous life-guiding and miracle-working force that lovingly guides us into the full abundance of what God has for us.

Think of *Future ME* like a mentor. The wise sage that gives us next-level advice, helps us transform panic into peace, and provides calm in the center of a storm. *Future ME* has a very simple, yet specific mission: *to guide us forward.*

As it says in 2 Timothy 1:7 (NKJV), "God has not given us a spirit of fear, but of power and of love and of a sound mind." Nothing of God is designed to make us fearful, weak, timid, or intimidated. Nothing. That's how we can tell *little me* from *Future ME.*

Future ME is focused on aligning us with God's plan, path, and purpose for our lives. She is responsible for reminding us how powerful we really are, how much God loves us, and what supernatural tools have already been made available to us. *Future ME* speaks life into our spirit and elevates our thoughts higher. *Future ME* is an iron-sharpener as well. She gives voice to the Holy Spirit, challenges us to believe bigger, and whispers affirmations of our worthiness and readiness. *Future*

ME is fully aware of our greatness, and is tasked with the honor of helping us uncover all of the incredible deposits and surprises God placed inside us. *Future ME* is passionate about us, wholly believes in us, and is committed to connecting us with every single part of the intended future awaiting us. *Future ME* isn't scared of reinvention and swallows disruption like a vitamin that makes her stronger. *Future ME* isn't scared of anything actually, especially not *little me*. *Future ME* is an expert navigator, specializing in the unknown, and knows that if we step into the future calling us, if we can become the women God always intended, we'll fulfill our life mission and become a catalyst that ignites others to do the same.

Of course, *little me* is fully aware of this as well. And so the two battle.

⟨ EMBRACING PERSONAL RESPONSIBILITY ⟩

Little me and *Future ME* battle all day every day for us—for our heart, our mind, our voice, and for our decisions. All the stuff that enables our inner incredible to produce outer impact.

> *Believing bigger is aligning with what God wants and where God directs.*

When God sends an invitation to upgrade and expand our lives in a bigger way, *Future ME* is the voice that says, "Let's try this." *Little me* is the voice that says, "Who in the world do you think you are?" The Bible makes clear that there is a "spirit of fear" and "spirit of faith." To keep it simple, when you think of a *spirit*, think of it (in part) as an influencing voice. As women, we must become skilled in distinguishing the voice of God from the voice of the enemy. Now, I'm *not* substituting *little me* for *the* enemy. However, *little me* (stinking thinking) is the primary messenger and strategy of the enemy. Likewise, *Future ME* (forward thinking) is the principal strategy of God.

We can't blame everything that goes wrong on the enemy. That's spiritually immature and completely ineffective. And centuries of sin-shaming is certainly not igniting us as women to enter into our calling. I refer to the voices as *little me* and *Future ME* for a reason: personal responsibility. Notice the word *me* is present with both. One invites us to shrink, the other invites us to grow. Without personal responsibility, we incorrectly see faith as something outside of ourselves that must be attained, and fear as an exterior attack as opposed to an interior awakening.

Future ME is how God equips us to align with the flow of the Holy Spirit, to move forward and to reap the fruits of faith-activated thinking, speaking, deciding, and doing. And *little me* is how the enemy hijacks our sacred beliefs and baits us into turning our own power against ourselves. Know this:

> *You are a target of the enemy because you are a threat to the enemy.*

However, that doesn't mean we have to live in fear and remain a perpetual victim of the enemy. God gives us free will and the power to choose, the autonomy to believe bigger. The enemy is going to do what the enemy does: pervert, manipulate, and sabotage. If the enemy can distort our thinking, the enemy can destroy our decisions. However, God gives us the final say when it comes to *our* decisions. *We don't have to believe everything we think.* We don't have to believe the whispers and lies. We get to choose what we believe. And, because we ultimately birth what we believe, the enemy unleashes *little me* to wage an all-out war in our mind.

You're carrying the incredible—precious cargo straight from Heaven. That's why the chaos came. It was an attempt to cripple your confidence. And that's *really* why disruption occurs—to do away with an outdated self-image, to retire our antiquated outlook, to show us what we possess deep within, and to allow what we're really made of—the unknown—to emerge.

Because we matter, and because the enemy is terrified of a woman who is clear about her purpose and confident in her mission, the enemy uses *little me* to lure us into second-guessing, doubt, shrinking, and self-sabotage. Yes, you are a target of the enemy because you are a threat to the enemy. That's how important, how critical, and how significant you are. *Little me* wants you to perpetually feel unqualified and unworthy—to settle for ones and to forget the fives. However:

God speaks in "cans" and not in "cants."

Remembering this core truth is key to identifying the methods, half-truths, and doubt-dipped whispers of the enemy. We'll talk more about this. For now, know *Future ME* (the invincible voice of faith) is the mouthpiece God uses to reinvent you and move you forward. *Future ME always tells the truth, even when you don't see it and even when it takes faith to believe it.* You were born beautiful, brilliant, and worthy. God has *already* given you permission to live accordingly. Stinking, shrinking thinking isn't from above, and it blocks us from entering our higher purpose. So as soul-shattering as my split-rock season was, I made a decision to journey through the valley of betrayal, heartache, and depression *trusting* and hoping it would make way for new life. For higher purpose. And for bigger to align me with *The Path*, not just a path. Hitting rock-bottom gives us a chance to look up. It might be intimidating, and even seem unfair, but challenges exclusively equip us with hard-earned insight on how to help others get through their split-rock moments, too.

intermission

DIVINE REINVENTION

**Disruption and destiny go together hand-in-hand.
Purpose, however, is not supposed to be a mystery.
God desires that we attain mastery.**

{ OUR NEXT STEPS }

Before we delve into the process of uncovering your purpose in Part II, I want to explain a few terms that often create confusion when I talk about discovering our life mission and true identity.

Later, I will share how I became a reinvention strategist and grew passionate about teaching faith, identity, business, resilience, and manifestation—the good stuff necessary to live a life worthy of the calling we've received.

But first, here are some key definitions I'd love for you to take in, record in your journal, and hold on to. These are my definitions—how I've come to look at divine identity over time. And we'll keep it pretty simple for now, but we'll be digging deeper into each principle as we go. Embrace 'em. Every one is a precious gem!

PURPOSE. Purpose is the natural impact your life and presence have on others. *Your* purpose makes God's plan for mankind more complete. And it reveals something in you that is unique about God. Your purpose is why you're here.

CALLING. Your calling is your assignment. It's a mission, an area, or an objective God is recruiting you to complete.

GIFTS. Gifts are your God-given endowments—abilities and attributes that improve the lives of others. Your gifts give your life focus, courage, and momentum. Your gifts clarify your purpose and focus your calling.

DISRUPTION. Disruption is an unexpected, inconvenient moment; an interruption necessary for course correction in your life. These are split-rock, life-altering, and defining events. Disruption is designed to realign us, elevate us, and propel us to become a stronger version of ourselves.

REINVENTION. Reinvention is coming into alignment with the original intention for your life. It is becoming new by removing the old. It is not about changing who you are, it is about changing what you do so you can become who you are.

You'll see that purpose and calling are related but not quite the same. Those are often confused, so I want to be clear about them.

Purpose is *why* God needs you and how God made you.

Calling is *where* God is sending you.

Purpose is more *personality* oriented, whereas calling is more a *path* and *place* of assignment.

I'll use an analogy to bring these big concepts together. Think of a tire. It's not a sexy example, but stick with me! *Why* does a tire exist? To roll, right? To make transportation easier. That's its purpose—to facilitate movement. It's how and why it's made.

But *where* does a tire belong? Not on a shelf. It belongs on a vehicle. That's its assignment. That's its place of utility and impact. Just as different types of tires go with different vehicles, your gifts will determine where you best belong and you uniquely roll.

There is something about your life, personality, and abilities meant to make things work and flow properly and smoothly for others. As you'll see, *belief* is like the fuel that makes everything operate. *Faith* is putting your foot on the gas pedal. *Fear* is slamming on the brake. Sometimes we do both . . . at the same time. *Disruption* is like engine failure and a car accident with no insurance. And *reinvention* is like the better-than-new restoration of a classic car.

You're on a journey, and you're being recalibrated so that you can take others on a journey, too.

Reference these definitions as often as you need to. I hope that you'll add these principles to your vocabulary as you elevate your life mission and step into helping others find and elevate their mission, too.

⊰ { THE PURPOSE MAP } ⊱

Now on to the main event! We're about to dive into what I call the *Purpose Map*: the five life stages of divine reinvention that position us on *The Path*—the one that aligns with our life mission. Each stage is part of God's master plan, and the Purpose Map helps us to see exactly how we fit into it and where we are on The Path right now. As you will discover, our master purpose (why you're here) actually never changes. Our assignment does. Like a soldier in active duty, we'll have multiple assignments (or deployments) over our lifetime. Our purpose naturally, almost effortlessly flows from us. It's our personality—an impact and essence that has been in place and part of us since before we were born. I'm not here to help you find it. I'm here to help you become more *aware* of it. We don't awaken our purpose—that's not possible. As my friend Dee Thompson says, "purpose never dies." We awaken our awareness—our thinking, our believing, and our choosing.

Don't assume you fully know your purpose.

None of us really know what God has in store for us. No matter how successful or spiritual we are, and no matter how accustomed we've grown to living for God, we'll never *fully* know every aspect of our purpose. Not while we're in this container called the human body. Walking with God is a never-ending adventure—one where we never stop discovering how He's handcrafted us in His unlimited image. Purpose can't be contained. Plus, God isn't seeking to give us certainty and results alone. He is seeking to give us connection and relationship first.

As you'll see, each of the five stages falls into one of three overarching zones:

+ The first two stages (Discovery and Talent) fall into the Comfort Zone.

+ The middle stage (The GAP) comprises the Growth Zone.

+ The final two stages (Gifts and Influence) comprise the Glory Zone. This is where your life mission and bigger calling awaits.

To move forward along *The Path*, then, is to move from comfort to growth, and from growth to glory. Glory is what it's all about. It's about moving forward—not just about being busy, but about changing position.

Your path isn't that different from mine, and mine isn't that different from yours. As each stage of the Purpose Map reveals, the details, experiences, and obstacles may vary for each of us, but the pathway of divine reinvention is fundamentally the same. We will breakdown each of the zones and stages in just a moment. For now, so that you have a visual, take a look at the Purpose Map and be sure to reference it back as we go!

{ HERE IS WHAT THE PURPOSE MAP IS NOT }

It's not a series of success steps. I'm not giving you a typical do-this-and-then-you'll-get-that type of formula. These five stages aren't steps, because the stages don't belong to us and we can't dictate their timing. These are stages God alone takes us through. Our role is to be present and participate in the process via surrender and by raising our awareness—not to dictate the process.

To best understand how these five stages unfold, think of 'em like the stages of a pregnancy. There are events that *naturally* unfold between conception and delivery. You can't control how pregnancy goes. You can interfere, but it's not a process you can control. While you may not be able to dictate the timeline, you can become more aware about what happens at each stage. Knowing what's coming gives you greater confidence, clarity, readiness, and resilience. It helps us as women to know what to prepare for . . . what to expect when we're expecting.

Entering destiny works the same way . . . only no one ever describes how a life of significance actually evolves—what battles you'll face, what feelings and doubts you'll encounter, what you can do to enjoy and thrive through the process. If you know a baby is coming, and that labor pains, cravings, and mood swings are part of the process, you're more resilient and able to press through. The abnormal is actually normal. Tears, hormone changes 'n weight gain come with the territory. But you wouldn't know that if you'd never experienced it or if no one ever explained it.

That's my mission with the Purpose Map. I don't want you to get stuck in the past, in betrayal, regret, self-doubt, or even something as tricky as success. I want you to maximize your life—fully unleashing what God has in you because He needs you. I need you. And others need what God has *exclusively* placed within you. Pregnancy is an inside job for sure. And no one can carry your calling but you. My intention is to walk beside you and help you gain greater clarity as to what you've been through, what you will go through, and what God has in store for you as long as you keep pressing through. It is also my mission to help you tap into (and unleash) your higher self by embracing the bigger belief system seeking to emerge through you right now.

Growing your relationship with God is not about steps.

The Purpose Map

Purpose is not an intellectual exercise. And it's not a checklist. We ladies love 'em—I know I do—but I'm intentionally resisting the temptation to only give you a list of tips for quickly getting from stage one to stage five. You simply can't rush your way through the stages and expect to arrive at your purpose. Growth, wisdom, spiritual resilience, and understanding are by-products of awareness, intimacy, and surrender. I really want your purpose to develop properly and make it to full term. Rushing puts us at risk of missing something significant to our destiny and development.

At points you may want me to hurry up the process. To give you some quick steps that hone in on exactly what *your* purpose is. I get it. And if I didn't love and believe in you so much, I would do just that. But my intention isn't to give you a quick fix when it comes to this purpose thing. Most people who have read books about purpose and heard sessions about it over the years still don't know what theirs is. I think it's because we've been unwilling to enter a process—one filled with pruning, patience, and *soaking* in the *heart* of God so that we can enter the *mind* of God. Thankfully, God has good breath! We need to be so close we literally feel God breathing new life upon us. That's where our purpose lies. His whisper is mightier and holier than anything I can tell you.

So, do me a favor. Resist the temptation to rush the process. To demand answers. As you'll see in the next chapter, that desire for certainty comes from our need to be defined and to have something to *do*. You'll want to know what your gifts are. What your voice is. Where you belong. It's all good. Desire is the beginning of destiny. But don't abandon the process. And please don't be too hard on yourself. We're going to figure it out together. Trust that the very act of your picking this book means the process has already begun. We're not connected by accident. Higher purpose brought us together for such a time as this in your life.

I promise to give you some very specific questions to ask, things to consider, and prayers to pray at the right time.

And, as we break down each of the five life stages within the Purpose Map, I'll pose one BIG question at the outset that will help you understand how purpose unfolds (or gets blocked) in that stage. I'm not here to add to your already overcrowded to-do list. I'm actually hoping to strip it.

The primary thing I challenge you with is self-reflection. Part II, which we are moments away from now, is essentially the examination to help you assess and realign your vision. It *is* a good idea to keep identifying your split-rock moments 'n disappointments and *little me* whispers, fears, and hang-ups now and every step of the way. In Part III, we'll put it all together with a way for you to understand your specific path and next steps. This is what I've seen work over the last several years in helping everyday women to find their extraordinary path, which is to take you through a process if you'll allow me and trust me. As we do this:

+ Highlight your *aha* moments

+ Jot down what you're learning in a journal

+ Meditate on revelations and reflect on critical questions

+ Turn your epiphanies into affirmations, declarations, and bold prayers

When we shift the way we think, we elevate the way we live.

Much like learning how the natural stages of pregnancy unfold, we're going to use the Purpose Map to explore the five stages of divine reinvention so you can prepare for the promise of what is coming and calling . . . your higher purpose.

❴ ONE FINAL DISCLOSURE ❵

I have two brothers and seven male cousins, and they all started a club called BAM (Boys Against Marshawn) when I was a kid. Until recently, I've had mostly male mentors, and I managed pro athletes (yup, more fellas) in the NFL and NBA for years. I've been a competitor my whole life. My point: I'm just a girl raised around a bunch of boys who has been knocked down and has had to figure out how to get back up. I'm a woman who loves long walks on the beach with the Holy Spirit, and I'm a straight shooter who believes Believers must adopt a winning mindset—the mindset and skillset of champions.

God built us to win. I was a baton twirler growing up, and was able to train under one of the best coaches in the world, Janice Jackson. I'll tell you more about that journey shortly. For now, know that the greatest gift she gave me wasn't the ability to get trophies and world titles. The most priceless principle she taught me was the power of *self-belief.* She was a straight shooter, someone God sent to help me develop *every* area of greatness, and that's who I'd like to be in your life, too. I have a feeling you could use someone in your life who is that passionate about you.

When I started down the path of reinvention coaching, embracing God's promise and forecasting that my pain would lead to changing the lives of women, I was told my message wouldn't work because it was *too big,* and (wait for it) that "the women would be *too broken* to receive it." I still have that email. The well-intentioned soul who shared that "wisdom" was a woman, not a man, and a woman of faith seeking to mentor and guide me. Listen.

> We've been mentored, taught, and conditioned to shrink and settle for generations.

That's not God's will or his plan for our lives. Those words play in my head on a daily basis. Not as a burden but as a call to action. I'm passionate . . . maybe slightly obsessed with your possibilities.

I've been told I need to "soften" my message, to make sure that it's not "too complicated," and that women don't like "leadership topics." (Sorry for the overuse of air quotes . . . but sarcasm definitely intended.) That we just prefer *stories*, not strategy. To avoid stepping out of line, we end up clinging to average. Hmmm. Okay. Well. I'm here for the anointed life . . . hope you are, too. So I won't be following any of that advice! That's not the voice God gave me, and I don't believe that to be true of you either. There is something *great* bubbling inside of you, waiting to burst out and bless the world. It's not generic. And I won't ask you to rise up while I water myself down. Ain't happening. I believe in God's mighty plan to propel and elevate women in new ways like never before. Specifically, I believe in you and *your* ability to rise to greatness. God only does BIG things, and I believe in your ability to handle everything God has for you. Call me crazy. Won't be the first, or last, time.

So yes, I am indeed in cahoots with *Future ME,* and I have every intention of conspiring with Heaven to help you maximize your potential, to believe bigger and live *bolder.* We can be full of God-soaked faith, yet stay stuck because we're missing a game plan. I am here to help you find yours. Just keep in mind that purpose flows from the Living God who sends us revelations about ourselves as a living, breathing, evolving, and course-correcting message.

> *So let's take the pressure off of having to figure it out perfectly and having to get this purpose thing just right.*

I've walked thousands of women, up close and personal, through the process of divine reinvention, and I've been through it myself. I know very well what happens when bigger is near, when your life is about to shift into dimensions beyond your comprehension. So I'll say it now and you'll hear me say it again later. As you turn these pages, you're not allowed to get in the way. You're not allowed to think you know it all. And you are not allowed to shrink, compare, doubt, or judge yourself.

Disappointment does not disqualify us, it anoints us. Doubt is what disqualifies us.

As we go through the Purpose Map, know also that at each stage we will see the battle between *little me* and *Future ME* intensify. The journey into significance is ultimately an ongoing, experimental quest in believing bigger. You can do it afraid. That's not a problem. Destiny is designed to stretch you in stubborn places so that the new, more limber you no longer recognizes the former, less flexible you. Believing bigger is a contact sport and it starts now. God is challenging you to become a fascinated student of you, and in the process, to get a God-painted picture of you and your future. Divine reinvention like that takes self-love. It takes patience, perspective, curiosity, courage, and surrender, not criticism.

Alas, disruption has called us out of hiding and onto *The Path* of purpose, an unpredictable purpose-paved path that travels through the land of reinvention. Just as an explorer discovers herself as she uncovers the unknown, we'll discover not only what we're here for and what we're made of, but the incredibleness we've always possessed (and perhaps been afraid to believe) all along.

PART TWO

Align

THE PURPOSE MAP:
FIVE STAGES
OF DIVINE
REINVENTION

1

Discovery
STAGE

Who am I supposed to be?

chapter four

STAGE ONE: DISCOVERY

As a woman thinketh in her heart, so is she.

—Inspired by Proverbs 23:7

The first stage in the Purpose Map's five stages of divine reinvention is called the Discovery Stage. Discovery is where the foundation of our identity gets pieced together.

This stage is where we initially learn what we like and dislike, what's possible (and what seems unattainable), how the world works, and what to believe about ourselves—our limitations as well as our possibilities. The day-to-day experiences in our life at this stage function like a series of seemingly random classrooms with a variety of teachers and moments that impress upon us *who* we can (or cannot) be, *what* we can (or cannot) do, and *where* we do (or don't) belong. Fresh on the scene, wide-eyed and malleable, we're the sponge. We're the student. We don't really get to pick our teachers, and because of our impressionability, we don't even get to choose the lesson. At least not consciously. We don't yet know how.

But impact is made. Values are established. Boundaries are determined. Our self-image is formed. And our beliefs get programmed. In essence, we learn how to learn. We learn how to think and not think, how to behave and not behave. We learn how to be loved and whether we're even loveable. We learn how to get others to love us or at least see us. We learn who to listen to, what not to say, and what we're supposed to believe. Most certainly, we master how not to step out of line. That would violate protocol . . . . *The Rules.* So Discovery is as formative as it is forecasting. This is where we develop a deep understanding . . . a guiding belief about where we fit and who we are good enough to become. We ultimately discover who we are. Well, strike that. We discover who we *think* we are.

⊰ MY FIRST TEACHER ⊱

The first person to really leave an impression on my life was my beautiful mom. My mom worked for the Social Security Administration. She had left behind a career in psychology and taken a job with the federal government to marry my dad and become a mother. Somehow she managed to part and braid my thick 'n curly hair every single morning before heading to work, while I was still sleeping. And she would tuck me in at night saying sweet prayers—specifically praying for protection and favor over me as I drifted to sleep. Half the time she would fall asleep, too! My dad (now retired) worked for the Federal Aviation Administration (FAA) as an air traffic controller—one of those guys in front of the large radar screens that talk to the pilots and help 'em navigate the great blue skies.

I didn't know as a little girl that they were both rarities in their field. That they were first-generation career professionals as African-Americans in the seventies. I didn't know that when they were my age, they could only use segregated bathrooms marked *colored*, or that their mothers (my grandmothers) both cleaned homes and bathrooms for *non-colored* people because those were the opportunities available at the time. I didn't know any of that. At least, I didn't learn those realities at home.

Our yellow brick home was very loving. Not perfect. My dad's job was stressful—but he was great at it. My mom worked long hours, too.

But I don't ever remember missing their presence. I remember playing horsey, riding on my dad's back when he got home after a long shift, and I remember my mom having open arms 24/7. I remember dinner on the table. We weren't a perfect family. My parents had seasons where they spent time apart, but they were always there for me and for my brother. There were nights with some drama. But we had each other's back no matter what. And I *knew* I was loved by my mother and adored by my dad. That was never in question. We lived in a nice suburban neighborhood, but I didn't realize until first grade that we were one of the only black families on the block. I didn't actually think about race or ethnicity at the time. I was a little girl living in a beautiful world.

But, then I turned six years old and it was time to go to school. We didn't live far away from the elementary school. I had been in day care, but school was going to be a new and exciting experience. The first day, Mom spent extra time on my hair, and I had a pretty, perfectly coordinated outfit, a new backpack, a lunch box with Strawberry Shortcake on the front, and a brand-new pair of lilac Coke-bottle glasses. My brother, Corey, was just one year and three days younger than me, so he would be starting kindergarten (something I hadn't done) that same day.

We took our Flintstones chewable vitamins, had some Aunt Jemima pancakes with Mrs. Butterworth's syrup, and then got buckled up in my mom's navy-blue Buick, nicknamed Kit. She liked the show *Knight Rider* at the time.

We went to the front office to check in and find out where each of our classrooms was located. The ladies at the front desk didn't ask us our name or welcome us to the school. They immediately explained that we were in the wrong place. My mom and dad proceeded to explain that we lived just a few blocks away. They insisted that we belonged at another school, about one mile in the opposite direction. My parents explained that *this* was our school and we had already been assigned teachers. My dad told them our home address. And then the women at the front desk asked for identification. We had to prove that this was where we belonged.

While all of this was happening, dozens of other kids were check-ing in and being escorted or directed to their classrooms. None of them had to show ID.

Apparently, the other school down the street was the one the majority of the kids with brown skin attended. The front desk ladies automatically assumed that since we were black (no one used the word *colored* in the eighties) we didn't belong. We couldn't possibly live in *this* neighborhood. But we did. This, whether they were ready or not, was where my brother and I belonged.

That experience. That was one of my first teachers, and I hadn't even made it into the classroom yet. That front office was a place I'd become very familiar with over the next six years. So would my parents. They had a lot of parent-teacher meetings . . . heck, they had a lot of parent-*principal* meetings. At home I felt like a sweet little girl—creative, help-ful, and talkative. At school I discovered I was just a stereotype. That first day really defined the next several years of elementary school. I learned I had to prove that I belonged. I'd thought I would be walking into a classroom, and I suppose I did—but not the type I'd expected.

{ WHEN LABELS STICK }

I really loved my first grade teacher. She had a sweet demeanor and poofy blond hair like the Golden Girls. I think that was a Texas thing. One day we were in the hallway doing a group reading circle—there may have been four or five other kids at the table—and out of nowhere, the door to the classroom directly across from where we were sitting flew open and I saw my brother's kindergarten teacher physically dragging him by one arm. He was crying uncontrollably. My brother used to cry here and there when he was little, but he was also incredibly shy and mild-mannered. I can still see his tears and the terrified look on his face to this day. And I remember the cold look on his teacher's face. I was only six years old at the time. Instead of doing something, I just froze. I was too afraid to speak up or stand. I still carry some guilt about that to this day.

What I remember most is that my teacher didn't do a thing. She just watched. She didn't intervene. She didn't call anyone. When they were gone, we went back to reading like nothing happened. This memory still boils my blood and at the same time breaks my heart. From time to time, people ask me *why did that happen* . . . the underlying innuendo being what did my brother, at five years old, do to deserve or warrant being dragged like an animal. That very question says everything about why it happened and still happens. My point is I learned that the people you trust may not be the ones that stand up for you, and may very well be the ones that mistreat you. Over the next few years, teachers and guidance counselors would try to convince my parents to consider putting us in another school—one more suited for kids like us.

I used to get in trouble for talking—a lot. I got to know the principal very well and was quickly labeled a problem child.

Once, in third grade, I got in trouble for accepting a dare from two boys who dared me to take things from some of the other kids' desks while everyone was at recess. I don't know why we were left alone in that classroom. We must have lost our recess privileges for some reason. Anyhow, I was *always* up for a challenge—especially one where I got to prove that I wasn't afraid—so I took the dare. I didn't think of it as stealing because I hadn't planned to keep that stuff. But the teacher and the rest of the class came back from recess before I could put everything back.

Kids started recognizing that things were missing, and the same boy who first issued the dare was the one who ratted me out. In fact, he escorted my teacher to my bag and showed her the goods! That was the day I learned what shame was. Having to face my parents that night in the living room, not the family room, but the living room, with the "good furniture," the room we only went in on special occasions, was the worst feeling I'd ever felt.

Teachers had *labeled* me a problem child, but that night, I *felt* like one. Shame is the worst. I understand why it's referred to as a cloak—it feels like skin. It's so heavy. So deep.

I had never seen my parents so stunned. They didn't yell. They didn't raise their voices. They didn't even punish me. They just asked me why. They worked hard. They provided me with everything and then some. I told them about the dare, and tried to clean up the story, but that bordered on lying, and I ended up digging a deeper hole. I couldn't deny the part that I actually did put the stuff in my bag. And then my dad said, "Your mother and I will *always* defend you. We'll *always* have your back and go to bat for you as long as you tell the truth! Talking is one thing, but the thing you can't recover from is if people look at you like a thief."

From then on I tried to get it right. I tried not to talk as much. I tried to make sure I did my homework and stayed out of trouble. But there was still this dark cloud that hovered over me. The worst part about others labeling you isn't the labeling . . . it's the believing. When I began to *believe* that I was less than, that belief conditioned my thinking and programmed my self-esteem.

Now maybe you can better understand why I chose the $1 bill instead of the $5 bill. I didn't feel as good, as likable or as worthy, as the other kids in class. And I didn't feel as smart as them either. I don't remember having the chance to take the tests for the gifted and talented kids. In fact both my brother and I were labeled antisocial and recommended for special education, which we didn't need. So when the "gifted" kids went off to the place the smart kids went, I always stayed behind and wondered what they did in Never-Never Land. (I called it that because I *never* went there.) Eventually, I stopped wondering and just embraced the reality that I didn't *belong* there. I wasn't smart. Neither was I gifted or talented. I was different, and not in a good way.

On top of that, I didn't feel like the girls at school wanted to be my friend. I remember asking a friend if she wanted to spend the night. We were on a soccer team together. After the game she went to ask her mom for permission, but she said no. When she asked why not, her mom proceeded to slap her in the face. She slapped her so hard in front of me and all of the other kids and parents that it almost felt like she hit me. In many ways she did.

My friend never came to stay for that sleepover. We never talked about it again. And, after that day, we were never really close.

That dark cloud never really left. Being one of the only black girls in the school often made me feel like a black sheep. I recall the day my fourth grade history teacher explained to the entire class that she was not ready for a black president during the 1988 election. I remember thinking, *What did that mean for me?* Was she saying I could never be president? Would someone who looked like me ever "belong" in the White House? And would the world ever be ready for me?

Let me say that there were plenty of amazing experiences throughout my childhood, too, and I was indeed a very, very blessed kid. I had two parents. I lived in a nice home, never missed a meal, and got to attend a quality public school and receive a stellar education. I'm fully and humbly aware that I'm not sharing a story of rape, abandonment, incest, physical abuse, sickness, or a sudden death of a loved one—nightmares that might be part of your reality. I used to feel like my story wasn't as traumatic and as devastating as others . . . and therefore not worth sharing.

But every story matters. Especially yours. We all have something that cripples our confidence. When we're transparent, I actually think it bonds us as women, because we each encounter self-doubt at different levels and at different periods in our life.

Being in an environment where she perpetually feels unwanted, unwelcome, and uninspired is crippling to a little girl's confidence. You not only learn how to survive, how not to disappoint, and how not to attract unwanted attention, you also learn the *protocol* for acceptance, approval, and attention.

EXTRACTIONS

Each of us has pivotal experiences, encounters, and moments that make an impression on how we think about ourselves. In some ways, experiences are some of the most impactful teachers in our lives. Experiences spark emotion; emotion glues us to a memory. That's why remembering how something made us feel is often easier than remembering what people said. After all, communication is only 7 percent verbal. The remaining, whopping 93 percent is nonverbal—body language and tone of voice. In other words, we don't remember most of what people say to us, but don't worry, others don't remember most of what we say to them either!

However, we almost always remember how someone else made us *feel*. Now I can't remember 99.9 percent of what I actually learned in elementary school. Sure, I learned to read, write, add, multiply, subtract, and divide. But, I don't actually remember the moment I learned that 2+2=4. I do remember that moment in the front office. I remember which school years were good ones and which ones I'd like to erase, and I certainly remember how I felt about my elementary school teachers . . . and how I thought they felt about me. And, I remember almost every time I was in the principal's office and the way the principal and those ladies at the front desk would look at me. My point is I remember what I *felt* in those moments, and those feelings shaped what I took away from each one.

> *learning isn't just about the information we receive, it's about the core identity we shape.*

When people say something that impacts us emotionally, spiritually, or mentally, *that* is what results in life-shaping impressions. That's what has shaped what we believe about ourselves right now in this moment.

This is how the Discovery Stage of life works. We get our internal programming, conditioning, and wiring. We're kind of like the blank hard drive on a computer waiting to be coded and commanded.

So how we view ourselves today, how we see others, how we approach circumstances, how we make decisions, how we believe, and how we interact with the world—all of that comes from influential people and experiences in our lives, and what we took away from those encounters. Said another way . . .

Who we are today was shaped by who and what we encountered in our yesterdays. And how we are (how we show up in life) was shaped by what we took away.

Much of our personality is shaped during childhood. It's certainly when we're the most impressionable. But, isn't it interesting that much of who we become is formed and fashioned when we know the least in life?

{ SELF-ESTEEM SNAPSHOTS }

What we take away from any person or experience (in the past or today) is really a snapshot of our self-image in that moment. If you're uncertain about who you are, like me as a little girl in the front office, an experience can sway your self-esteem one way or the other. My take-away that day could have been very different. Wisdom comes from learning *how* to process different encounters. There are some beliefs we've held on to that we would be better served by throwing away. When we hold on to the wrong lesson, it stunts our growth, dents our self-esteem, damages our ego, and skews our vision.

Let's say I'm at the customer service desk in an airport for example. If I feel like the attendant is ignoring me or giving me a hard time, I might assume it's because the attendant doesn't want me there or doesn't believe I belong there. Because it reminds me of a familiar experience, I might draw a familiar conclusion. But is the experience really similar or is that just my view of it? Sure, I could go on and on about how many times it has seemed that someone treated me (or my friends and family) differently because of skin color. But what if that isn't what the attendant is actually doing? What if my past experience shaped how I'm seeing what's happening right now?

This is why it's so important to uncover what lessons we absorbed in the Discovery Stage. It's where *little me* first found its voice and made its way into our heads and hearts.

Future ME tries to focus us on the lessons and habits that move us forward. But *little me* is tricky. *Little me* is a master at messing with us by sending mixed signals to our mind. Again, let's take my first day at school. My mom poured an incredible amount of time, attention, and love into getting me ready. My dad told me over and over again how pretty I was and how wonderful my hair looked. I even had two parents take me to school! I didn't just feel loved that morning. I *was* loved. I knew I was lovable *and* loving. But then, in a matter of moments, I got a mixed, contradictory signal. One experience in the front office caused me to question my worth and my relevance in just an instant.

Little me then used that first mixed signal to reroute my attention to more damaging beliefs. At home I was always affirmed. I had structure and discipline and a healthy self-image. But at school, my mind (over time) became programmed to believe I was a troublemaker. So the fantastic wiring at home got scrambled and mixed with the faulty wiring I extracted from school.

Every time my name was on the board, every time I went to the principal's office, and every time I saw the look of disdain in a teacher's eye, *little me* seared that impression into my soul. It reinforced faulty wiring, making it more normal and eventually instinctual.

{ STUDENT OR TEACHER }

I remember sitting . . . well, really sinking and shrinking, in my chair during sixth grade homeroom. I raised my hand and asked a genuine question about that day's lesson. My teacher's answer felt dismissive (my experience . . . probably not her intention) and I felt like the dumbest kid in the room in that moment. Again.

That's when I had my first lightning bolt moment. It was an AHA . . . a moment of revelation and clarity. I promised myself this:

> *One day, I am going to become a teacher.*
> *Only my students will never feel incapable or unwanted.*
> *My students will feel like they can do anything!*

It was more revenge and ego than altruism, but that was the moment I became passionate about others' feelings and their esteem. And I was going to show the teachers how this thing should really be done. In retrospect, though my eleven-year-old self had no clue at the time, I can see that it was actually a prophetic, purpose-clarifying moment.

Of all the things we learn, there is still something no one tells us as kids:

At any given moment, we are either student or teacher.

So it's not just *that* we're learning . . . it's *how* we're learning. During Discovery, we don't yet know that the ultimate calling and intent for our lives is that of teacher.

Let that sink in for a moment. It's big.

No one tells us that teaching is tied to our ultimate calling. But that's because few realize it. Becoming a worker is what's socially prized, and that shapes how we direct our lives. No one ever teaches what comes after that. Who are you without a title? I missed that class in school. We're directed and molded without ever knowing that the purpose of working (becoming good and proficient at something) is to develop wisdom that will be needed later for teaching and leading. We're simply taught to provide, reproduce, and then retire.

We're *not* taught that one day our calling will call us to step up. To lead. And that our season of Discovery is about preparation for eventual deployment in a larger destiny. One day the student is *supposed* to become the teacher.

This is a life-shifting, mind-elevating truth. It's one that will really help you understand purpose, calling, and your true identity as we move forward. *You're a teacher—in some way.* God has a plan for you to impact others with *who* you are, *how* you think, and *what* you know. That's what God intended you to become before you learned what you were *supposed* to be.

Let's pause and reflect here.

Who were your most influential teachers? What are the experiences and people who made a lasting impression on your self-esteem, your beliefs, and your possibilities?

+ *Which ones taught you to believe in yourself?*

+ *Which ones introduced doubt?*

Did you ever feel like a problem child? Like an inconvenience? If so, in what way? How did that shape your personality, relationships, decisions, ambition, and beliefs?

We all learn different lessons during this period of development. But few of us really reflect on *why* we believe what we believe to be true, appropriate, good, or bad. Few of us really think about the way our early experiences influence who we are at work, or even the way we act in relationships . . . whether we're an encourager, a pleaser, a disciplinarian, a doubter, or a firecracker!

This is what we're going to dive into in the next chapter. We'll look at how we've all internalized lessons about what we *should* become and what path we *should* take. Understanding this is the first step on your journey to divine reinvention.

chapter five

IDENTIFYING YOUR RULE MAKERS

The Discovery Stage is all about how the experiences, lessons, and people we encounter add up to and result in what we believe about ourselves and our future. And the Discovery Stage is where we develop what I call *The Rules*. The Rules are like a personal manifesto, a check list of dos and don'ts that have been guiding you through your life—probably without your even realizing it. Essentially, we each have a little rule book inside our heads dictating what we think, feel, believe, and do. When we're "thinking," we're really consulting our personal, internal rule book.

In the context of the Purpose Map, The Rules are your compass, helping you navigate what to do, where not to go, and how to secure arrival at your intended destination. In this chapter, we're going to look at the rules you've been following in your life, understand how you came to internalize them, and see how you might break free from them and embrace the purpose God has in store for you.

Again, the Discovery Stage is all about figuring out . . .

1. Who you are *supposed* to be

2. Where you fit in

3. What it takes to survive and thrive

As we uncovered in the last chapter, many of us go through the Discovery Stage of life deeply wounded and severely doubting ourselves. This isn't your fault, and it's not just one thing that causes it— it's a series of experiences. We're subtly taught to doubt ourselves . . . especially as women. We're taught to fear failing and to silence and submerge the part of us that is most in tune with our greatness and significance.

The primary reason we miss our purpose in the formative years of life is that we believe the false lessons we're taught, and those steer us *away* from our purpose instead of *toward* it. Instead of learning the courage and curiosity that would allow us to pursue our purpose, we learn a set of dos 'n don'ts. Our experiences lead us to develop a sense of what we *should* and *should not* be doing, and we adopt protocol—what we think is an *appropriate* way of living, believing, and deciding.

The Rules are made up of the dos and don'ts we consciously and subconsciously learn and live by that allow us to fit in, to please others, and to protect ourselves from failure, rejection, or ridicule. Over time these rules become the beliefs, expectations, and core values that guide us. The Rules we live by determine our core values and beliefs, and ultimately influence all of our decisions and relationships.

Don't get me wrong. A disciplined system for living your life is incredibly important. We all need to have a barometer for what's right and wrong, for what to do and what not to do. *The problem is that many of the rules we learn are not all good, true, or from God.*

Let's revisit my first day of school. At six years old, I couldn't even see over the front desk. I don't remember the ladies' faces, but I remember their words and how I felt. That experience, combined with some of the other embarrassing and shame-inducing moments I shared with you, led me to believe that I was unwanted. That may not have been anyone's intention, but that was my experience, my conclusion, and therefore my reality.

I then adopted a belief that I wasn't worthy of friendship or affirmation. It wasn't until I started making good grades that I started feeling validation. The better my grades got, the more praise I got. And then I started getting academic awards, and that was a huge adrenaline rush and a reliable ego boost. So I learned the following: *In order to be accepted I need to achieve.* That was my experience . . . my truth. It became a guiding belief shaping my identity, my relationships, and my approach to life. That's what I took away from how people interacted with me. I could influence their behavior and affection with my performance.

Achieving was also a way to reshape the "problem child" perception others had of me. I shifted from a problem to a performer. From an inconvenience to an inspiration. That gave way to perfectionism, which I also viewed as an asset. In church, leaders called it a "spirit of excellence." For me, it led me to become a prover and a pleaser. But this paradigm worked for quite some time, which only reinforced that my broken belief system was healthy and even impressive.

The specific rules you live by are going to be different than mine, but we've all got 'em. I've discovered three primary drivers that most shape the rules we adopt and live by.

Rule Maker #1: Affirmation

If we experience or see something that gets rewarded, we want to experience more of those rewards. So we tend to do stuff that gets us smiles, hand claps, positive attention, and praise. For me, that was getting good grades. That became a must-do. That got most people off my back! *What were some affirmation-generating "must-dos" for you?*

Rule Maker #2: Consequences

If we see that something gets punished or criticized, we tend to actively avoid that situation in the future. We tend to stay away from things we think will be too hard, too controversial, too isolating, too painful, or too unfamiliar. These are also the things people actively or inadvertently steer us away from. We're taught to avoid risk and to play it safe—and here safe means "acceptable and predictable." We become risk managers as opposed to risk engagers. This is where we're told what not to dream and what's not a worthy path . . . but paths never explored could well be connected to your true gifts and higher purpose. *How did the threat of consequences, including fear of failure or rejection, shape your rules?*

Rule Maker #3: Repetition

If we experience or see something over and over, we tend to adopt that behavior or belief until it becomes a habit. This is why our school-teachers make us memorize certain words and force us to add 2+2 so many times—at some point, we instinctively know it equals 4. The knowledge becomes automatic. Our response becomes subconscious. You're no longer actively adding 2+2 because you've memorized it. Driving can be the same. Remember when I shared that I made it to the airport to confront the soon-to-be-ex about cheating, but I didn't remember the actual driving, exiting, or parking? The things we don't even think about doing, but still do, significantly shape our personality and our way of living. Things like listening to the same teachers or mentors because we always have. Or reciting scriptures on cue without really thinking about the meaning or listening for fresh revelation beyond what we've been told. How we consistently react to people or circumstances . . . the routines in our lives . . . become rule makers, too. We adhere to them and even fight for them. They give our lives predictability. *What are the things you do simply because they're what you've always done?*

⧼ PINPOINTING YOUR RULE MAKERS ⧽

To determine the rule makers in your life, let's reflect on a few questions.

+ In terms of *affirmation*—What makes you feel important? Accepted? Loved? Validated? Smart? Necessary? What are the things you've pursued in search of praise?

+ In terms of *consequences*—What haven't you done, tried, or pursued because of perceived negative or unwanted consequences? What are the things you learned *not* to do? What rules or norms are you most afraid of breaking or disobeying? And who are you most afraid of disappointing, going against, or even offending? Why?

+ In terms of *repetition*—What are the things you've mastered over time that are just automatic for you now? What are the habits, beliefs, attitudes, or even skills you've learned that taught you how to navigate life?

+ For now, take a moment to list 'em out. Don't be shy. It's just me and you. We'll soon figure out how these are showing up in your life and how they might actually be the very dams blocking your higher purpose, new season, or next level.

⧼ WHAT TO KEEP AND WHAT ⧽ TO KICK TO THE CURB

We've looked at our *rule makers*—what beliefs and lessons have been at play in building our current life. Not all of these rules are bad. Some of them are very important, and others are false narratives we need to get past in order to get to our bigger, more blessed life.

Which are the experiences (and people) we ignore that we should pay attention to, and what are the things we pay attention to that we should really ignore? How do we know the difference? Well. The best way to figure out what to keep and what to kick to the curb is to put our major life lessons into one of three "information buckets": *Blessed*, *Bad*, and *Broken*. Let's look at each one.

Bucket #1: Blessed Information

Much of the information we get from others is what I call *blessed*. It's heaven-sent. It's true, and right, and helps you and others. And it doesn't necessarily have to be spiritual in nature. For example, say you learn to change the oil in your car. That's blessed. Say you learn to pray. That's blessed, too. Both are productive and move you forward in some way. Both help others. Blessed information and teaching enriches our life, our self-esteem, our abilities, our opportunities, our knowledge, our outlook, and our decision-making capacities. Blessed is good. Blessed is very, very good. We most certainly want to hold on to lessons and nuggets that fall into the Blessed bucket.

Bucket #2: Bad Information

At the other end of the spectrum is *bad* information. We've all gotten bad information before. For instance, you ask for directions and get misled. Someone gives you their opinion about your clothes or your hair, but it's all wrong for you. I believe that by and large people mean well. We're all just doing the best we can. There are sho' nuff some that couldn't give a flying fart, and we all encounter a person here or there that is out to sabotage us. But, for the most part, people mean well when they give us advice. But some of the things we are taught are just flat-out not true. So let's stop and pause for just a moment. If I could get you to underline this and have the words flashing on and off in bright red lights right now, I would:

Not everything you've learned will get you where you need to be.

Even if it's been working for you so far, what got you here won't necessarily get you there. And what got you out of Egypt won't get you into your promised land. When we consciously *and* unconsciously take bad information and put it in the Blessed bucket, we end up headed in the wrong direction. An example could be the popular mantra "if you want something done right, you've gotta do it yourself." That ain't wisdom. It's bad dressed up as blessed. It keeps us isolated and overwhelmed. The Bible talks of wisdom being found in the multitude of quality counsel. Even Christ needed a crew, and so do you. Bad information can include mistaking humility for hiding—a common lesson that many of us are taught. Believing that caring for yourself makes you selfish. Believing that being ambitious means you're greedy. All of the things we're told about what women can't be or shouldn't do. It's bad teaching. It's not blessed.

Bucket #3: Broken Information

Somewhere in the middle between blessed and bad is *broken* information. Broken info is like a part in your car that may have worked just fine for a while, but eventually breaks down and needs to be replaced. Most broken information comes from opinions and traditions.

OPINIONS: Many of our closely held beliefs are opinions we heard and adopted from others (and now pass along). This is why it's so easy to end up following someone else's dream, and living someone else's life, without even knowing it. Others' views become your views, their voice your voice, and their example becomes your road map. It may start you off in the right direction, but soon you'll start to feel discontent, unsatisfied, or just out of alignment, and you won't know why—because you did all the right things and followed all of the right advice.

TRADITION: Tradition is the second source of broken information. By this I'm referring to all of the teachings that have been passed down to us about culture, religion, and family history. A lot of it is good. But a lot of it is junk. Some of what we've been taught to believe, be, and do has nothing to do with what God actually wants for us. It's just a passed down "rule" that people follow because they've always done it, and now they expect you to do it, too. Tradition largely exists to maintain the status quo.

Eventually, convention conflicts with calling. God isn't limited by or even interested in the way things have always been done. God is a God of firsts. He is *the* Creator in Chief. He intends that we create new ways of being, doing, and thinking. That we evolve, mature, and renew our minds. That's the only way to create a new movement. That's why God is the Living Word. That's what makes belief in Christ unique. It's the principal of newness.

When tradition crossbreeds with opinion, we end up adopting strongly held beliefs—ones we'll fight to keep alive. Here is another hard-truth moment: We don't always like to *actually* renew our thinking. It's easier to simply recite scripture as opposed to being stretched by it. Again, not all messages are bad. But the broken ones are dangerous.

Here is a super-simple, almost silly example. As a teenager, I wanted to shave my legs. Leg shaving, however, was not something the Louisiana-born ladies on my momma's side of the family did. To some that may sound odd, but whether you shave or don't shave, it's still just a tradition—a practice that you either follow or you don't. Momma told me that if I shaved my legs, the hair would grow back thicker and prickly like a cactus. She told me what her momma, my grandma, had told her. That was their opinion passed down as wisdom. But the cool girls at school all shaved their legs, so once I snuck into my parents' bathroom while they were both at work, took a razor, and shaved my legs for the first time. (I wish I had known that in addition to water, shaving cream was a part of the process!)

I truly believed for years that it was wrong (borderline a sin) for me to shave my legs. That's what I was taught—it was a passed down belief. If that's not silly enough for you, I also believed for the longest time that it was wrong for me to wear open-toe shoes because my toes weren't straight. This, too, was advice I received from my sweet momma because her toes looked about as scrunched up as mine! It wasn't bad information, it was just an opinion mixed with tradition and conventional wisdom. It was protocol. As you can see, different strokes for different folks doesn't mean that folks are right or wrong . . . it just means it's a chosen way of living or doing.

Oh, in case you're wondering, Momma and I both let go of the you-can't-do-this baggage. Yes indeed, we shave our legs and wear open-toe shoes whenever we feel like it now, honey!

But there are other, more serious traditions that I've come to realize are broken, too. I was taught in church culture that money is bad and the root of all evil. Believing that and hearing that replay in my heart for years caused me to shrink when it came to deciding what I wanted to be. For a while, I pursued juvenile justice as a career path because it seemed like the *right* thing to do. Even though I came out of the womb setting up lemonade stands, I had been told girls just didn't go into business. I never heard a woman in church, in school, or even on television encourage me to become a CEO. The opposite was true. I was always encouraged to make a difference, to be beautiful, to give back. I was told that money wasn't important. That men were best suited to handle and lead in the area of finances. That money was dangerous, synonymous with being unscrupulous.

However, today, I'm keenly aware that one of my divine gifts is moneymaking. That's a large part of my calling—teaching others how to maximize their divine gifts in the marketplace. It comes as naturally to me as flapping does for a butterfly. As a kid I sold lemonade, not just from a stand, but door to door. When I read the word of God, I don't see a message that encourages us to build the world's dreams as opposed to our God-given ones, nor a call to limit our earning capacity when we serve an unlimited God. Eventually, I started to see the truth about this woman in Proverbs, chapter 31, known simply as The Proverbs 31 Woman. She was a revolutionary, gifted, and globally dominant businesswoman. She also happened to be a mother, wife, and a creative force of nature that reflected how endless potential and possibility lives within. Go figure! The wise man who wrote this part of the book didn't even give her a name. But we know of her works. Would we if she had "stayed in her place" and merely followed convention, protocol, and tradition?

It's the broken beliefs that break our confidence. Confidence is critical to unlocking our true calling.

APPROPRIATENESS: We've talked about the opinions and traditions that lead to broken thinking. The idea of what's "appropriate" is also in this bucket. Let's go back to the babysitting story I shared earlier. I didn't ask for the money I knew I had earned because I was afraid—afraid of coming off as greedy or selfish. I felt like I should take the smaller bill because it wasn't appropriate to ask for more.

As women, we've been shoulded on quite a bit.

We've been told lots of "stuff" about what we should and should not do, about where we belong and what's appropriate for a woman to learn, master, become, and even desire. Most shoulds are passed down as wisdom—but it's really stuff somebody decided about what is appropriate. Others were wounded by rejection, isolation, and failure, and their opinions get passed down to us as advice on how we should navigate *our* lives. Most shoulds, then, are based on little more than fear. The same well-intentioned men and women that taught us to believe in God didn't always know *how* to teach us to truly *trust* God in bold, peculiar, and brazen ways. They had wounds and worries, too. Maybe it seemed easier or wiser for them (and us) to play it safe and call that faith. So now our faith-wiring has been short-circuited by faulty thinking and hidden fears masquerading as solutions.

Not all information about what's appropriate is broken, of course. But it can be tricky to discern the blessed and bad from the broken. Often, we think we're hearing from God, but in reality, opinions, traditions, or ideas of appropriateness are sneaking their way into our heart, mind, and soul. The key to elevating your life is being open to the possibility that some of your steadfast beliefs were built with misinformation, passed-down regret, faulty thinking, or a desire to conform. This is a big deal because what we believe makes us who we are! It sets our personal reality. *Beliefs either expand or limit our horizons.* Our ability to fulfill our purpose begins (or ends), then, with our beliefs. However, *God's truth always trumps tradition.* We just have to be willing to see old things in a new way, and release what God is trying to reinvent.

Right now, I want to invite you to open your heart and allow God to show you The Rules that have been consciously and unconsciously navigating your life. Remember, there is no self-judgment or criticism here. This is simply a chance to let God speak to you and reveal a few false ideas and truths you've internalized and other rules you've now outgrown. Don't overthink it. Pause and just jot down whatever comes to mind—what are the passed-down opinions, traditions, and fears you've adopted that may no longer serve you? Once you identify the belief, pinpoint where it started and then determine whether it belongs in the Blessed, Bad, or Broken bucket.

List Your Rules Below

(It's okay if you need to get another piece of paper!)

Rule	Rule-Maker	Belief Bucket
(Belief)	(Who Wrote It?)	(Blessed, Bad, Broken)

{ RULE BREAKING }

I bet some of the life choices you've made were because you, too, were afraid of truly pursuing your passion and failing. I know some of mine were. And each day I meet women who also pursued a career path because it paid well or just because it was the natural next step based on the major they chose when they were eighteen. They were afraid they would be unable to make a living doing what they truly loved. Maybe they have even forgotten what they once loved. We're taught that getting to *love* what we do is a luxury, not a necessity for a Believer. Broken thinking, my friend.

It's also hard when we see others make what we think are mistakes. We end up vowing to never be like them or do what they did. Sound familiar? Avoiding mistakes isn't necessarily bad, but *preventing* disaster is not the same as *pursuing* destiny. There is a very big difference.

We're not here to live as others think we should.

Though we become masters at it, life is far too short and precious for conformity. We're here to live a life that glorifies God while defying the impossible, and to inspire and invite others to do the same. That's what it means to *live* in God's image.

Instead of letting a bunch of accumulated broken philosophies from grade school, Sunday school, your momma's kitchen, or childhood determine what constitutes a blessed, appropriate, God-touched life, I'd love for you and God to develop your own, unsullied theory. A new level requires fresh thinking. Set religion aside. Take off your culture and disrobe from the conventions and traditions you've learned to wear so well. Purpose can't be written by man! It's not one size fits all.

God wants to break up the ingrained belief system blocking what He is ready to build anew in your life. As a woman thinketh, so *is* she. Thoughts don't just shape our reality, they reveal it. It's Manifestation 101. If we think we can, we do. If we think we can't, we don't. The same God that said *all* things are possible wants His daughters to be *fully* aware of what we think *and* why we think it. The limited thinking of yesterday can't take us into the unlimited realm of tomorrow. Thoughts and beliefs establish who we are, and who we have yet to become.

Purpose and belief go together like seeds and soil. Belief is the soil and purpose grows out of it. God is seeking to water thoughts that are *truly* fruitful so that you can live a faith-bearing life overflowing with multifaceted fulfillment. God needs your participation so He can make room for a new thing to blossom and bloom.

2

Talent
STAGE

Who did I decide to be?

chapter six

STAGE TWO: TALENT

*When you don't have a clear vision,
any vision will do.*

In the Discovery Stage, we were introduced to the rules that govern our behavior. Uncovering your rules, the real captain navigating your life choices, is an ongoing, intentional process of self-awareness. At this point, I hope you are better able to understand why you believe and do the things you do.

Stage two, the Talent Stage, is where success guides our steps and approval paves our path. This is where we turn our beliefs about where we think we belong into choices that set us on a particular path. The Rules have spoken. We have listened. It's best to play it safe and find a hideout called predictability or success. So we pick a lane and that lane becomes our life.

In our discussion of the Discovery Stage we asked, Who did The Rules say you were supposed to be?

In the Talent Stage, we ask, Who did you *decide* to be?

{ BATONS A-KNOCKING }

My parents were wonderful about giving my brother and me opportunities to explore our interests and develop our abilities. I was a cheerleader in elementary school and junior high, and played soccer and softball through junior high. I also picked up the nontraditional sport of baton twirling, as I briefly alluded to earlier. I actually first got into it when I was in day care! These ladies would come by the day care a couple of days a week and teach baton twirling lessons. I love looking at pictures from this time—I had big poofy cotton-candy hair with those infamous lilac Coke-bottle glasses, and would wear a classic eighties white T-shirt with red trim around the collar 'n sleeves along with super-tiny little red shorts. We even had recitals to showcase all that we'd learned.

After I left the day care and enrolled in school, I practiced baton on my own. Then my mom discovered that a lady at the end of our street, Ms. Caffey, taught baton twirling lessons in her garage-turned-dance-studio. After about a year, Ms. Caffey pulled my mom aside and suggested I find another teacher. I was picking up the tricks and combinations really quickly—much faster than the rest of the kids. She couldn't spend the one-on-one time with me to teach me the more complex, higher-level skills. She also suggested we consider me twirling competitively, but it wasn't her area of expertise.

But where exactly does one go to find a competitive baton twirling coach? This sort of thing wasn't really well advertised. Gymnastics and dance—that's pretty easy to find. But twirling not so much.

One day we were in the parking lot of the elementary school I attended. They had a huge covered area in the back of the school where the playgrounds and soccer fields were. But this day, something fascinating was happening. There was a teenage girl there with her mom practicing baton twirling. She was amazing. The best I'd ever seen. She'd throw her baton in the air, spin around four or even five times, and catch it under her leg . . . or behind her back! She could juggle two and three batons at the same time as well, and she incorporated dance and acrobatics. I was absolutely mesmerized. My mom and I got out of the car and just watched from the parking lot. We watched her the next few weekends, and then my mom asked whether she would be willing to coach me. She actually said yes!

Her name was Kathy Gilbert and she was about fifteen years old. Get this . . . She lived on my street, too! Her house was at the opposite end of the block from Ms. Caffey. I had never seen her outside playing. Now I knew why—she was always practicing. Her house was filled with trophies . . . They took up the entire living room and entry hall of their home, and many were taller than me! I wanted to be like her. I wanted to keep getting better so I could win some trophies like those, too. However, one day Kathy *also* said it would be best if I started working with a more advanced coach . . . her coach. And, that's how I *almost* met Janice Jackson.

I say almost because you didn't just automatically get to work with Janice Jackson. You had to audition. She didn't teach fundamentals—you had to be competition ready. So I "tried out" with Susan, who was a twirling and dance instructor at Janice's internationally renowned Dal-Star Studio. She had been on one of Janice's world champion teams when she was my age—I noticed her in the team portraits hanging next to the massive international trophies in the studio lobby every time I walked in. I would be in very good hands. They made champions here.

The studio accepted me as a student, but I would have to master more fundamentals, my technique, my skills set, *and* my dance abilities before I could take private lessons. I worked hard. I'm thankful for Susan and how patient she was in getting me ready to move on up. When I started training with Janice, my life, even as a young teenager, went to a whole different level.

Twirling competitively gave me an escape from the low expectations of my schoolteachers. I was surrounded by people who actually believed in my potential. Other than with my parents, I'd never really experienced that before. And although there wasn't much ethnic diversity in the sport—I don't remember seeing very many black girls—Janice and her staff never once treated me like I was different. That, too, was a first. That studio was like a church for me. It was a place where possibility and hard work intersected to ignite new horizons. I kept competing and eventually started winning. The more I practiced, the better my results, and the more trophies I won. My confidence grew. Finally, it was nice to be known for my triumphs and not for my troubles.

Twirling eventually led me into the world of pageants. Someone gave me an application for one while I was at a twirling competition and explained that twirling could be my talent. Twirling competitions also have a pageantry element already intertwined—complete with gowns and interviews—so I was used to that. I gave it try. I don't think I even placed in my first pageant, but I kept going. I had gotten a taste of what it was like to win, and I wanted to see how far I could go.

⌈ THAT TIME PURPOSE TRIED TO SPEAK UP ⌉

I eventually won a few preteen pageants here and there. Pageants get a bad rap, but learning how to carry yourself on stage, communicate with confidence and charisma, and perfect and perform a talent is no small undertaking. I enjoyed competition, but what I really loved was the opportunity to make a difference in the lives of others. As a title-holder (that's what they call you when you win a crown), I was able to travel to different schools, conferences, fairs, nursing homes, rodeos (yes you heard that right), hospitals—every kind of event you can imagine. When I visited elementary schools and day care centers, I'd read a short story from an illustrated children's book about the importance of having confidence and a positive attitude. There is nothing more adorable and exciting than seeing a room full of kindergartners hanging on your every word. (And, by the way, nothing more disappointing than having to tell 'em that, no, those aren't real diamonds in the crown . . .)

When I turned thirteen, a dear Italian woman named Benna helped me get ready for the Miss Teen Texas competition. She had been around pageants longer than I had been alive, and she was the woman who first taught me how to *properly* Texas-tease my hair. I was in a salon chair when Benna explained I needed to choose an official platform for the competition. A "platform" is basically an issue or cause you are passionate about championing as a part of your service to the community. I *immediately* knew what I wanted to concentrate my advocacy efforts on.

"I'd like to focus on building self-esteem!"

Benna looked concerned. A little wrinkle formed in her forehead as she said, "That's not a real platform, honey. Self-esteem is nice and important, but it's not a *real* social issue. You need to pick a cause that has more meat to it. Something like cancer, AIDS, adoption, or crime."

I listened to her, politely nodded, and soaked up her advice like a sponge. I always appreciated when adults were willing to shoot straight and share wisdom with me. It's better than being brushed off, and I'm just wired to learn. She went on to explain that "fluffy" topics like self-esteem weren't taken very seriously.

Now—I didn't know exactly *why* I wanted to focus on building self-esteem. I just knew. I wrestled with self-doubt—largely due to feeling left out and overlooked at school. Believing in yourself was the topic of the children's books I instinctively picked out and read when speaking at elementary schools. And this is what the books I picked out for myself were about. Odd, I know, for a teenager to be reading self-help and personal development books, but I did.

Inside, I took a deep sigh. You know—the one when you're thinking, *Where do I go from here?* I loved sharing the power of positive thinking with audiences. I had come up with all of these activities for kids and had figured out how to adjust my talk for adult audiences, too. I would have to really think about what else would work that would also tap into my passion. It took me another year or so to figure it out.

My focus came together as I started getting involved as a volunteer and student leader with youth violence, crime, and drug prevention initiatives while in high school. The first big project I worked on was a campaign with the State Bar of Texas called "Stop the Violence." I remember it well. Thankfully, I didn't have to deal with the fear of dodging bullets and gang warfare every day. I grew up in a beautiful neighborhood in the suburbs of Dallas. But, for some reason, I was drawn to help others whose circumstances were dramatically different than mine. I had this deep appreciation for the blessings I did have, and felt compelled to do what I could for other young people who didn't have the same opportunities as me.

So youth crime prevention through leadership development became my platform. I knew better than to use self-esteem in the title, so I ended up incorporating the phrase "leadership development" instead. That one seemed to work! I had found the right words and the right lane—one impressive enough and therefore good enough.

❴ WHAT *IS* THE RIGHT LANE? ❵

The right lane is the *paved* path. It is the acceptable, *right way* of doing things, and going down it leads to an approved life. One that is socially desirable, stable, and viewed as successful. The right lane has an insanely strong pull, so strong that it's the path most people—not just women—travel. After all, it's easier and less intimidating to walk down a road that's *already* been paved . . . especially in high heels. And because well-meaning friends, family, and mentors who want the best for us don't want us wandering off on a dark road all alone, they steer us as best they can onto what seems like the best or "right" way . . . the path least likely to cause us pain . . . even if it's crowded.

That's what Miss Benna was trying to do in steering me toward a "proper" platform. She wanted me to have the best chance of winning, and helped me find the most predictable path that would get me there.

This is not necessarily a bad thing. But the Talent Stage is where we're taught how to pick and stick to a lane. We choose who we're going to be and what we'll work toward becoming.

The question is, are we equipped to pick a path aligned with our destiny? It's hard to pick a path you don't even know exists, and it's incredibly unlikely that you'll pick a path you don't believe you belong in or deserve.

❧{ SETTLING VERSUS MATURING }❧

The decision to choose the "right" lane at fourteen years old later turned out to be an incredibly influential choice. It shaped the focus of my life, my decisions, my schooling, my goals, my time, and my spirit for the next eleven years. I went *all* in. I spoke about youth empowerment and investing in young people, sometimes sixty to seventy times *a year*. I ended up majoring in political science and criminal justice, and then went to law school with the intention of becoming a juvenile court judge, and one day Attorney General of the United States. Being an advocate no longer had anything to do with pageants. That's what got me in the game, so to speak, but it was passion and conviction that kept me in it for over a decade. I cofounded a federally funded organization called the National Youth Network at sixteen, and went on to spend much of my time lobbying legislators, speaking at Department of Justice conferences, and organizing youth empowerment events in conjunction with local police departments around the country.

Then Governor (later President) George W. Bush appointed me to the Texas State Advisory Group at the age of nineteen, to consult on juvenile crime issues, and the US Justice Department's Office of Juvenile Justice and Delinquency Prevention later blessed me with the Strengthening the Voice of Youth Across America Award. All this time, I was still training as a competitive baton twirler, going to school, getting straight A's, and applying for and winning awards and scholarships, all while making seventy-plus motivational speeches a year.

Why am I telling you this? I often think back to that salon chair moment. What would have happened if I had just stood firm in my desire to choose self-esteem as my platform? Would I have racked up frequent flyer miles in my teens? Would I have traveled the world and fast-tracked my leadership acumen at such a young age? Would I have met and worked with the then US attorney general, the late Janet Reno, and other world leaders? Would my poli-sci and criminal justice major in college have been different, and would I have even gone to law school?

I don't know. I'll never know for sure.

This I do know for sure: *purpose made itself known very early.*

The desire to focus on self-esteem back then foreshadowed my commitment to encourage you to believe bigger now. It started with that first lightning bolt moment where I vowed to be a belief-elevating teacher. My point is that it's who I've always been. Even if we don't always see or understand God's hand in the moment, or miss the clues about how He's prewired us to impact others, divine providence is always working. God clearly planned for me to become a baton twirler. He didn't just plan it—He put me smack in the center of it. I was literally surrounded by it—not just at the day care, but my first two coaches lived on opposite ends of the *same* street where I'd grown up. How crazy is it that these two women lived just a few feet away? They had been there all along—well before I was born and before my parents picked our yellow brick home. Think about how God has prewired you, your personality and your natural interests, too.

God most certainly placed early purpose clues and destiny-developers in your life, too. Can you think about what they were and what impact they had on you?

To be clear, my life purpose was not baton twirling. That's a skill. I happened to be more natural or gifted at it than most. However, *purpose is more about your personality and about how you show up in a way that improves the lives of others.* It's about your natural impact. And, as you'll discover, *purpose is also about a larger message your life is meant to convey.* However, baton twirling was a maturity mechanism and skill builder on *The Path* to higher purpose for me. It certainly gave me discipline and dedication.

God knows exactly what He is doing and places us in certain environments for a reason. I didn't always understand the lack of diversity in my neighborhood or at my school, but perhaps God wanted me to develop resilience, self-motivation, and drive. And maybe he put me right where I needed to be to uncover a hidden talent. I had no idea when I picked up that baton in day care that being able to twirl would take me fifteen years later to the Miss America competition, winning talent, interview, and $80,000 in scholarships. That faith journey is another story for another day.

We must remember that all things work for good when we're called according to (aka, fulfilling) God's purpose (Romans 8:28).

In hindsight, I have absolutely no regrets about following Benna's advice. I have every confidence the path I took was indeed one God intended for me to travel, because His fingerprints are all over doors only He could have opened. For a young brown girl living in the South, labeled a problem child, the granddaughter of housekeepers and the descendant of sharecroppers, to have ended up where I was—yes. God was all up in it.

And yet, this was my first experience of trading passion for approval. It's the first time I can recall that I picked what society and the powers that be told me would be the "right" lane. It was a mixed bag. Nothing to be ashamed of, but more so something to be aware of. Much of activating our true calling is about awareness anyway.

The key takeaway here is that purpose showed itself early in my life. It had been there all along. The topic of thinking bigger, growing confidence, and believing in yourself flows through my veins. It always has. Even though I didn't know it, self-esteem building was *always* my mission. *We can't change who we are.* We can hide out, but our divine purpose and natural inclination to impact others is always with us.

We can't pick it—God places it in us and it manifests unconsciously. During those early years of doing juvenile advocacy work, I was really helping young people find their core of possibility, positivity, and self-esteem, and encouraging them to believe beyond their circumstances. Back then, I was doing it by speaking to kids in gangs and juvenile prisons. Now I'm blessed to speak in front of millions. It's the same message, just in a different format.

The same holds true for you. Your ultimate mission, your purpose . . . your thing. It has always been there, too. Natural purpose isn't something we have to work hard for; it just flows. We can't help it, but over time, we can learn to harness it.

> *The obstacles you've faced are really about the obstacles you're assigned to.*

Looking back, I'd say God (and maybe Miss Benna) knew that those kids needed my message the most back then, and that was why it was channeled in that way. But my purpose was always there.

What about you?

What purpose clues showed up in and around you?

The best way to look for clues about this is by going back in time.

Think for a moment about the early, pure dreams and desires you had as a kid. The stuff you wanted to do before others told you who you needed to be or to focus on something more practical, stable, and acceptable. Was it singing? Was it drawing or dance? Was it being an astronaut? A fighter pilot? Sewing? Designing? Playing an instrument? A TV host, an engineer, or the best mother on the planet? What was it?

God places early desires in us that most reflect His desires for us. Those desires know no limitations until someone talks us out of pursuing them.

What is something you've always naturally done?

Is it encouraging others? It is strategizing? Creating or crafting?

Is it organizing, mentoring, coaching, or teaching?

Conversely—what is something you always wanted to do but never had a chance or the courage to do or explore? What problems did you want to solve? What difference have you always wanted to make? Why do you think that initial desire was there?

Just take a moment and do an inner assessment of things you've always done, things you've always loved, and things that have always come naturally to you. Also think about things you didn't do or ideas or interests The Rules talked you out of pursuing.

This exercise isn't about nostalgia or rehashing a painful season of life. It's certainly not about blame or regret. That comes from *little me.* Refuse to allow stinking thinking to hijack this moment. Reflection is an invitation. Remember, *God speaks to us from the future to invite us into untapped promise and provision.* It's about hearing God's whisper for what He wants you to know about His master plan for you *now.*

I know without a doubt that purpose has often raised her voice and made appearances in your life, too.

chapter seven

MASQUERADING AND MOUNTAIN CLIMBING

{ THURSDAY NIGHTS }

I picked my career path early. I was sitting in front of a two-hundred-pound box waffle-wrapped in yellow wicker, with a screen tough enough to withstand karate kicks and flying soccer balls. We called it a television, but it was more like an elephant with knobs. It was bigger than me, and probably heavier than me, my brother, and my momma combined. But right now it had my full attention. Thursday night was when the entire family gathered 'round to watch *The Cosby Show*.

As you know, I grew up in a predominantly white neighborhood and went to what was essentially an all-white school. When I picked up a magazine or turned on the yellow elephant, every woman I saw in television commercials was also white. When I did see someone who looked like me on television, a woman who God had also chosen to wrap in brown skin, she was always serving someone who didn't have brown skin or she was struggling. But not on Thursday nights.

On Thursday nights, I saw teenagers that looked like me and my brother. I saw the only woman who was half as beautiful as my mother. Clair Huxtable. She was a lawyer married to a doctor, and she was the epitome of a supermom. She had a successful career, a thriving family, a beautiful house, a charming yet no-nonsense personality, and a husband who drooled over her. And her brown skin looked just like mine!

During one episode in particular, I watched her walk through the front door of their expensive brownstone in New York City with poise and a briefcase in tow. Her hair was perfectly layered, and somehow, at the end of a very long workday, she looked happy and refreshed . . . fully ready to shift from superwoman to supermom. That's when I decided who I would become. I would become a lawyer, too. I had never seen or even heard of a black female attorney. I didn't actually meet one until I was nearly twenty-one. But Mrs. Huxtable looked important, polished, and admired. I knew then that I, too, wanted to be seen, significant, and successful.

Thursday nights gave me something to look forward to. That show gave me a chance to dream, and I took it. Seeing Mrs. Huxtable, I didn't want to be the problem child anymore. Now I knew what I wanted to be. I just needed someone who would give me a push to become it.

{ DESKTOP WHACKS 'N SMACKS }

Let's back up just a few years. Yes, we're going back to elementary school one more time. In the fifth grade, Mr. Eger was my homeroom teacher. He was a tall, slender man, with dark brown hair and a pointy nose, very funny . . . fair but also no-nonsense. He walked around the classroom with a yardstick and would smack it on your desk if you were talking or not following class rules. However, on this day, I didn't even get the pleasure of a desktop smack. I probably had said something smart-alecky in front of the class and pushed his buttons— I don't remember what. But his faced turned redder than I thought humanly possible, and he told me to meet him in the hallway.

"Why do you act like this?" he said. "You can be so much more than you think you can. You just have to start believing you can."

And there it was. My sign. A big *aha*! That lightning bolt moment. This was the first time in my life that I could recall someone other than my parents specifically telling me *I mattered*. That *I* had a worthy future and opportunities beyond my past and present experiences. And it was a schoolteacher at that!

Coach Janice, Miss Benna, and Clair Huxtable—they inspired me, but they didn't know problem-child me. Mr. Eger did, but he didn't seem to look down on me like the other teachers. He had transferred in just a few months prior and this was his first year at the school. I will never forget that hallway moment of awakening. It was as if someone splashed cold water on my face, waking me from a trance. It shook my spirit and my size 6 shoes to the core. I was used to seeing angry adults glare at me with disdain. However, as I looked at Mr. Eger, I only saw the eyes of love and of God looking back at me.

❧ SUCCESS CONDITIONING ❧

That hallway chat was more than just a chat. It was a *catalyst conversation. This* is when I started working hard in school. I was gonna show those know-it-all adults who said I needed to be in special education classes. I went from having good grades to having great grades. I started winning academic awards and then started excelling in both school and leadership activities.

When I brought home my report card, it no longer had problems listed, only praise. My dad would give $20 for each A and $10 for each B. He was the first person to invest in me! So now I had a double incentive to stay focused, get better, and succeed—a good showing would mean either applause or a sweet payday! Eventually, I became hooked. I'd finally found a way to fit in. I'd found a reason to be liked. And I'd found a path that would at least give me a shot to prove I was worthy—that *I mattered* and had something to offer.

I was smitten with success. Achievement became my drug, and it was the type of habit everyone around me encouraged me to continue. People *love* to be around achievement. So, just as I was saying goodbye to low self-esteem, my battle with success addiction began. I became an overachiever and a $200,000 scholarship-getter who lived on the honor roll. I graduated college *magna cum laude* and went to one of the best law schools in the world. I was a long way from being the problem child now. And I liked it that way. Actually, I *loved* it that way. Voted "Most Likely to Succeed" in high school (*take that, haters!*), I was on my way to becoming a high-powered lawyer, a real-life Clair Huxtable who was getting to make a real difference in the lives of young people who were less fortunate than me.

Helping others became my obsession. There is sometimes a thin line between service and success. My passion was sincere, but it was also another form of accomplishing and striving. In retrospect, I see that everything I did was obsessive. In truth, I was just scared to death of failure, rejection, and being invisible.

Inspired by Clair Huxtable and one teacher's comments, I had picked my lane—success by any means necessary. So tell me . . .

What's your lane?
Do you remember when you picked it?

⸙ LANES, DRUGS, AND MOUNTAINS . . . ⸙ OH MY!

Once an addict, always an addict. Well that's what they say. I kinda know what they mean. Over time God helped to wean me off the achievement drug and the *need* to feel important, but the urge never really goes away. Keep in mind I have had Christ at the center of my life since I was a toddler. Believing in God and loving God doesn't automatically mean that your life is perfect. Don't let others sell you that bag of lies.

Spiritual growth comes from perspective.

As an adult, I can see now that much of what I did was in response to me clinging to The Rules and running from the *little me* whispers of insignificance and self-doubt. I'm not sure I wanted to be successful . . . I just didn't want to be alone. I certainly didn't want to be invisible. *My* escape was achievement. I mastered the art of looking impressive. I figured out how to get people to like me, pay attention to me, and applaud me. I never used drugs—that would have been against The Rules—but achievement was just as addictive. Today in my life work as a mentor, strategist, and spiritual teacher, I find that every woman on the planet has a drug. That includes you, sweet friend. The question is, what's *your* drug of choice?

Your drug is something you've come to cling to. We all have an addiction to something . . . an underlying need to showcase and validate our worth, to be needed, and to prove our relevance. None of us as women are exempt. You may not be willing to admit it just yet, that's okay. I didn't like being called an addict either. It's cool. Just stay with me.

Most women I know tend to strive and define themselves in one of five areas. I call them the 5 Success Mountains—not to be confused with the five stages of reinvention we're unpacking. Each "mountain" simply represents a goal, responsibility, or lane that we choose to live in that gives us meaning, focus, and a sense of identity. Understanding what type of mountain climber you've been and what hidden addiction has led you up it (what you're really running from) is key to discovering where God is trying to lead you next.

Mountain #1: Marriage. The Marriage Mountain is one that we're taught to climb as little girls adorned with dolls and fairy tales. We're programmed to search for Prince Charming. Being pretty becomes a priority, and we soon learn that's also who and what Prince Charming wants. On the Marriage Mountain, we find our identity and sufficiency in being a wife and having what we believe to be a successful marriage that others admire and want to emulate.

Mountain #2: Motherhood. The Motherhood Mountain is where our identity is attached to our children. Even if you don't have children, you might believe that part of fulfilling your calling as a woman means having children and being celebrated for it. Oh, how addicting this one is! I loved being a bonus mom. It was something I'd always wanted . . . so badly that it created blind spots that kept me from seeing that infidelity was all around me.

Mountain #3: Money. The Money Mountain is defined by work, career, and building a professional legacy. On this mountain, we find our value and worth in our work, the titles we earn, the checks we make, the suits we wear, the office we hold, the awards we win, the perceived impact we have, and how impressive we look.

Mountain #4: Mending. The Mending Mountain is tied to our inner Miss Fixer. It's the reason we end up trying to be all things to all people. We find validation in being able to help others solve their problems, being reliable and dependable, and sacrificing ourselves for the sake of saving others. It feels good to come to the rescue, and to be a perceived master at holding it all together. It makes us *feel* useful, needed, and relevant.

Mountain #5: Making a Difference. Giving is godly, but when our core identity gets defined by the act of serving and sacrificing, giving is no different than greed. Though our efforts seem noble, truly we want something in exchange. We want praise. We want validation. Underneath the service there is ultimately a burning desire to satisfy a void by *being seen* as a servant.

You may identify with one mountain in particular, or maybe more than one. I have always gravitated toward the Money, Mending, and Making a Difference mountains, in that order. Those tend to give me my fix. I was often not really sure that I'd have what it took to be a mother or to be selected as a wife, so I inclined toward the ones that I could control . . . the ones that didn't rely upon other people. Hey—it does feel good to *feel* like you can fix folks! We just have to be conscious of the temptation to try to "be" something for ourselves or for others that really is just our addiction in action—an attempt to feel important . . . and worthy.

Which mountain do you most gravitate to? How has it defined you or even confined you?

As women, we don't just want to be *on* the mountain, we want to look like we've *mastered* it. So we keep climbing, fitting in, and doing whatever it takes to get to the top. That's what happens in the Talent Stage—*you become good at what you do until what you do eventually defines who you are.*

But look. The mountains aren't the problem; it's how we climb them. Success isn't solely about accolades. It's about appearances, how we want to come across to others, and it's about whatever we believe validates our identity.

The things that we're climbing toward on those mountains often have very little to do with our anointing and master purpose, but we're too focused on our goal to see it. If you think you're a struggling artist, and God is telling you that you're a wealthy engineer . . . that's going to seem crazy. If you think you're "just a mom," you might miss that God is calling you to be a media mogul, an international speaker, a creative entrepreneur, or a multimillionaire. You end up ignoring the call, the signs, and God's will for your life.

We can miss who we're called to be because we're addicted and attached to who we've decided to be.

When the bigger vision doesn't make sense, we tend to look the other way. Don't get me wrong. Each mountain is a divine gift, and God *loves* to give us the desires of our heart. In fact, I believe each mountain represents a desire God placed in us for a reason. Mountains give us an opportunity to impact others, develop our potential, and find our way. There is tremendous purpose in each lane, but each still has its limits.

Limit #1: First of all, attaining success on any of the five mountaintops is contingent on other people. I don't believe that God intends for our core identity to be attached to or predicated on anyone else but God. Look at Mary. She's known for motherhood, the Immaculate Conception, and giving birth to Christ. But, in essence, she was really just a woman on an intimate faith journey with God where the two of them conspired to do the unthinkable and birth the impossible. That's who Mary was. That's who Mary is. A faith-walker . . . and unleasher.

Limit #2: Second, what do you do when disruption strikes— when the marriage fails, the kids grow up, the job (or paycheck) ends, your advice is no longer needed, or those you serve take you for granted? If Mary's whole life was *only* about being a vessel for the birth of Christ, which was her mission, what was she to do when Christ grew up? Did her life cease to matter? Was it time for her to retire and live the rest of her life going down memory lane? Absolutely not.

God calls us to reinvention, not retirement.

Being a mother and a wife is a blessing and a divine opportunity, but if you don't get married and don't have children, you *still* have an incredible core purpose that is larger than any one title. Being able to help others improve their lives, to serve, and to do work that matters or earns a living is also a blessing; however, it may have nothing to do with where God needs you next.

Most of us suffer from what I called *RVSD—Random Vision Selection Disorder.* We don't necessarily pick our path because it's what we're called to do, but because it was available, attainable, and seeable. *When you don't have a clear vision, any vision will do.* So we pick a lane and make it our life based on one of the following reasons:

+ **Proficiency:** *We're good at it*

+ **Passion:** *We love it*

+ **Praise:** *We're celebrated for it*

+ **Pay:** *We can make a living at it*

+ **Pressure:** *We had to do it*

+ **Protocol:** *We're supposed to do it*

That's all good. But . . .

Notice that very few of us picked our present path because of *purpose*—what we were called by God to do. We don't know how.

❦ DEVELOPMENT VERSUS DESTINATION ❦

Ultimately, *your talents are the sum total of what you've learned to do via exposure, training, and practice.* They are those skills and abilities that with time, training, and practice you turn into proficiencies. Naturally, there are some things you do better than others, and so often the things we've focused on the most become the talents that define the scope of our beliefs and dreams. We not only bypass our purpose, we never see it coming.

The Talent Stage—where we master a path, develop a proficiency, and adopt a chosen identity—is a necessary part of our divine development, but *it's not the final destination.* Sure, our talents are areas of strength, and strengths make us *feel* safe, capable, competent (which we love, right?), and secure. But your talents are not the final destination.

God is not confined by your career or your choices, but He is *obsessed* with ushering you into your calling. Most women (and men) live their entire life in the Talent Stage. They retire here and die here. Let's not be counted in *that* number. Let's not leave behind untapped potential and untapped purpose. Purpose goes beyond a career path . . . it goes wherever God flows. That's where and who we want to be. Wherever God is.

The Talent Stage can be comfortable. It's where you do what you're good at. In this stage of my life, I went all the way from lilac Coke-bottle glasses to the Miss America stage, one of the top law firms in the world, to appearing regularly on television, and starting my own professional sports agency. But the drug of success is dangerous, too. When you're caught up in whatever you've chosen to do, there's rarely quiet. There's rarely time to think about what you're doing. *Noise feels natural.* Silence can be frightening, and it's intimidating, but that's when you ask yourself, *Who am I* really? *Who do I* want *to be?*

Who is the woman that I will no longer allow myself to be?

Hmmmm. When you start to ask these questions, that's when you start to move beyond the Talent Stage.

The Talent Stage is supposed to be merely a season of your life, not the whole shebang. If we're really serious about following God and discovering the unlived life Heaven has for us, then we've gotta become comfortable with disruption, with letting God take us beyond predictability and titles that can become idols, to a place where we enter our purpose and assignment.

Change is God's specialty, and interruption is God's area of mastery.

Before you move on, though, it *is* valuable and helpful to purposefully uncover and take stock of your talents—your skills, abilities, achievements, and what you're good at. So . . .

What are your talents?

What have you learned to do really well?

What impact have you made at home, in your community, in the lives of others, and/or in your career 'n journey thus far?

And what are the things you enjoy doing?

Don't be shy. God wants us to look at our talents with a healthy sense of accomplishment and gratification—just as God looked proudly upon His work after creating the world. However:

Our true identity is attached to God's divinity, not activity.

The Talent Stage can be dangerously *task*-driven, urging us to contribute to society in a useful and socially productive way. Talents may be our beginning, but they are not supposed to be our ending. As we will soon discover, *gifts*, on the other hand, guide us into a dimension far greater than where talent can ever take us. Gifts are not task-driven, they are *testimony*-driven, designed to unleash the glory and goodness of God in us, through us, and around us.

So, my beautiful friend, here's the conclusion; here's what I (a recovering success addict) now believe in my heart of hearts to be undeniably true: the skillfully manufactured faux-significance we've found through goal-slaying, mountain-climbing, and identity-creating can never satisfy us or fully glorify God.

For that, we need to allow God to lead us out of the Talent Stage and into what I like to call *The GAP*. Tapping into the God-made, purpose-soaked future awaiting you is the only *real* path to fulfillment. So let's enter it. Shall we?

3

The GAP
STAGE

What is happening to me?

chapter eight

STAGE THREE:
THE GAP

{ EMBRACING IN-BETWEEN }

The big mission inside of you is seeking expression. When God calls you to something that is not on your radar, embrace it.

As you now know, the purpose journey begins in the Discovery Stage, where we are bathed in The Rules, and later we make decisions about what kind of life we're going to pursue in the Talent Stage. But after a while, many of us start feeling uncomfortable there. Our inner rebel gets tired of the old, bored with the predictable, unsatisfied with the superficial, and ready to relinquish our identity addictions. That's when the really good (and scary) stuff begins. When we're done, God gets started. Heaven unleashes its Holy arsenal and uses everything at its disposal to move us from our Comfort Zone into the Growth Zone—or is it a war zone? Probably both. *Little me* isn't going to let your higher purpose unfold without a fight.

As comfortable, familiar, and maybe even exhausting as the Discovery and Talent stages are, they can't compare with the more fulfilling life that awaits. But what *is* that exactly? We feel something greater in the future calling to us. It tugs at our soul and agitates our spirit. But we can't quite see the bigger picture . . . and, we're not 100 percent sure we want to either.

What was once stable is now shaky. People you trusted are now letting you down . . . deeply. Your job suddenly ends. Your kids go off to college. You lose a loved one, or something unexpected intrudes upon your plans and dreams. Your life somehow gets flipped upside down. You ask . . . *Who am I now and why am I feeling this way? Where did these tears and this newfound fear come from? Why is everything changing around me . . . everything I worked so hard to establish? What does all this mean? What do I do now, and where in the heck am I going?*

What. Is. Happening. To. Me?

God must be trying to get your attention. And now you find yourself in a peculiar place. A wilderness and place of transition. A place in-between where you've been and who you're called to be. That place is probably extremely uncomfortable, because you're no longer in control. Welcome to stage three of the Purpose Map. Welcome to *The GAP.*

❧ THE GAP ❧

I don't like change. I never have. I love predictability and I love a good plan to follow. Give me a checklist and a strategy, and I'll give you results that'll wow you. I doubt I'm the only one who wrestles with God for the steering wheel. I want Him to drive, but I still secretly wanna know what He's doing, where He's going, and how He plans on us getting there!

But then disruption comes in and changes everything. It disturbs our attachment to predictability and anything that has too much of our heart and attention. God is actually trying to get us to shift. Here is why.

God won't bless where you no longer belong.

It's the principle of *here versus there*. God can't bless you *here* with what He has for you *there*. If He gave you your *there* blessing, you'd never move from *here*. You'd stay. So sometimes the reason God seems like He isn't answering your prayers is that the provision doesn't fit with where you are.

God isn't being mean. He is being a parent. You never learn how to walk unless you take forward steps. If you're always carried, or if everything comes to you, then you never find your legs. You never learn what it takes to get up from where you are to get to where you could and should be.

God isn't holding a blessing hostage, He has just put it *there*—smack in the center of the place He wants to get you to. However, the place in-between your here and there is The GAP.

It's that obscure place of transition. It's when you know it's time to leave where you've been, but you're not completely sure where you're going.

Sometimes we *choose* to enter The GAP. Desire leads us to do something new and different. Sometimes we get *frustrated* into it. We can no longer stand our circumstances and we just know it's time for a change. And other times we get *split-rocked* into it.

But this in-between place of uncertainty isn't supposed to be permanent. And it's not supposed to be punishment, although it can seem like it. Being in The GAP is like moving from the womb to the birth canal. At a certain point, the womb gets too small and it's time to move on. You can't stay in the incubator forever. But the canal is tight, dark, and uncomfortable. You're being pushed, pulled, squeezed, and poked all at the same time. Naturally you wonder why in the world your mother is doing this to you. Everything was going just fine before! But this transition is necessary for your new season to begin. New experiences. New possibilities. Ample room for growth. The danger is staying where you've been. It stunts your growth and limits your future. If you stay, the womb becomes a tomb.

The best is on the other side of birth.

There is a reason babies comes out crying. They're mad! They've not known anything other than the comfortable warmth of the womb. The unfamiliar is almost always unwanted . . . at least initially. And there is nothing sexy about birthing. Even deliveries without the intense pain aren't pretty—beautiful but not pretty. It's messy. Most things that matter are.

But this is how the shift into higher purpose and a season of calling happens in our lives, and it might be what is happening to you now. You're being evicted from *here* and relocated to *there*. And just because a life shift is messy, that doesn't mean it's not majestic, too.

⊰ WHY ARE YOU IN THE GAP? ⊱

If you're in The GAP, it means you have outgrown your Comfort Zone. It doesn't mean there is anything wrong with where you've been. You may have been very successful there. But we're not interested in mere success; we want a life soaked in significance. You may have been sensing that it's time for change, though you may have been ignoring, delaying, procrastinating, or avoiding it. Maybe you haven't been able to decipher what the change should be. Or maybe you've been too busy to focus on it . . . to listen . . . to surrender . . . to make room for more.

You're not and never will be invisible to God. You're necessary for His master plan.

What are you hiding from exactly?
Your calling.
Your *true* calling.
Your higher purpose.
The GAP is God's way of moving you from your Comfort Zone into your purpose.

It's time to find your voice. It's time to discover your new possibilities, resurrect dormant dreams, and step into a new season of impact, influence, leadership, giving, love, and service.

First, you'll have to unload a few of the beliefs, people, and attachments you've been holding on to. This won't be easy. So take a deep breath. Now take another if you need it.

You're in The GAP because you're somehow unsatisfied with where you've been. Not necessarily unhappy, but you're *hungry* for more. You are no longer content with where you've been and what you've accomplished. And, God needs you in new place.

Let me pause to say that discontent, too, is a mixed bag. If we're unsatisfied because we're *never* satisfied, then that's a different thing. That's chasing after the wind—a search for meaning found in doing. As a seasoned striver and achiever, I know that breed of discontentment very well. It's rooted in trying to *prove* worth and significance. *Embracing* significance, however, is very different. It's surrendering to truth. The truth is you are *already* fearfully and wonderfully made—beautifully complex, permanently loved by God, and necessary to Him and therefore humanity. There is nothing for you to prove.

Disruption comes to replace discontent with destiny—to draw us into a deeper dimension of living, giving, and flowing.

There is, however, something bigger for you to unleash. When destiny begins to brew and bubble in your belly, it's time to get ready for a new kind of delivery. That's a healthy discontent; the sign of a healthy, supernatural pregnancy.

I know many of us have been told that only some people are called to lead, and that the rest of us need to grow where we're planted.

Not so. While it's true that grounding yourself is key for development, the question is, *what are you being developed for?* I mean . . . why grow your faith anyway? *Are we supposed to be trees planted in one place? Or are we supposed to be fishers of men like Christ? To get out of the boat?* The GAP is about finding the courage to take that step. After all, we're more like eggs than seeds. Both grow, but only one can move. The only way to move into your purpose is to travel through The GAP.

The GAP is also about gaining an appreciation for your gifts and your voice—learning to tap into the good stuff God gave you and to actually start flowing in it . . . not just having drive-by experiences with your God-giftings. The GAP is like a classroom that teaches you to live at a higher level and in a higher frequency . . . one capable of attracting what you need and accelerating who you truly are. On the other side of The GAP, you'll learn to activate your voice, gifts, and influence, but this time is about paying attention, unlearning, and discerning what new season God is calling you to enter. *Purpose always leaves clues.* But for now, understand that there is a destination. A *there* awaits.

Being in The GAP can be scary, because you're not in control. When things outside of your control start happening, God is reminding you who is really in control. You can't keep clinging to the stuff that's been keeping you *here*. So, if you won't just go *there* . . . then God has to start emptying out and stripping down your *here*. Cue the split-rocking, quaking, and life-shaking.

Warning. Regret, resentment, shame, and self-doubt will certainly sprout. *Little me* will lure you into blaming yourself for events that have been happening around you . . . the things you feel you've lost or just messed up. Remember that God did not bring you to this point only for you to live under the weight of past regret, shame, self-doubt, and blame. Blaming yourself is only going to prolong your stay in The GAP and cause you to miss the new opportunities God has coming to you. Stinking thinking is a trap.

God doesn't live in the past. Regret does, but not God. So let's leave regret behind, too.

God has already planned a future bigger than your past decisions.

This growth stage is also about realignment. Alignment with God is necessary for our divine assignment. The GAP gives us a chance to get an overdue adjustment while God brings all the skewed parts of our life into proper, powerful, and purpose-ready order. Think of it like going to the chiropractor—it's about getting everything working the way it's supposed to.

Higher purpose is always on the other side of a process.

God sends his promise by way of a process, which is why we miss it! We think it is going to fall out of the sky like manna from Heaven, but The GAP is where we must *go* to enter it . . . our purpose, more provision, more healing, and even more miracles. It's all on the other side of process. *This* is what comes after your split-rock moment. The GAP is your wilderness between Egypt (what you've known) and the Promised Land (what you've been praying for and are destined for).

What we're moving toward is not necessarily a bigger house, more money, less stress, or better relationships . . . although I have no doubt that *everything* is better on the other side of surrender. God doesn't leave our heart's desires behind as He ushers us into our destiny. But a shift isn't about stuff. It's about exchanging your current plans for the life God is calling you toward. And, it's about getting where God needs you to be in order to accomplish something new that Heaven is seeking to do. It's a great question to ask: *God, what is the new thing you are leading me to?*

The Word says God's yoke is *easy* and his burden is *light*. That sounds like a new and *better* life to me.

I'll share how I found myself in The GAP. Hopefully, it will make you feel more at ease about what God is doing in your life, how he tends to do it, and how he specifically uses life circumstances as an interactive classroom preparing us for a larger mission.

❧ THE SHIFT BEFORE THE SHIFT ❧

While infidelity was certainly my awakening, it wasn't actually the beginning of my time in The GAP. It was really more in the middle. It was what awakened me to a shift already in progress.

I knew well before that curbside chat with God that my life was not my own. I didn't know how I'd gotten *here*, sinking in shame as a woman scorned, but I knew I wasn't meant to stay here. If you recall, I asked God one simple question, *Why did this happen to me?* And, God answered, *You're going to be able to change the lives of women like never before.*

Over the next several months, I had a chance to really marinate in those words. At first I was thrown off by the focus on women. That wasn't my desire—not consciously. Outside of my close circle of girl-friends, I didn't always have great experiences with women profession-ally. There was an esteem-wounding tension there. But what was really significant wasn't the focus of my new assignment, it was the process of getting there. God said I would be *able* to change the lives of women like never before. I realized that that meant I *wasn't* able to yet. Said another way, Marshawn *here* was not at all ready for God's *there*. Not her heart, attitude, or skill set. I can see now that it was true.

I knew the Holy Spirit. God and I had had some awesome adven-tures. But it was time for something higher. The old rules I'd lived by couldn't go with me into the new place, and neither could my addiction to success. I needed to learn something new called *flowing*. It's surren-dering to God's leading in real time . . . letting go of *my* normal and *my* way for *His* new and *His* way. There was indeed a shift already in progress.

{ THE STRUGGLE TO LET GO }

It's *time*. That was the message I kept hearing in my spirit. But it didn't make any sense. I had worked hard and found myself sitting in a fancy office on the twenty-first floor of a luxury high-rise office building, doing what I'd always said I wanted to do. I was a fully-licensed-to-practice, real-life Clair Huxtable. My law firm was one of the best in the country and one of the biggest in the city. It was prestigious, it paid insanely well, and it was what I had always wanted. But I felt like a prisoner trapped in a palace. I certainly couldn't complain—I had a wonderful job, I'd bought a home, and I had my own smartphone. (Having one was a big deal back then; for some reason, it seemed to really represent that I had made it.)

I had an office with a view, a secretary, a baby-blue paycheck that came every two weeks, benefits, *and* my BlackBerry. It had only been a year and a half since I started at this firm. So why in the world was I feeling trapped? Why was God telling me it was time to make a change when I'd only just gotten started?

It turns out I loved the *look* of law, but not the *life*. I liked wearing the suits and having the business cards. I loved the way people were impressed when they found out I'd gone to Georgetown. But actually *being* a lawyer was not fun. Not for me.

I didn't love my work; I didn't even like it. It wasn't nearly as exciting as the law and order shows I watched on television. It wasn't even as interesting as *The People's Court*, and they don't even have lawyers. While I had some awesome days and wonderful experiences here and there, I had started praying about the tension and dissatisfaction that was growing greater by the billable hour. I was incredibly grateful for my job. I knew it was a blessing and a rare opportunity, and I didn't want to grumble. I, too, had been taught over the years how important it is to *bloom where you are planted*. Now I know why this was such a popular sermon topic. It's tough to get up day after day when you don't really like what you do. The Rules I learned said that getting to love what you do is a luxury, not a necessity. So I learned to hush 'n buckle up, and to stick it out.

But I wasn't fulfilled. Thankfully, during my first year of practicing law, I had negotiated an opportunity to enter a six-month fellowship working at a legal aid office. My firm basically paid me my big firm salary, but "loaned" me to the legal aid office so that I could gain experience and provide free services to those that couldn't afford legal representation.

Now, legal aid was different in every way. My legal aid office didn't come with a high-rise view of Midtown or a U-shaped maple desk with a new laptop. My legal aid desk had seen its day . . . maybe a few decades in fact. It had carvings in it and came with a wooden chair (try sitting on a tree all day) and a chunky, white-turned-dingy old school desktop monitor that looked like one of the first computers ever made. There was a break room, but no fancy futuristic instant coffee and tea makers. On the first day, I went to heat up my lunch and just assumed there would be paper plates like at the firm. No ma'am. I used two or three coffee filters and bootlegged a plate. (Don't judge me . . . I was hungry!)

My job was to represent tenants being illegally evicted by their landlords, some of them slumlords, and to represent people unlawfully fired from their jobs.

Providing free legal services to the poor was some of the most rewarding work I have ever done. It was not glamorous, but it was good. I helped a single mom to stay in her home after the landlord tried to evict her because her son was mentally disabled. There was another mom who worked two jobs, still making less than a livable wage for her two children, who was being evicted because someone randomly mentioned her name in a police report as being involved in a crime that happened at her apartment complex. She wasn't even at home that day. She was at work. The police never followed up with her, and they never arrested her. However, because her name was on the police report given to the landlord, the landlord evicted her. She didn't have a voice and she didn't have the money to move. When I visited her apartment, there was mold in the ceiling and air vents. It was everywhere, and she had young kids. These conditions were unlivable and illegal. So not only was I able to help her win her case, we countersued the landlord and won $5000 for the deplorable conditions, and she was able to use the money to move into a new place.

There was an elderly woman who was being kicked out of her home because she kept falling. She was physically disabled and severely obese. Her family lived in the area but almost never came to check on her. When she fell out of the bed, sometimes she'd be stuck, alone, on the floor for days, unable to get up . . . and unable to go to the bathroom. To get up, she often had to call the fire department for assistance because of her size. The landlord found this to be too big of a burden. I visited her apartment as well. The smell of dried urine and roach infestation was almost unbearable, but *she* was absolutely adorable. We were able to secure daily in-home assisted care and some special accommodations. Landlords can't evict someone with a disability *because of* their disability.

Dozens of stories like that came in daily.

At the end of the six months, I returned to my high-rise office, and everything was just as I had left it. As my assignments started to pile up, I realized it wasn't that I didn't love the law—I didn't love *where* I was. I didn't enjoy pouring my talents into places empty of purpose. *This* is why I was tired. *This* is why *I* was unsatisfied. There was nothing wrong with the firm, it just wasn't where *I* was supposed to be. It may have been purpose-full for others, but it was not fulfilling for me.

I can't tell you the details of any of the big corporate matters I worked on. I still draw a blank. I know there was lots of money at stake, I know I billed a ton of hours working tediously, yet none of it sticks with me. But I remember the legal aid cases. I remember the people . . . the women I helped. Their eyes. Their stories. Their humility, and each woman's desperate desire to find someone who would listen and help. We all need someone. Being able to be *that* person for those who didn't know where else to turn was God's way of holding up an identity-revealing mirror to me.

The legal aid experience showed me what I've always known to be true: *I was built to help people.* I didn't know at the time that it was women in particular. I didn't even realize at the time that almost all of my legal aid cases were representing women. I didn't have eyes to see or discern that clue back then. But I did know I was created to serve, to be an advocate and to help others overcome the obstacles that stand in their way. I wasn't built to help enormous corporations make more money or cover up their mistakes.

We're all built to fight, but when we fight the wrong fight, we begin to break. You can't bloom where you're not supposed to be planted.

Toward the end of my time at legal aid, the mother of a disabled son came by the office. She had brought me a large cup of mixed fruit, some plastic utensils, and some paper napkins in a white plastic grocery bag . . . probably from the corner store. She was originally from Ethiopia and explained that although she didn't have much money, she wanted to thank me for helping her stay in her apartment. She was so insistent, but we weren't allowed to accept gifts or payment of any kind—not even fruit. But her offering was far greater than any paycheck I had ever received. She didn't give out of her surplus, she gave from a place of sacrifice.

My craving for success, the need to *look* the part, started to subside. I realized I wanted to do work that mattered, not just to *look* like I mattered. I wanted to be in the trenches with others in need, and I wanted to be the bridge to a better future if it was in my means. *That* feeling changed my life. Back when I was volunteering in juvenile detention facilities, I'd had *that* feeling. At the fancy law firm making a fat check, that feeling was nowhere to be found. I'd climbed the money mountain, but the view at the top wasn't as impressive as it seemed.

I found myself at odds with my boss. She was a well-connected female partner at the firm, someone I had hoped would be my mentor, but . . . let's just say it didn't work out like that. Just about the time I started at the firm, I was on *The Apprentice* (more on that below), and she didn't seem thrilled that someone so young in her legal career was on a major television show. One day during a mentoring session, she mentioned that I had the name recognition some lawyers work their entire lives for. She implied I was *supposed* to be a run-of-the-mill first year associate who was *supposed* to work her way up the ranks like everyone else, like she did.

While I can appreciate the bigger picture today, her words really broke my heart at the time. I had been looking forward to having a female mentor—it's something I think all of us women secretly crave. We want to be believed in and poured into by a woman who is where we want to be, and who not only sees something great in us but is passionate about unlocking that greatness, too. Her being a successful woman with brown skin only made her approach toward me more difficult to swallow. It felt like hazing. I realized I wouldn't necessarily be welcomed here, either. I'd have to shrink to belong.

The work environment became toxic and stressful. I felt like I was back in elementary school again. I avoided the hallway that required me to walk by her office. Anxiety set in, and I started losing hair and losing weight my already thin frame didn't have to lose. When our body starts breaking down, that's God's final warning. I felt like one of the people in the hostile work environment cases that I worked on as an employment lawyer!

Looking back, I can see that I had placed expectations on the shoulders of someone else who was not in a position to give me what I was hungry for—mentorship and having someone who believed in me wholeheartedly. Someone simply cannot give what they don't possess. But insecurity takes on a mind of its own, and I didn't have the tools to understand that at the time. I take responsibility today for how I viewed that time of my life. In some ways, I suppose she *was* my mentor. Maybe not the one I wanted, but in retrospect, she was what I needed. Without that friction, I wouldn't have felt the tug of discontent—a labor pain indicating the time to move was drawing near. It can be unpleasant, but it's still divine providence at work.

We must focus on flow, not fault.

So maybe it *did* make sense. Maybe I kept hearing *It's TIME!* in my spirit for a reason. But time for what? I didn't feel led to go back to legal aid, though I loved the experience. And, I didn't know what I would tell others if I left the firm since I had just gotten started.

As I prayed and really surrendered myself to the possibility of doing something new, I started having new dreams and desires. While I was in law school, one of the ways I supported myself was teaching communication skills and seminars to pageant contestants, professionals, and some politicians. I did some copy writing, speech writing, résumé writing, and built what I called "platform messages." Basically, I helped women figure out what they needed to say, to take their desires and give them organized direction and the best presentation possible. Today, we call it branding. Back then, it was just called communication! I was really good at this brand-building, message-making thing, but I stopped when I started practicing law because I didn't need the side income anymore.

But now God had my attention. It was time for a change, so what exactly was I supposed to do?

{ THE APPRENTICE }

Now, I promised I would tell you more about how I ended up on television, and I want to do that here, because it's a part of what was happening to me in The GAP.

When I was in my last semester of law school, I auditioned for a television show called *The Apprentice,* airing on NBC. It was a blockbuster reality show about business. The contestants would compete on various business and marketing tasks proving that they had what it took to be the protégé of a prominent real estate tycoon named Donald Trump. This was twelve years before he became president of the United States.

People always ask how being on the show came about, so I'll share a bit about that here. Honest moment: I often shy away from telling this story because I've never wanted to be defined by it or to have my life viewed through the lens of one fleeting season. But it was an epic, life-expanding experience and part of my unconventional shift into higher purpose. It taught me about gifts and abilities I didn't know I had. And it's a chapter in a larger story much bigger than me. All of our chapters matter. So here we go! I invite you to view this through your purpose lens as a fellow teacher in training, too, okay?

I got an email announcing the casting for the first season of the show during my first year of law school. I knew I wanted to audition. In fact, I knew that I wasn't only going to *audition for* it—I knew that I was going to be *on* it. I can't explain why—I just knew it. The problem was, I had just started law school at Georgetown and didn't want to interrupt my studies. It's hard enough to get admitted in the first place. But I embraced this belief as a certainty anyway.

Two and a half years later, I was ready, and I auditioned, just like everyone else. I didn't have a hookup or know anyone on the inside. I stood in line in the parking lot of a Mercedes-Benz dealership in Alexandria, Virginia, to wait for my turn. NBC and Mark Burnett Productions were actually casting for two versions of the *The Apprentice* that year—one hosted by Donald Trump and a new spin-off hosted by Martha Stewart. I was standing in line for the Trump audition. The line was really long, and I heard the Holy Spirit tell me to get in the other line. It was cold, and I was standing outside in heels. So between the chilly wind gusts and having walked with God long enough to move when He said move, I got in the shorter Martha Stewart line.

Once I made it inside the dealership where the interviews were happening, I was seated at a table with ten other people, including one female casting director. She was petite and thin, with short brown hair, and she had a total poker face. The casting director threw out questions that would naturally spark debate, to see which voices and personalities were unique enough to stand out. In about ten minutes, we were done. She took our applications and said we would hear by end of day if we had made it to the next round.

I went back to my apartment and literally waited by the phone all day. I probably should have been studying, but I didn't want to miss that phone call. Six p.m. came. I figured they were still working. I made a sandwich and reflected on how I did during that interview. And then 10 p.m. rolled around. I figured I would get ready for bed, but I wouldn't shower until the next day so that I wouldn't miss that phone call! At midnight, the day was officially over and I hadn't heard anything. Tears started to well up. I'd been holding on to this vision for two and a half years—but maybe I was just dreaming. I turned the lights off, plugged my cell phone into the wall, and tried to go to sleep.

It was pitch-dark in my apartment bedroom when the blue light started flashing on my phone. The casting director was calling. Hallelujah! I played it cool. She had no idea I was laying my head upon a soggy, tear-soaked pillow. She invited me to the next round of auditions. I had made it in after all.

For the next four weeks I went through the entire casting process, auditioning for the Martha Stewart version of the show. I had to do interviews and put together videos. Back then there were no video cameras on cell phones. I had to use actual film and tapes. I kept advancing from one stage of the audition process to the next. Finally, the casting director called to say the network wanted me on *The Apprentice*—only they thought I would be better suited for the Trump show. The one I had initially planned to audition for.

This experience always reminds me of how reinvention really works. Reinvention isn't always about doing something new or getting instant results; it can be about following an unconventional process to get to God's *original* intention for your life. Purpose doesn't always seem to make sense, but if we follow God's voice, we'll still get to *His* intended destination.

I was still in law school at this point. It was my third 'n final year, and I had held on the entire time to the vision that I was going to be on the show. I'd had absolute certainty about it—it wasn't stubbornness or arrogance, but an inner assurance. Maybe that's what faith is really about. I structured my entire class schedule around when I *estimated* the casting would take place and when the upcoming season would start taping. I didn't actually know when or where the auditions would be, but I chose courses and clinics representing clients in legal matters in my final semester that wouldn't require me to be on campus to finish final exams and to graduate. With no exams, I could turn my papers in early and finish my clinical work, too. That was the plan. And that's exactly what happened. Sometimes our guesses are really divine guidance.

> *Faith is making room for what you're expecting to experience even if you have no clue or zero control over it actually happening.*

I was on the show for ten out of thirteen weeks—almost making it to the very end. I learned how much we can actually accomplish in short periods of time when we commit to bringing our best. If it interests you further, you can learn more about my incredible experiences on that show, along with business advice for how women can elevate our approach to sisterhood and career success, in my previous book, *S.K.I.R.T.S. in the Boardroom.*

Here is the cool thing. While I was still taping the show, the network flew me to DC so that I could walk with my graduating class, which I didn't think I'd get to do when I committed to this plan! They flew me in on a Saturday morning and then flew me back that same evening to New York City to finish taping. I didn't have to abandon my degree or my dream.

On the show, I discovered I wasn't just a good speaker with the gift of gab. I had the ability to put together and lead major advertising campaigns for companies like Lamborghini, Bally Total Fitness, Dairy Queen, and Under Armour. I even did a campaign for *Star Wars*! I came up with our team name (*Capital Edge*), taglines for most of our projects, and was always the team's go-to presenter when it was time to show our work to ad agencies or in the boardroom for final judgment. I was using the same skills I used to help Miss America and Miss USA contestants come up with their platform messages, and now I knew I could do more . . . be more.

Exposure expands our expectations.

New skills and untapped abilities emerged, and my existing strengths found an elevated home. All of that increased my confidence but also my understanding of potential. We don't know what we're really made of until we're tested, stretched, engaged, and challenged. That's when your gifts, your voice, and signs of your next-level calling sprout and stand out.

IS THAT LIGHTNING?

The morning after my last day on the show, I woke up frustrated and shell-shocked that *I* got fired. But then a lightning bolt of clarity struck my soul again. And with it, there was an out-of-the-blue desire to start working with athletes. This was not something I had ever even thought of before. I actually remember listening to my peers in law school fight over the few seats available in the only sports law class offered, and knowing I wasn't at all interested. But now, a couple of years later, I wasn't just interested, I was fascinated. Certainty struck again.

I immediately called my mom and told her that I didn't know how this was going to happen, but that this was what I would be doing. I'd be helping athletes to communicate better and to build a future off the field. I probably sounded nuts! That's why I called my mom. She pretty much always supports my off-the-wall visions . . . and even prays in agreement with me for this crazy stuff to come true. My dad, over time, became the same way.

So though I had no idea *how* this was going to happen, I spoke it into the atmosphere with full conviction that it was going to take place. Now, it's two years after the show, I'm dissatisfied and physically and emotionally stressed in this high-rise law office, and that off-the-wall desire to go into sports was coming back. That blurry vision I had been carrying became a bit clearer. The desire started turning into vision. I started getting specific ideas and strategies and a new picture of what my impact could be. I shared my idea with my mentor in the firm—and, well, you can imagine how that went. The firm wasn't open to my idea because they said I was too young. I was thinking a little too big for my britches. Apparently, I didn't need to focus on generating business or making relationships (the stuff that all of the successful partners had mastered to become partner). I needed to do what first year lawyers do, which is research and networking with other lawyers . . . not prospective clients.

Oooookay. I've always been good at high-level networking . . . like meeting people impossible to meet and closing deals with companies that seem way out of reach. But that was not valued here. I mustn't step out of line or get too much shine. Perhaps you can relate? I needed to stay in my place, keep my head down, and keep my ideas and opportunities (even for the firm) to myself.

While this was going on at work, I started actually meeting new people that happened to be in or connected to the pro sports world. It had taken two years, but I had arrived in an oasis of opportunity. If the firm wasn't going to be open to this, I decided I would just start my own agency. I didn't debate this for too long. I often get a "nobody puts Baby in a corner" burst of motivation that drives me to ignore critics, separate from the pack, and do my own thing. Waiting for approval and permission has never been my strong suit.

Picking myself has always paid off.

I continued to do my work at the law firm, which required a minimum of sixty hours or more per week. In the evenings and on the weekends, I worked on my business. I started with a name for the business, a website, and some business cards. I'd call it EDGE 3M, which stood for Expect Dedication Genius and Excellence, and would focus on representing athletes in media, marketing, and management opportunities (hence the 3M). It started with communication training, but it evolved into so much more.

I had my first order of self-designed business cards shipped to my law office, which was a really dumb idea! The box arrived with a sample of the card taped to the *outside* of the box! My heart stopped, but I walked over and grabbed it like it was no big deal. Thankfully, I spotted it on the edge of my secretary's desk before anyone else saw it . . . I think!

That *same* evening, I was slated to go to the opening ceremonies for a major convention for minority MBAs. That night I met someone who worked for the global sports apparel company Russell Athletic. I exchanged business cards with the gentleman and followed up the next day. He not only became a good friend, he agreed to sponsor one of my then pro bono athlete clients with a product endorsement deal. I had taken on a few pro athletes who weren't yet paying me, but having them as "clients" gave me the experience and the time to develop key relationships with media outlets and corporations that could lead to more endorsements, TV contracts, and marketing deals. I was willing to get the experience to get in the door.

It was working. Slowly but surely, it was working. So I put my exit plan in place. I would start charging the pro bono clients, keep working on nights and weekends, save up more money, and eventually make the leap.

❴ THE TIME COMES WHEN YOU ❵ LEAST EXPECT IT

I'd estimated I had about six more months to go before making the big leap into entrepreneurship, when the word *TIME* started flashing in my dreams and interrupting my plans. I kept hearing this as a recurring message when I read my Bible, went to church, when I brushed my teeth . . . everywhere. Then the final sign was when someone gave me a book that had the word *TIME* in large bold print at the top. That was my tipping point.

Now God *really* had my attention! Seeing that title wigged me out for sure. But what was He trying to say or get me to see? As I stared out my bedroom window, the Holy Spirit sweetly said this to me: "It's TIME. TIME stands for (T)otally (I)n (M)y (E)lement as long as you (T)rust (I)n (M)y (E)xperience."

I was floored, intimidated, and intrigued. The Holy Spirit regularly speaks to me in acronyms . . . but c'mon! Two for one this time?!

I didn't feel ready to make the leap to go out on my own just yet, but clearly God was saying I was. I wanted to save up some more money. I wanted more paying clients. And I wanted more time to get ready and *make sure* this was the right decision. I had a mortgage, bills, and no roommates that I could split expenses with. I wasn't on my parents' health or car insurance anymore. The realities of life went through my mind just like they do for everyone considering making a leap and major shift. While I was scared, I was absolutely certain this was God's voice, and I knew I had a small window of opportunity to listen to it. As with the *Apprentice* audition, it was time to get out of the predictable line.

The next day, I gave my two weeks' notice. Some of my coworkers were naturally confused at why I'd give up a cushy six-figure job for the chaos and uncertainty of entrepreneurship. I didn't really have answer, so I simply said, "It's just time."

After all, I had some prospects on the table and was hopeful they'd soon become paying clients, though none had come through yet. And I had one solid consulting contract that had been in place six months, with an investment firm. I used the money as starting capital, and I figured it would get me by until I inked a management deal with an actual *paying* pro athlete. At least, that's what I thought until disruption bulldozed my doorstep. The company that had me on a retainer lost its $50 million credit line. Fifty million dollars! They immediately canceled all of their contracts, including mine, with no advance notice. I couldn't reach anyone . . . no one was answering the phones. It was like they disappeared. Deep breath.

I had just finished the last day on my job! I didn't have that biweekly blue check to fall back on. In fact, all of the stuff from my law firm office was still in the trunk of my truck. I was glad I'd gotten a few extra pens and pads of paper before I left, because I was going to need every dime I could spare. I didn't have the luxury of panicking. I had bills, and I sho' nuff wasn't going to ask for my job back! I knew I'd have to focus.

New dreams must turn into new decisions to form a new reality.

I got so stinkin' focused and I ended up signing my first *paying* client (hallelujah again!) just a few days later. He was a pro football player who had just signed the highest-paying defensive end contract in NFL history at the time, $62 million. And now I was *his* marketing agent. I'd be able to afford pens and paper now . . . and keep the lights on . . . and probably more. All of the free work and trust-building paid off—not with everyone, but with the right one. I guess it was indeed *TIME.*

⁍{ MAYBE YOU'VE BEEN CHEATING, TOO }⁌

I was running EDGE 3M—which was becoming the fastest growing woman-owned sports agency in the country in less than a year—when I met the man who later became my fiancé. That's significant to note because I was already in a shifting phase, but didn't realize it. I didn't realize that I was most passionate about working with women because I still had that inner tape playing in mind that said, *You don't like women and women don't really like you. And they don't get you.* So, I hid out in the sports world.

Think about it. *What old inner tape, plans, or limiting beliefs might be blocking your bigger?*

I didn't realize at the time that my career shift wasn't about a job, it was about moving one step closer to my higher purpose . . . to *there.* I didn't fully realize I had a *gift* (not just a talent) for branding and messaging that was transferrable. I didn't realize that branding, business, and law would also be necessary for my future assignment. And I also didn't realize this was just a pit stop—I planned to retire in the world of professional sports—but that I would use those skills for a bigger, yet different purpose. The leap from law to sports got me out of an office, but it wouldn't get me *fully* into my life mission.

leaping must become a lifestyle.

I just didn't know exactly where else I belonged . . . so it seemed easier and more comfortable to stay. Perhaps you can relate? That unsettled feeling starts to taunt you and haunt you. Inside you know there's more for you to be and do, and you're right. What's on the inside, the rebellion ready to cause a revolution, is persistently trying to get out.

I started the sports agency years before I got engaged, but in both scenarios cheating was front and center. In my relationship, I was being cheated on, but at my job, I was cheating on my calling. And in both situations I knew deep inside that I was in circumstances where I didn't belong permanently.

So I'm curious. Before we move on to learning what it takes to get out of The GAP and actually enter your calling, what parallels have you found in my story?

What unlikely messes and naysaying mentors can you now be thanking God for?

What frustrations have you been feeling that might indicate it's TIME for a shift?

What dormant desires or blurry visions have you been carrying for far too long?

What broken perspectives from unpleasant experiences have been holding you back from entering (or even recognizing) possibility?

What is it that you now realize hasn't happened to you but for you?

chapter nine

MAKING THE SHIFT

God calls us to shift us.
The interruption is the invitation.

We know The GAP is a growth zone, full of both obstacles and opportunity. During this season, God's goal is very simple: to make us into a vessel *capable* of carrying something greater, and capable of impacting the lives of others in a new way. He does this by stripping us down, realigning us, and preparing us to cross over to the other side. In essence, we've gotta travel light! We need to empty out before we can elevate and accelerate. You won't exit The GAP until a shift happens in your thinking.

Letting go is not easy! Many never emerge from The GAP stage because we don't want to give up the familiar! Gappers aren't willing to be uncomfortable. They aren't willing to invest in themselves. They aren't willing to let go of the comfort zones, toxic relationships, or self-sufficiency. They struggle with pleasing and not disappointing others, and aren't willing to make the unpopular, tough decisions. When I say "they," I'm talking about me and you!

Folks stuck in The GAP tend to be content with merely *talking* about what God is *going to do*. Gappers can be very optimistic, but not very practical. They expect God to do all the work while they quote Scripture and tout affirmations without changing any behavior.

Capacity building precedes a bigger calling.

It is in the release of the old *and* the response to the new that we receive clarity, fresh vision, direction, and inclination. God begins to pour newness into us like fresh wine into a new wineskin. Don't forget that during this season, God's goal is very simple: to make us a vessel *capable* of carrying what God has and *capable* of changing the lives of others in a new way . . . to get us to make a shift. Heaven doesn't want us in The GAP forever.

❦ HOW SHIFT HAPPENS ❧

Again, The GAP is like a birth canal—we decide whether it's a passageway or a purgatory. When God calls you, He starts tugging at you. He's seeking to bring forth the new you and unleash the new mission inside of you. *The Tug* is what we feel when God's plans and our inner purpose start communicating about what's next.

But to get to the other side, we must choose to push—to surrender to and flow with the divine force making all of this happen . . . It's the power of *shift*. The same energy and breath of God that created the heavens and earth is the divine force being used to bring our life into higher order . . . into alignment.

The Tug is a sign that we are not only in The GAP but it is indeed time to shift—to move from *here* to *there*. If The GAP is the birth canal, then the shift is the push and The Tug is the contractions. God is seeking to manifest something new, and His next vehicle for delivery happens to be you. To make sense of and actually experience a shift, you can't ignore the core of why you're here . . . not if you want to make it out of The GAP.

You know shift is happening when God starts giving you new desires, ideas, dreams, confirmations, urgings, longings, and vision. You start getting pulls and nudges that can *only* come from God.

> *If you've prayed for God to use you, then you've prayed for God to shift you.*

Shift is what we're really praying for when we ask God for a change, better circumstances, healing, companionship, opportunity, favor, protection, or guidance. I think of shift like God's hands tenderly reaching into our womb to help facilitate a precious, very important delivery. God's part is the shift—the splittin', strippin', and realignment . . . everything used to get us to the point of delivery. When we feel The Tug, our job is to push. Don't give up. The pain is really a loving pull. It's time to move. To go with His flow.

Let's pause here for a moment of important reflection.

What recurring whispers, nudges, and tugs have you been feeling, hearing, or sensing?

What signs indicate a shift is either coming or already in progress?

⊰ UNLOCKING *YOUR* INNER VAULT ⊱

Self-discovery is the secret to a major life shift. *A new season doesn't happen to you, it comes through you.* As you reflect on your nudges and tugs, one other thing I'd love for you to do is what I call a *Blessing Dump.* A Blessing Dump is where you list out everything you can think of in terms of your abilities, lessons learned, accomplishments, education, know-how, experiences, and unique character traits. Think about the things people compliment you on, and the cool 'n quirky things that make you you. This is a great time to add in the listing of talents and areas of impact you reflected on earlier, too.

And don't forget the things you like about yourself. You can list anything that comes to mind, no matter how big or how small. Give yourself permission to dote upon yourself unapologetically. A Blessing Dump is a spiritual practice and something of a life inventory rooted in appreciation. You're going to look back over your life and experiences during the Discovery and Talent stages of life. *What did you pick up along the way? How can it serve you moving forward?* God takes our experiences and attributes and mixes them like secret ingredients to make a marvelous meal . . . one that will amply feed us and those assigned to us, too.

Blessing Dump

Next, write down your attributes and abilities, in what I call the *Inner Vault* (see next page). You see, your treasure is already within you. As you do this exercise, you'll discover how much you have learned and gained, the good and the ugly—it all matters. Be sure to silence the *little me* whisper that says you have nothing to offer or very little to list. *Dig deeper. That's where the Holy Spirit is.* And fight the part of you, your ego, that wants to skip this exercise altogether and just move along. *If you don't value process, you can't truly value purpose.*

Believing bigger isn't possible without believing in yourself and appreciating . . . really *valuing* . . . your journey at a higher level. A vault contains your valuables. A shift requires us to let go of dismissing, minimizing, rushing, and devaluing ourselves. Proverbs 25:2 (CEB) says, "It is the glory of God to hide something. It is the glory of kings to discover something." God hides his gifts, promises, and abundance *in* us. The enemy has no authority here. It's an airtight vault. God's path to our promised land is *in* us, which is why *little me* seeks to turn our thoughts against us . . . to keep us from looking inside the vault . . . to keep our gift box closed and shut tight. We glorify God, and experience expansion, influence, and greater power in the Glory Zone when we do the work to dig deep, go within, and search out the secret provision already within. We'll go deeper into how your abilities, experiences, and characteristics will help you pinpoint your gifts and life mission in the next stage. For now, don't move on until you've filled the entire space. And feel free to get more paper. You serve an unlimited God who has gifted and purposed you in infinite ways. This is your chance to embrace them and enter them. Self-discovery moves us from gapping to shifting.

My Inner Vault

Attributes:

Abilities:

Accomplishments:

Know-How:

Experiences:

And More:

In a world that feeds upon your self-doubt, believing in yourself is a courageous act!

{ FROM GROWTH ZONE TO WAR ZONE }

God calls us to a bigger, bolder life, but He cannot make us want it, and He will not force us to enter it. We always have the choice to say yes to purpose. And *little me* isn't letting you leave the Comfort Zone without a fight. So as you get more serious about your calling, your Growth Zone will quickly morph into that war zone we talked about. All of your insecurities will rise to the surface, totally unashamed to kick, scream, and shout. *Future ME*'s leadings will make you think you're nuts, and *little me* will pull out all of the stops, making you feel more like an ant than an elephant. You'll be flooded with distractions, disappointments, delays, possibly depression, and most certainly doubt. It's okay.

Know that new dreams come with new nightmares. That's inevitable, and normal, too. Fear will mess with your mind. That doesn't mean you don't have faith; it's an invitation to build it at higher and deeper levels. A big shift is *supposed* to be uncomfortable . . . just like pregnancy. Think about it. Without the discomfort how would you know and *believe* that you were indeed pregnant? You *need* the signs.

{ WHAT'S BLOCKING YOUR SHIFT? }

Shifting is largely about letting go. Letting go of relationships, rules, titles, successes, safety nets, and whatever is stopping you. *What you most cling to controls you.* The thing we're most afraid to let go of represents the captain navigating your ship. *It* becomes your idol. The thing you *think* you need to survive and thrive is the very anchor keeping you stuck. Deep breath!

What's beautiful about *divine flow* is its naturalness and ease of movement. Moving water is majestic and life-giving. When flow becomes difficult or stagnant, it can turn toxic. It's a sign of a problem . . . a blockage. There's a dam blocking streams that are meant to flow.

Flow is the current of the Holy Spirit. It's what the *split rock* was seeking to release. Flow is the way God aligns us, guides us, and guards us. Purpose is designed to flow . . . it *is* flow. It is like a current we get to be a part of. In it is everything; apart from it, we're lost.

The question is:

> *What beliefs, bonds, and behaviors have you built up over time that are now blocking your __natural__ flow and taking you out of the current of where God wants you to go?*

Is it your career or another mountain you're clinging to? Is it financial security or fear of not being seen? Do you fear being invisible or not looking like you're relevant? Is it the fear of doing something new? Is it a relationship? Your reputation? Worry about disappointing others? Do you think you're too old . . . or too young? Lack of support? Do you feel unprepared, incapable, or not good enough? Do you fear failure, success, or rejection? Or is it just a lack of clarity about exactly what to do?

Anything we struggle to release is a sign of deeply seated doubt. It could be about a career, a relationship, or any of the mountains we discussed earlier. What we cleave to exposes our deepest fears, and showcases where and how we're unable or unwilling to fully trust God.

I don't doubt God's ability (well, maybe on occasion), but (let's keep it real), I do doubt God's willingness to come through for *me*, sometimes.

When an obstruction (a dam) is in the way, our current (our flow) can get misdirected and start filling up places we don't belong. It's like pouring water into a small ditch and hoping the ditch becomes an ocean. A ditch can never become destiny. If it's a ditch, it's a dead end. The ditch will only get deeper. You may feel like you're swimming, but you're sinking and settling.

A man-made ditch is manufactured, and it's certainly never going to be an oasis. It may be an oasis for someone else, but if it's not where God desires you, for you it's a ditch.

Eventually, limiting beliefs and behaviors become *Blessing Blockers*—self-sabotaging habits that get ingrained into our personality, attitudes, outlook, and choices. There are a ton of 'em, but let's talk about the most common ones that keep us stuck in The GAP and see which ones relate to you.

Blessing Blocker #1: Self-Doubt

Doubt and destiny are like two sides of a coin. Most of our self-doubt comes from lessons we mislearned during the Discovery and Talent stages. Again, quite often, our struggle isn't to believe in God, it's to believe in ourselves. That we're good enough, loved enough, worthy enough . . . just enough. And that we're important enough to be a priority on God's radar. When your deepest desires still feel off in the distance, it's tougher to have that *me-faith* certainty; the knowing that knows God will come through . . . not just generally for others, but specifically for you no matter what it looks like.

> *Instead of doubting yourself, start doubting the voice that says you're unqualified. It's the liar. Doubting yourself is really doubting God.*

Ouch! This one always stings. I don't like to admit that there are areas where I doubt God. But to exit The GAP, we'll need to commit to expose those very insecurities and say goodbye to self-doubt.

What about you? Let's call it to the carpet.

> *In what areas do you doubt God will use you, bless you, heal you, restore you, shift you, or come through for you? Be honest. Gotta face it to fix it.*

Blessing Blocker #2: Isolation

Isolation is really a fear of trusting others. As intimate as a walk with God is, it's not meant to be done alone. For years, I struggled with trusting others. Okay, I still do, but I'm getting better. Mistrust comes from extracting more of the wrong lessons in the Discovery and Talent stages. When people let us down, we vow to never let that kind of disappointment enter our lives again. We withdraw and become more skeptical. And we start to look at our now moments through the lens of yesterday. In doing so, we bring the past into the present, and that pollutes our future. This isolation and mistrust thing is really prevalent with us as women.

Skepticism and mistrust aren't the same as discernment, though we often try to dress them up as such.

They're just another excuse to stay to ourselves as opposed to risk the vulnerability found in trusting others. Isolation is a trap. God wants us to be in community with others, especially other women who can support our growth. Otherwise, he wouldn't have given us gifts and the good stuff that *others* need. Our lives are intentionally interconnected. The very wisdom you need to make your shift will likely come from a messenger you're least likely to expect or appreciate.

Now, sometimes God calls us into a season of incubation, where he needs us to be free of distraction. *But* (big ole but here!) if that's been your lifestyle, it's a *Blessing Blocker*, not a builder. Betrayal and disappointment come with the journey. They might feel like manure, but they are really maturing mechanisms. You can't change what's hurt you in the past, but you can invite a new future by reframing how you see what's occurred. When we look at what's happened, good and bad, as lessons, we can see that God was preparing us for something better in the future.

> *What disappointments or betrayals from your past have caused you to pull away from others?*

> *How has isolating yourself cost you support, opportunity, connections, or even love?*

Blessing Blocker #3: Comparison

As hard as it may be to believe, what God is doing in the lives of others has absolutely nothing to do with what He is seeking to do in you! Ummm . . . let's just underline that, shall we? Comparison cripples our confidence and compromises our calling. When we obsess about what others are doing, we extract a lie . . . another limiting belief enters our mind and *little me* waters it and gets to whispering: *You're not doing enough. You're behind. It's too late. You're not as talented. You're life isn't as pretty. You don't have enough. You just aren't enough.* Social media fuels these toxic comparisons every day. We see airbrushed images of children who don't cry, women who wake up with perfect lashes, flawless skin, and lots of vacations. While you're working, trying to pay the bills, keep the kids from tearing each other apart, and somehow squeeze in a bath, it seems like everyone else is living a perfect life. Remember, the enemy will indeed use anything to exploit an insecurity that *already* exists. So, when you're asking God for a husband, of course all you're going to notice is engagements! The goal of the enemy is to get you to shrink, to lose hope, and most certainly, to doubt.

Doubt is kryptonite to your destiny.

The other danger of comparison is ego. It can lead to competition and arrogance. We can start to feel like we're better than others because our life seems to be better. Or, in an attempt to keep up, we start striving, proving, and showing off. No matter how you slice it or dice it, there is nothing good that comes from comparing. God wants us to look up, not around.

How has comparison crippled your courage, clarity, and confidence?

Blessing Blocker #4: Indecision

I've met women (and plenty of men, too!) who were afraid to move until they heard God speak. *But what if good is good enough for grace to make up the distance?* What if God speaks most powerfully by saying nothing at all? The belief that we have to get it right or that we'll somehow step out of grace stems from the fear that if we're not careful, we're going mess up our lives. Mess up someone else's life. Or severely disappoint God to the point that we'll have to face His wrath. That's our real guiding belief.

When you're faced with a choice, it is easy to find yourself facing paralysis. We over-think, over-pray, and over-research our way out of opportunities. And we over-question, trying to discern if something is God's will.

We become watchers instead of leapers. We keep waiting and waiting . . . and waiting on the perfect time. Waiting on God to move.

While there are times during a shift that God asks us to get still, to wait on him and His timing, there are other times when God is waiting on us to do what He has *already* said! To do what's *already* written in His word. To meet a need we can *already* see. We don't need to hyper-spiritualize the obvious. If someone is hungry, feed 'em. If you want to learn a new skill, take a class. We won't always know 100 percent of the time exactly what God's will is. And, we don't have to pray about every single thing, looking for confirmation in every possible way. That's fear, not faith.

> *If you wait for perfect conditions, you will never get anything done.*
> —*Ecclesiastes 11:4 (TLB)*

That scripture literally means that if you wait for perfect conditions, you'll never sow *and* you'll never reap! So hear my heart here. Prayer is essential. But it can become another hideout. An excuse not to make a bigger, bolder decision.

How does fear tend to manifest as indecision in your life?

Blessing Blocker #5: Facts

Singer Crystal Lewis has a beautiful lyric in one of her songs that says, "Only fools believe in only what they see." Facts may be true, but they aren't necessarily the whole truth. God operates in the unseen. That is the very nature of God—to create something out of nothing. God is not limited by . . . well, anything. The big vision comes from above and belongs to us to hold on to. The details? The how? That stuff belongs to God. Miracles are His domain. And God loves to surprise us. Believing only in what we can see, quantify, and prove is often just a way that *little me* gets us to embrace a rational lie.

So what facts have been blocking you? How is what you're seeing blocking what God is actually showing?

Facts don't tell the full picture—especially when God is writing the story. Remember the little boy with two fish and five loaves of bread and thousands of hungry people? Facts said there was no way that food was enough for thousands of people. But it was.

God creates something out of nothing.

Facts have little to do with how real faith and supernatural manifestation works. A key secret to a major life shift is speaking faith and not facts. When we trust in the unseen and expect what we haven't experienced, that's the very invitation God responds to . . . and the type of next-level, bigger belief He's been waiting on.

Blessing Blocker #6: Hoarding

So much of The GAP is about emptying out. That's partly because by the time we get to The GAP, our life is usually full of *stuff*. It can be physical stuff we're attached to that makes us feel or look important. It can be achievements and accolades. It can be memories of the good ole days. And it can be any places, prizes, protocol, or people we cling to and find refuge or significance in. We can even hoard unforgiveness, regret, and cynicism. Hoarding is just another way we hold on to the old—the old ways of thinking, living, and finding significance. Whatever we hold on to the most has a hold on us. Our stubbornness most reflects our areas of distrust, and what we hoard ends up being what God asks us to surrender to Him.

Can you think of something—a relationship, a situation, a belief, a behavior, or even something physical—God is leading you to let go of?

We must be willing to unlearn and unload in order to uncover (and make room for) our larger mission—one that requires a new mindset and new way of being and believing.

Blessing Blocker #7: Distraction

Focus is probably the most important skill you need to enter a bigger future. *Little me* is a master of distraction. It's the most effective weapon in fear's arsenal. Ever wonder why it's easy for you to finish the insignificant things, but you procrastinate when it comes down to your big dreams and desires? Distractions are a doozy. One of my clients, Dr. Fred Jones, says, "Distractions are the death of your dreams happening in slow motion!" Whoa! And distractions are intentional— a stealth form of resistance designed to block your bigger. The key to making a shift is to pay attention to the truly important things, and to learn what (and who) to ignore. *The greater the significance, the greater the resistance*—and *the more susceptible we are to self-sabotage, doubt, and succumbing to distractions.*

Opportunity can be a distraction disguised as destiny.

Everything that looks good isn't necessarily God. As Reverend Campbell B. Singleton III, one of my spiritual mentors says, "Even Jesus ignored people to stay focused on His mission." When you're in a shift, it's especially key to be on the lookout for distractions. They will be coming. When you get new opportunities, new ideas, and new invitations, ask if these things are in alignment with what you feel is God's *new* vision. And, know what normally trips you up.

What distractions usually take you off course?

What distractions are stealing your attention right now?

Every *Blessing Blocker* is rooted in some form of fear or inadequacy, which influences our beliefs about *who we are, where we belong,* and *what we deserve.* These blockers, consciously and subconsciously, are why we cling to our *here* and don't shift into our *there.* Once we know what's been blocking us, we're able to build from a better belief system.

So, which *Blessing Blockers* resonated most to you?

- ☐ Self-Doubt

- ☐ Isolation

- ☐ Comparison

- ☐ Indecision

- ☐ Facts

- ☐ Hoarding

- ☐ Distraction

Check all that apply! You might have immediate connections to the ones I've listed above, but I also encourage you to pray about these and proactively look for other fears and blockers that might be showing up in different areas of your life.

Here's a simple prayer that I pray when I'm working on my own self-examination. You might find it useful as well as you work through your own blockers.

SIMPLE PRAYER
God, show me how I'm getting in my own way.
Help me to see how my habits and hang-ups are harming as
opposed to helping.

⧼ THE EXODUS—EXITING THE GAP ⧽

We've talked about some of the things that keep us stuck in The GAP, but how can we get out of it? How do we actually exit The GAP and enter our calling? Here are some steps you can take to help you get there, as well as some *simple prayers* you can pray.

Step 1: Get a Bigger Vision

I use the phrase "get" a bigger vision as opposed to "wait for" one because being proactive about your destiny is a sign of commitment and maturity. Part of the reason The GAP becomes a purgatory instead of a passageway is because we don't have a big enough vision—big meaning a vision (B)uilt (I)n (G)od. I'm not just talking about a vision blessed by Him, but one bathed in Him.

Our vision becomes our compass. Our certainty. And if it's a *faulty* vision, one being held together by insecurity, outdated rules, guilt, fear, and shame, it's time to retire it. God wants us to have a *fantastic* vision. One guided by love, joy, impact, possibility, and fulfillment. God's bigger vision is always about making sure you have a greater impact. It's where you thrive, not just survive. Also, it involves unspeakable joy. When your vision touches upon those things, you're on the right path. When it's about avoiding risk, play-ing it safe, or doing "the right thing," you're not even in the ballpark. Your bigger vision *should* excite you and at the same time shake you up, make you nervous and be a stretch. And it should make you question, *How in the heck is this going to be possible?* That's a ques-tion God loves to answer.

SIMPLE PRAYER

God, please give me a bigger vision for my life.
Help me to believe that my purpose is bigger
than what I understand,

*and to trust that your view of me and my future is bigger than
what I externally see.*

Step 2: Let Go of the Past

If we're going to be transformed by the renewal of our minds, we've gotta look at the faulty beliefs and lessons we've accepted over the years, and do the deep, intentional work of shedding these. They no longer serve us and they're blocking our bigger. Again, this is a process, but being intentional and paying attention to faulty thinking invites transformation to start happening in real time. Simply ask: *Is this thought connected to the past or my future?* Whatever we think on we bring on, so awareness allows us the chance to interrupt our old patterns, reactions, and habits. That's what it means to take our thoughts captive.

This may mean you have to make a difficult decision. It may mean ending a relationship. It may mean trying something new, outside of your comfort zone, so that God has a chance to show up in a new way. Whatever it means for you, remember to look forward. *New dreams and new decisions unveil a new path.*

> *Dreams are not just to be longed after,
> dreams are meant to be lived.*

SIMPLE PRAYER
*God, give me the courage to let go of
whatever you ask me to release.
Help me to do it quickly, wisely, and lovingly . . .
but with certainty.*

Step 3: Speak What You Seek

When we speak what we seek, as opposed to what we see, we activate possibility and operate in the power of *certainty*. Certainty is a steadfast commitment—a belief so strong that we've locked into it, where nothing can deter us. It's a commitment to and trust in an eventual outcome, not appearances. To the end result, not the process. It's faith.

When we are operating in certainty, we naturally create the same way God creates. We give voice to our expectation and use our words to spark something new in the atmosphere. God said let there be light, and there was light. God didn't *ask* for light. He activated it. He spoke what He fully expected to appear, even though it had never actually existed before. When we speak what we're seeking, we are telling God that we're ready for the new and that we are on board with His new agenda. *We don't have to see it to believe it. We have to believe it to see it.*

Notice that I'm not merely suggesting that we pray for it to happen. We speak as though it's already *happened*. This is shifting from begging to building . . . from asking to activating. We act *as* if, not *what* if. And we make plans accordingly and wisely.

It's not wise to shirk responsibilities you've already committed to, but it is necessary to plan your transition, prepare, and put things in place if you're serious about surrendering and shifting into something new. *Plan for what you're praying for.* In that regard, actions speak even louder than words, and Heaven most certainly sees and hears that you're making room for what's coming.

SIMPLE PRAYER

Lord, help me to speak what I seek until I see what I've said.
I give you thanks for the manifestation of this
vision already in progress.
Give me wisdom, humility, and certainty as I make room for
what you've said is for me to become, have, and do.

Step 4: Invest in It

What we invest in shows what we're truly committed to. Words without action just aren't enough. When God starts giving us new ideas, new desire, and a new vision, we need to put a deposit down on it. Why? Well, it says in Matthew 6:21 (KJV), "where your treasure is, there will your heart be also." God knows whether our heart is really *in* something . . . and so does *our* mind!

What we invest in, financially, emotionally, spiritually, *and* intellectually, most demonstrates what's important to us . . . as well as what's merely lip service. Lack of investment, an unwillingness to make a *full* commitment, is one of the primary reasons some can get stuck in The GAP for decades. They're waiting on God, but not willing to invest in what they're waiting for. If you're not truly invested in your future, The GAP can end up swallowing your potential, and snatching the best parts of life away.

Investment is a catalyst to calling. Yet most never invest in their purpose. I'm not talking about attending church, tithing, and offering. This is different. If I wanted to becoming a doctor, I would need to invest in medical school; becoming more skilled at whatever God is leading you into also requires intentional focus, investment, and development. Investment isn't always about a degree. It could be investing in a new interest, a gym membership, a training class, a new skill, new community, a counselor, coach, or mentor. Making a new investment is one of the best ways that we can give ourselves permission to do something new. *Water whatever you want to grow.*

SIMPLE PRAYER
God, make me a woman who puts my money where my mouth is.

❧ ONE MORE SHIFT SECRET ❧

While God has given you many gifts, the core thing that God has created you to do is to *be* in relationship with Him. To be. Not to do.

*Our being must precede our doing;
otherwise our doing will destroy our being.*

So The GAP is designed to reconnect us with our sense of *being*. God is seeking to equip us for our larger mission. Turn our mess into a message and change the lives of others like never before. You're reading and hearing this right now because it *is* time for you to shift in some way.

If you've been looking for a sign, this is it.

The Tugs and nudges we feel, those are God's way of getting us back into alignment and inviting us back home. But not back to a familiar place. Our all-things-new Father is calling us back to a new place in the future not the past. *Home* is back to the heart of God, to a deeper place of communion and connection. This is the essence of divine reinvention. *Being.*

Stillness is what best orders our next steps. God is trying to get us into alignment with *His* next assignment. It may not be what you'll be doing forever, but He needs you to take some new steps now. At the time, I didn't know why I needed to get in that audition line for the television show. It didn't make sense from my limited ground's-eye-view. But only God has a clear, higher view. We have to learn to trust His peculiar leading anew.

Shifting into your higher purpose is a life-changing process . . . a season of development. I can't tell you the timing, or how long your stay in this stage will last, but I can tell you that God's timing is perfect. The way through it is by taking one faith step after the next.

chapter ten

ENTERING THE GLORY ZONE

When we do something we've never done, we find something inside we never knew we had.

Before we move on to the final two stages of the Purpose Map, let's do a recap of the first three stages. We started off in Discovery, learning about how The Rules enter our life and condition our thinking. I shared my elementary school experiences to help you connect with how The Rules you learned may have shaped your perception of yourself and where you believe you do or don't belong.

Then there is the Talent Stage. Here we pick a lane to travel, a mountain to climb, and a path or career that becomes our identity. For me it was achievement—winning competitions, getting good grades, competing on television, and becoming a lawyer. I challenged you to think about what path-picking looked like for you.

Next, we stepped into The GAP together. This is a season of transition—a place known as the "in-between." Most women I know are in (or about to enter) The GAP right now, but the goal is for it to become a space that equips you to shift—a canal that advances us into our calling, not a purgatory. My shift began with leaving my law firm, starting a sports agency, and trying (unsuccessfully) to make that mountain my new identity. Then betrayal *forced* me out of my Comfort Zone. In The GAP, we have to do the work of unlearning and letting go of whatever's blocking our bigger.

As we escape from The GAP, shifting our way through the Growth Zone, we eventually cross over from *here* to *there*, and enter life in the Glory Zone. While the Comfort Zone, comprised of the Discovery and Talent stages, was about who we've been, the Glory Zone, comprised of the Gifts and Influence stages, is connected to who we are becoming . . . our calling and higher purpose.

You're entering your *where* . . . your promised land, space, and place. You discover in the Glory Zone that you possess what you never *fully* knew you had. You're brilliant in areas you didn't know existed, and needed in ways you couldn't have calculated. When you surrender your agenda and exchange ambition for anointing, there are no limits to what God will do through you. None.

In the Glory Zone, we learn how God has uniquely *pre-equipped* us to bless others and to change lives like only we can.

❧{ MAKING ROOM FOR DESTINY }❧

When I called off my wedding, I had already shut down my sports agency. Though I'd found myself with my back up against the wall a few times in life, this was different. I felt empty. Incapable. And wounded.

I knew that I had to forgive my ex-fiancé if I wanted to move on. *Forgiveness is the only way forward.* I believed that . . . but I couldn't *do* that. Not right away. Don't let people or religiosity make you feel guilty because it doesn't happen in an instant. *Deliverance isn't magic.* I kept showing up each day. I kept committing to dumping the dirt out of my heart. I discovered that forgiveness isn't *just* about focusing on forgiveness. This was big for me.

Forgiveness can become a self-defeating obsession, especially when everyone is telling you over and over how you have to forgive, but no one tells you *how*. I wouldn't say I'm an expert on this topic. But I found that when we replay our worst memories, we re-wound our self-esteem and re-anchor ourselves in the past. Replaying, masked as trying to forgive, is why it can be incredibly hard to get unstuck.

The key to forgiving is to stop praying about the problem and to start visualizing the solution.

I asked God to give me a new vision of myself and to make me a woman *able* to walk in forgiveness and trust, and not bitterness. Forgiveness is more about the future than the past. And I stopped setting a timeline. Being patient with yourself, yet still intentional about how you approach each day, really works. Progress, not perfection.

I'm not advocating ignoring your hurts. I put my little tush in therapy every week, sometimes twice a week, for over a year. But I focused daily on a new vision, not on the past. Moving forward was a better investment of my energy and put me on the path of healing and elevation.

It might seem too soon after heartbreak or disappointment to start praying for a bigger vision. You'll feel like the right thing to do is pray about what just *happened to* you. That's a trap. Pray for what you want to *come to* you. Don't keep rehearsing what's already been removed! We know God uses disruption to get us to His greater, so pray for a *bigger* vision. A vision *bigger* than blame. *Bigger* than the mess. And *bigger* than your feelings. Feelings aren't fact . . . they're fickle.

Your future, however, that's eternal. You have to speak life into what you seek—not the suffering you've seen.

SIMPLE PRAYER
God, show me your bigger vision for me.
Show me the higher version of me.

I prayed that prayer day in and day out for ten months. It wasn't pretty. And I didn't feel like it most days. Remember, I wasn't sure how I was going to pay my bills. But just days after the "almost-wedding," new started to knock at my door. Unsolicited speaking engagements started coming in. I had been a paid speaker for years at this point, but that same year I called my wedding off and closed my sports agency was the year my then management company mismanaged and spent the money *I* had earned that year! They ran into some hard times, but didn't let me know until it was all gone. So I wasn't making money from my sports agency because I had followed God's leading to close it down . . . and the money I *had* earned wasn't available because of mismanagement. It's water under the bridge now, but it was a tough year. A **really** tough year.

So when speaking engagements, well-paying ones, started coming in the door, I knew I could indeed take the time to heal. God provided. He was able to work with seeds I'd *already* planted over the years. That's the beauty of obedience; it positions us to experience overflow right when we need and least expect it. I didn't have a gazillion speaking gigs—I wasn't traveling every day of the week like I had been in the past—but I had more than enough. I made enough with just a handful of bookings in the first three months of the new year to ensure I'd be able to pay my mortgage and keep the lights on for the rest of the year.

That gave me peace of mind. It also gave me room to heal and to discover new passions. And a chance to just hang out with God and myself. I didn't go *seeking* purpose. I wasn't in a hurry to figure out how to help others. That's not how I found my calling. I needed a break. Too many of us rush into "rescuing the world" when our inner world needs recharging first. It's our inner mountain-climber on autopilot.

We have to manually override our default "do more" setting. I committed to self-care, learning how to smile (yes, that takes intention!), and how to have fun again.

Having fun is important, because finding your calling starts with committing to joy. Take that in for a moment. Joy is our most beautiful and most dangerous asset. Now that might not be what you were expecting to hear, but finding joy is how I tapped into God's business plan for me. It turns out entering God's business is exactly what He intended . . . literally.

GOD IS IN THE BUSINESS OF BUSINESS, TOO

After my failed engagement, I spent ten months bathing in self-care, reading books about identity and God's voice, sticking with my therapy sessions, going to the gym, discovering new restaurants, finding a new church named Victory (go figure!), reconnecting with friends, going to every movie on the planet, and just living. It was difficult at first to know what to do with my time. I only knew how to fill my plate with projects and goals. I didn't know how to live my life. So it took a while to detox until I entered into a place of enjoyment.

I was thirty years old at the time, and I can honestly say living for enjoyment was a first. Enjoyment was different than the thrill of achievement. Enjoyment, however, creates a new, optimistic, and centered state of being. If we commit to entering it, it travels deeper than achievement and busyness, and it's stronger. It's healthier, divinely stimulating and cleansing for the soul. Soon I was hopeful about the future, and I started to dream again.

And then another lightning bolt struck my soul, while I was in my kitchen. It was two words: *Marketplace Women*. I grabbed a pencil and piece of paper and jotted them down right away. I made the "t" in the word *marketplace* a cross. And I felt a stirring for helping women to be successful in business. Specifically, women who loved God and wanted to fulfill their calling. Initially, I assumed it would be a ministry of some sort, something I would do on the side. I had been successful in various businesses, and during this time of self-reflection, men and women alike were constantly asking to pick my brain over lunch.

I had been doing regular commentary for CNN, Fox Business Channel, and ESPN—and I taught myself how to book television appearances. How to pitch producers, craft talking points, and how to get rebooked and become a regular. I had inked endorsement deals with major companies like Rolls-Royce, Nike, Tiffany & Co., Sprint, and PepsiCo for my athlete clients. I hadn't had any previous experience in this, but I figured it out because that's what the clients needed and *I* needed to keep my clients! In the process, I uncovered a skill and a knack for branding and business that I hadn't known I had. And other people started noticing as well.

I saw all of the "can-I-pick-your-brain" requests as a sign that I *did* have something valuable. It just so happened that my *real* sweet spot had nothing to do with my degree. I continued to ask God to reveal his bigger vision for my life and my next step. With that lightning-bolt *Marketplace Women* revelation in the kitchen, it started to come together.

I was preparing to deliver a keynote for Doreen Rainey's Get Radical Women's Conference. My product table was set with my books and I was ready to go, but I felt a wave of emotion and knew I needed to go up to my hotel room quickly. I started to cry—I can't tell you why. That just happens when you're heartbroken and emotion sneaks up when you least expect it. I didn't have much time, so I got myself together, put some eyedrops in, and touched up my makeup. I suited up again—put on my smile, headed back down in the elevator with my head held high, took the stage, and talked to the women about *reinvention*. God definitely showed up and grace carried me through that talk. It was the first time I'd ever given a talk on the subject of reinvention—and it wasn't what I had planned to speak about at all! But during that little trip up to my hotel room to get some tissue, my message became clear. I remember one key statement in particular—it was something I still say and teach—but it was fresh manna delivered in real time while I was on stage that day:

My goal isn't to change who you are. That's not what reinvention is about. My goal is to help you change what you do so you can finally be who you are.

When I finished the keynote, I rushed to my book table and hugged hundreds of women—selling out of books, too! That always feels good.

On the way home, I told my good girlfriend Valorie Burton (who was also speaking at the conference) that I felt this next season of my life was going to be about reinvention—helping women to reinvent their lives. I knew this was a divine thing. Remember, I had never wanted to work with women in the past. But now I couldn't wait to help women step into their full potential and align with God's original intention for their lives.

I had no idea how to make this happen. But I said it out loud. I said it on stage. I said it to Val. And my pencil became my microphone as I sketched the phrase *Marketplace Women* on a random piece of paper alone in my kitchen.

Giving fresh voice to a fresh vision is the way we give that vision permission to grow.

A few days or weeks later, I got an email from a friend of mine, Jonathan, who was passing along a video series he felt would be valuable to me and my future. So I watched the videos. I didn't just watch them . . . I devoured them!

I pulled out a baby-pink spiral notebook, a blue ballpoint pen, and then stayed up all night in my home office taking notes. I didn't sleep. I had been chillin' for months and I'd finally found something that sparked my attention! At some point in the wee hours of the morning, I started seeing blueprints in my head. That's often how vision comes to me—I see blueprints.

So I did what I always do. I grabbed another pencil and drew out boxes, arrows, sequences, and lines—whatever I was seeing my head and mind—and mapped out my vision.

I started learning about the world of life and business coaching. I had always thought life coaches were silly! At the time, I didn't see it as a "real job" and certainly not an elite profession. I didn't understand what they did, and I had no clue what went into business coaching. But I realized I did have insight valuable to offer, and needed to be open to a new way of sharing beyond traditional speaking. I had success in getting sponsorships, getting high-net-worth clients, securing media and publicity, negotiating contracts, landing corporate clients, and branding and marketing. I gave really great advice that actually got results. Plus, I had been doing communication and presentation training for Miss America and Miss USA contestants and pro athletes for years now. What did I have lose? I started with what I had and with what I knew, and trusted it would be enough.

Others saw it—but now I was starting to see it, too.

I taped the piece of paper with the pencil-sketched blueprint of my big vision to my bookcase and saw it every single day for the next several years. I never moved it. It was my road map. On it, I'd drawn plans for events, mentoring programs, products, books, television, and even a publishing and apparel company. It was the blueprint for an entire empire on a single piece of paper drawn with a #2 pencil.

It was not a *formal* business plan, but this was *the* plan. Fresh from Heaven.

I started planning a women's conference for the next year. The desire to do something like that kept coming into my spirit. I hadn't ever held a conference before, so I figured I'd just put together a small workshop for about fifty people in the interim. That way I could start making some money, start helping people, and get my feet wet before launching bigger.

The workshop was called ME University—The Ultimate Business & Branding Bootcamp. I can't even begin to describe how nervous I was in putting this idea out there. Normally, I would have been out there guns a-blazing, but I was hesitant. I needed a win. I didn't know if my heart could survive another failure when it was just starting to beat on its own again.

I contacted a colleague I'd met while speaking at another conference a few years prior—actually the same event I met my ex-fiancé
at, come to think of it! My colleague's name was Brian Tippens, and
he was in leadership at HP—Hewlett-Packard. He was always polite
and insightful but had never green-lighted anything I pitched . . . yet.
Maybe this time would be different and he'd consider HP sponsoring
my boot camp! I knew from landing and negotiating endorsements
and sponsorships for my pro athlete clients that these deals are very
much relationship-driven and that they could take time. Which it did!
Five months of back-and-forth . . . of checking in and hoping for a yes.

I was pretty darn good at putting sponsorship proposals together,
but on this pitch I created a mock flyer so Brian could see how we
planned to integrate HP into our marketing and branding of the event.
I look back at it now and realize how gutsy 'n risky that was! It could
have come across as really presumptuous. After all, we didn't have the
deal or the commitment—but I believe in vision and making it clear so
that others can literally see it and connect to it, too.

And, then on August 13, 2010 (I still have the email!), I got a yes!
HP was, at the time, the eleventh largest company in the USA on the
Fortune list. They were investing in me financially—and they donated
computers, training materials, bags, staffing, and more. I booked the
W Hotel the next day as my venue, and the boot camp was officially
on! Now, I just needed to actually get some attendees.

❧{ THE NEXT YES }❧

I aimed for fifty people to attend that first event. The first person
to buy a ticket was a longtime family friend, Phyllis Jenkins. I called
her Mrs. J for short. Listen—I would have *given* her a ticket. She had
known me since I was five years old. But she didn't ask for a hookup.
That ticket cost $1500 (way more than I'd ever charged—or invested—
at the time!) and she paid for it in full. I can't put into words what that
did for my confidence.

She was an elementary school librarian at the time but had a dream to start sharing her message in a much larger way. The yes from Brian and HP had given me the courage to take that final step and commit to the hotel contract. The yes from Mrs. J let me know that I had taken the right step. At least one person would be in attendance! About thirty-five more yeses came through. Not bad—especially for my first rodeo. It looked like we would have a workshop on our hands!

I'm sharing this with you because people often think entering your calling is easy or is just about an epiphany. But, it's not.

Awakening must be followed by action.

It's scary and at moments it can be snot-flinging ugly. If it's not stretching you, you're not fully on that higher path. But the process of trying something new showed me that people couldn't say yes to something I had never offered. They couldn't say yes until I put myself in position to receive a yes. And you'll be shocked and blown away by those that believe in you and have been waiting for you to come out of *hiding*. Mrs. J was the first customer to invest in what would later become my seminar and coaching business.

I put that other big women's conference on hold and felt the Holy Spirit leading me to focus on what was immediately in front of me—growing ME University. It wasn't just supposed to be an event—it was to be a full-fledged enterprise. That initial two-day event with thirty-five people grew to over one hundred the next year . . . two hundred the year after that. Then it grew to three hundred and four hundred attendees, with everyone investing thousands of dollars each to listen to *me* teach and train. I never had *any* of this on my radar.

I had sold-out conferences. A new team of staff members. Mastermind coaching groups where I'd mentor women (and some men who weren't afraid of pink) on how to brand themselves in the business world. That first sponsorship deal with HP (later HPE) would continue for seven years (and counting). I signed other corporate partners, like Home Depot, Office Depot, Ernst & Young, Delta Air Lines, Black Enterprise, and more. I couldn't see this life and these possibilities on those days I wrestled with depression . . . the days where it was almost impossible to get out of bed. They hadn't been on my radar, either.

I went from not knowing how I was going to pay my bills to running one of the highest earning coaching companies in the country. *The money isn't at all the point.* It's certainly a blessing to be able to pay your bills, give bigger, support missions (which I love to do!), and live without financial stress. *The point is the power of purpose.* When you dare to believe bigger and take a step, even if it's shaky, it's amazing how radically different your life can become even when it seems in shambles. And it's amazing how your purpose really does make appearances earlier in life.

As a child, I used to get in trouble for talking. That caused me to doubt my voice, but it turns out my voice was the very bridge to my calling and this season of next-level assignment. And I didn't initially want to work with women because of the lack of support I'd experienced from women in leadership, but they were my calling. You might be missing your mission because of a mess and bad memories, too.

> *Greater purpose is almost always hidden behind a place of pain.*

God embeds purpose in the last place we'd think to look because it takes faith and trust to go there. Let that sink in. *The unlimited is hidden inside the unlikely.* And it confuses *little me* and the enemy, too. *Little me* thinks your wounding is a sign disruption is winning. But it's not. It's developing a next level of destiny within you.

{ YOU KNOW IT'S A GIFT, RIGHT? }

When God moves, the process is unpredictable, but the outcome is impeccable.

In the second year of my coaching and seminar business, I led ten women in a business mentoring retreat. The retreat was supposed to be an intimate professional gathering, but really it turned into a revival. The women (myself included) each left with clarity and newfound, fresh focus. Some were stay-at-home moms seeking more meaning, while others were career women ready to shift into their calling, and monetize their insight and talents. All were in transition—they were in *their shift.*

"You know it's a gift, right?" That's what Judge Eileen Olds, one of the women, told me during the morning bathroom break. I just kept saying, "yes ma'am" and "thank you." She kept saying it all day. Truth is, I didn't know what the heck she meant! I figured she was just being polite and was giving a you're-doing-a-good-job compliment. And, at the time, I believed I was *just* teaching business principles. Really, I was *unlocking.*

That's what I call it now. Today, I can see that Judge Eileen was referring to the way I could easily help people figure out the best way to say something . . . pretty much anything. Whether it was coming up with the perfect tagline or title, or helping them to clearly identify and communicate in a compelling and captivating way what value they offered to the world. I didn't have to prepare. It flowed effortlessly. The moment anyone shares what they are struggling to do, it goes into my brain like a complex code and comes out simple and clear. I was always good with words—coming up with my platform back when self-esteem wasn't "good enough" actually helped me to figure out messaging. I know how to say stuff in a way that works and gets to yes in almost any arena—especially business.

That's how I ended up with $200,000 in academic scholarships—learning how to get to yes and craft messages that mattered and resonated. I call 'em *money messages*. I paid my way through law school by coaching Miss America and Miss USA contestants with their platform messages, résumés, and interviewing skills, too, with a company called Communication Counts! Still, Judge Eileen's compliment took me by surprise.

I saw message crafting as an ability (something I *could* do), but I didn't really understand it as a gift (something I was *called* to do). It came so easily that I didn't know to truly *value* it.

As the day went on, there were tears . . . lots of them. It kinda freaked me out. There are no tears in business—at least that's what the fellas had taught over the years! But God unleashes things you never imagined or intended. This retreat became such a spiritual experience . . . and in a *boardroom* of all places. Mushy stuff is *not* what any of the women came for. They came to talk about business—how to make more money. Instead, we discovered something better than business. We found destiny. I say *we* because I unlocked it in myself, too. Let me tell you something.

Destiny discovery is totally unpredictable.

This little boardroom had become a delivery room. It was a safe haven to shed fears, dream forbidden dreams out loud, and to give ourselves as women guilt-free permission to be strategic about ourselves. This was *destiny-mapping*. And God loves destiny. He *planted* eternity in our human hearts for a reason:

Yet God has made everything beautiful [and appropriate] for its own time. He has planted eternity in the human heart, but even so, people cannot see the whole scope of God's work from beginning to end.

—Ecclesiastes 3:11 (NLT).

Here's the really crazy thing. While I was helping these ladies find *their* path, I stumbled upon mine. As I was helping them to believe in the beauty and rarity of their voice, I found my own.

You don't find your calling on the sidelines. You find it once you're in it. It's not something to be explained . . . it's something to be explored. Destiny is not an intellectual exercise. It's experiential.

God reveals your brilliance *while* you're building the bridge . . . not once you've gotten to the other side. The act of building up and pouring into others creates benefits for all. As you help others discover something new, you discover something unexplainable in yourself, too.

Over time, I realized that messaging—helping others find their voice personally and professionally—was a *gift*. A spiritual gift at that. It wasn't listed in the Bible with the gifts and fruits of the spirit. I thought divine gifts were limited to healing the sick, giving, prophesying, and speaking in tongues. No one in *all* of my thirty plus years of church had ever taught me differently.

But the truth is, *there are no limits as to what God is able to do in us and through us.* Just because our eyes have not seen, ears have not heard, and minds have not yet comprehended the anointing and immeasurable hope to which we've been called, that doesn't mean we haven't been called to it. Remember, God doesn't want our purpose to be a mystery. He *wants* us to have mastery. The key to understanding and entering our calling is found in *unlocking our gifts*, sharing them with others, and *then* developing them. Catch that order. We develop our gifts *as* we share them, not before.

So you see, we don't "find" our calling. God calls us, not the other way around. Our role is to get out of our way long enough to hear the call and surrender to it. Entering your calling doesn't happen in theory or by doing research, it emerges in the stretch and *during* faith steps. That's how you end up in the thick of it.

❧ CALLING SIGNS ❧

So this is how I found my calling—or how I got out of the way so it could find me. In the process I learned a few things.

+ *First*, I am a teacher. I never realized and internalized it before. I heard Heaven whisper it when I was stewing at my desk at eleven years old in the sixth grade. But now I understand that "teacher" is at the core of my identity, and I believe it to be at the core of your identity, too.

+ *Second*, calling (our mission and specific assignment) becomes clear when we're giving, serving, or imparting something . . . when we're making others' lives better. It's not an intellectual exercise, it's engagement.

+ *Third*, we each have a voice, and our voice unlocks the voice in others. When I did work for legal aid, I was serving as the voice for those that didn't have a voice. Later, I was helping Miss America and Miss USA contestants, pro athletes, politicians, and even big brands figure out how to get their message across—how to share their voice in a way that communicated the depth of their vision. I gained an appreciation for voice and how divine it is. More on that in the remaining chapters.

+ *Fourth*, we can't be intentional about something we don't realize we have. This is huge. And this is where accessing our *Inner Vault* comes in. I didn't value this "messaging thing" because it came naturally. I wasn't trained in it and I didn't go to school for it. We often overlook our area of significance because we don't think of things that come easy as being connected to our calling. We tend to value what we have to struggle to acquire. That's why we esteem degrees and careers—things with clear titles and things we had to *earn*. But, as we'll soon see, gifts aren't earned. And, titles can become idols. Gifts have to be developed, but at the core, they were given in grace before we took our first breath.

+ *Finally*, mentorship is at the heart of higher purpose. Sharing what we've learned, putting our insight and genius to work, and sharing our story and abilities with others—that's the ticket into the promised land . . . both for you and those you're assigned to.

People often ask how I knew I was actually *in* my calling. That can be a tricky question because I firmly believe you can be in your calling or on assignment (meaning you're where God needs you at the moment) at different times in your life. Entering a *season* of calling doesn't necessarily mean you were in the wrong place before. It just means you've been recruited to go and serve someplace fresh . . . and you're being *invited* to experience something awesome and new.

Calling is an opportunity to become intentional and to exit randomness.

I'll share in the next chapter more about your master purpose and how it, along with your gifts, guides you in this season of calling. But how did I know I wasn't just in another random lane this time? These indicators helped me to know that I was in my assignment:

1. **UNPREDICTABILITY.** It wasn't on my radar! God loves to surprise us. Calling—your specific assignment—isn't predictable.

2. **CONFIRMATION.** It aligned with the new vision God had been hinting at for some time—esteem-building, branding, and business training for women. There was convergence of both passion and proficiency.

3. **IMPACT.** I was making a real difference in the lives of other women. This was what God meant when he said I would change the lives of women like never before. Well, I had indeed *never* done this, yet their lives were elevating and transforming in dramatically different ways. And it wasn't just what they were learning about how to start and grow a business—it was their walk with God that was growing, too.

4. **JOY.** I loved the chance to love on women. To help them believe bigger and live bolder. I loved the rush of ideas I'd get for others, I loved praying with them, I loved teaching and mapping out business strategies and messaging. And I loved discovering I was a coach at heart—*unlocking* my ability to do what my twirling coaches and mentors had done for me. To push others past their blocks and fears and to find unique ways to pull out greatness. I loved it and still do.

5. **RESULTS.** I was good at it. Coaching and teaching seminars were new to me, but they ignited and resurrected my original spiritual gifts—things like messaging, packaging, and presentation. And it gave me a chance to discover my spiritual walk as a catalyst and teacher, too. *When your gifts unlock others' gifts, then that's when you know you're in your calling.* Give yourself a chance to explore the untapped parts of you.

6. **FREEDOM.** I didn't need permission to do it! I didn't have any rules I had to follow. I only needed God's voice. *We don't need permission to do the thing God has already commissioned.* Jesus was a rebel and a threat because He didn't idolize protocol. He didn't fit in, nor did He try to fit in. He followed the Holy Spirit, which isn't usually the same thing.

I finally understood that moment in my kitchen, when I'd made the "t" in *Marketplace Women* a cross. *Business really was God's business.* It was and is an avenue for us to cross over into His higher purpose. God anoints whatever *He* wants—even the realm of business—to fulfill a purpose and plan only He can orchestrate and amplify.

Getting to love what you do isn't a luxury for a Believer, it is a necessity.

It's like air—only we don't know it until we've breathed it. I'm not talking about career, mind you. You can have career *and* calling at the same time. Careers are man-made. Calling is God led. For Mary, carrying Jesus wasn't a career! It was being available for the unpredictable—that's calling, honey. It's being in alignment with where God needs you. Calling calls forth the best of who you are . . . not just what you've learned to do. It will intimidate you, but alignment brings you joy and fulfillment—a sense of significance success can't even touch.

I'll say it again—God *loves, loves, loves* to surprise us and to send us to places that seem out of reach. That way we rely on him to give us eyes to see, ears to hear, and the type of supernatural strength for the next level that can only come from cleaving to *His* voice and being in *His* presence.

4

GIFTS

STAGE

How did God really design me?

chapter eleven

STAGE FOUR: GIFTS

Gifts are those deposits within you that bring the best out of you and improve the lives of those around you.

Discovery, Talent, and shifting through The GAP have now ushered us into stage four of the Purpose Map, which I call GIFTS. The GIFTS stage is where we find our voice and discover our super-powers—the keys we'll need to fulfill our calling and change lives. Here, we'll use all we've learned and all we've been given, the good with the bad, to elevate and accelerate the lives of others. It's time to use our wisdom, intellect, personality, story, creativity, and God-given genius to help others tap into their own.

Life has been grooming us for this very season and for such a time as this. The drama 'n trauma, the wins and the losses, the trophies and the trials, selection laced with rejection, and the love 'n heartbreak, too—it's all been the master class for your life mission and message. But what is the mission? What is the message?

YOU.

God has already deposited His message, along with super-attributes and special abilities you'll need to fulfill His larger mission, *in* you. They're in your *mouth* (your voice), *muscles* (your talents), and *divine DNA* (your personality). These are your gifts.

Gifts are the agents of purpose, and the bedrock of calling. They exist to provide laser focus in your life by showing you what your life is really about. We're here to teach, to serve, and to gift out what's been gifted in us. The exciting thing about the GIFTS stage is discovering hidden abilities and supernatural proficiencies you didn't even know you had. These super-abilities and super-powers serve a purpose larger than ourselves.

WHAT ARE GIFTS?

Simply put, gifts are what you've been given to give to others. Your gifts help *fulfill* God's game plan. Gifts *move* others forward (into their *there*). And gifts *improve* lives. Note these words—fulfill, move, and improve. These are the results your gifts are designed to produce.

+ Fulfill God's game plan.

+ Move others forward.

+ Improve others' lives.

To understand your gifts, you've gotta understand what I call the *law of interdependency* and God's game plan. Purpose begins and ends with its Creator. Everything created has purpose—a reason for being. The air, the trees, the birds and the bees. Everything in our ecosystem is interdependent—it all works together . . . this for that, and that for this. God's infinite intelligence and intentionality was at work when He created me and you, too. We're designed to be interdependent. Just as the bee needs the flower, I need you, and vice versa. The bee has the special ability to extract pollen and produce honey. The grasshopper can't do that and isn't supposed to. Neither is the ladybug. But the bee knows its mission because the bee knows it has the ability to fly, to see what's *in* the flower, and to transform those raw materials into miracle food. The bee knows that it's not a swimmer. It's not a writer or a soccer player. Unlike us, it can't be what it is not. But the power and the beauty of the bee is the bee knows what the bee is.

You see, the bee knows how to focus because the bee uses what's been given. Nothing more, nothing less. And that's how our gifts are supposed to work. They are to anchor our identity and give us focus— the type of focus that creates momentum and impact. Improving our lives as we improve the lives of others. Though our gifts differ, you need me and I need you. The gifts (super-abilities) you've been given enable me to move forward, and my gifts do the same (albeit in a different way) for you.

But you're not a bee. You have many talents and interests. And that's where confusion comes in. The endless possibilities can be overwhelming. We're full of potential. So the question is, how do we focus *our* lives? That's where our gifts come in as guides.

> *Gifts align us with the best parts of ourselves that bring out the best in others.*

Our gifts advance us. They operate in flow and forwardness. Tapping into our gifts is one of the most sacred, humbling, and God-glorifying things we can do. He has designed our lives to bring glory to Him by depositing within us God-glorying abilities and propensities. Everything from our personality to the way we're built to think, solve problems, and create is *specifically* purposed (in some way) to connect others to God and his bigger plan.

Each person is given something to do that shows who God is.
                            —*1 Corinthians 12:7 (MSG)*

When you think of a child who does something that reminds you of his or her parent, you see the DNA passed down into that child's behavior. God's DNA works the same way. God deposited his DNA— Dynamic Noteworthy Attributes—into your being. When you speak up, use your voice, shine, and walk in your brilliance, others don't actually see you. They see the God in you. It's your "It factor," an unexplainable, magnetic essence about you. There is a part of God's DNA, a unique strand of supernatural ability, God exclusively placed inside you. It holds the answers to your life's purpose.

Your spiritual DNA holds the roadmap to your destiny.

The GIFT stage aligns us with the essence of who we are, who we've always been, and the "who" we've been running from becoming. Our life plan is tied to the gifts we've been given. When we understand our gifts, we better understand God's goals for our life. And what *isn't* his intention, also. It's no wonder the enemy loves to keep us busy, distracted, and spending precious time on things, people, and places that have nothing to do with our core purpose.

When we're out of alignment, we're like a grasshopper trying to make honey, or a bee trying swim in the Olympics. Or like a lawyer who is really supposed to be a painter, a customer service rep who is really a worship leader. When in alignment, however, we're like a river that finds its way to the sea. We're unstoppable.

❧ GIFT BOXES AND LIFE GUIDING KEYS ❧

My love for the topic of gifts was spawned while I was managing pro athletes. This was well before the infidelity. While sitting with God in prayer, I had a vivid revelation but didn't fully understand what it meant back then. I did know it had something to do with the future, and I knew this wasn't just pertaining to *my* future; it was about you, too. It was about the way we're collectively supposed to look at the future. As I sat in stillness in my prayer closet with my eyes closed, waiting for what God would say next, an acronym dropped into my spirit: GIFT stood for (G)od's (I)ntended (F)uture (T)reasures.

Years later, after I started to grow my coaching company, I reflected on that revelation. God took me back there, but to a deeper place with more direction. As you can tell by now, I have a sacred appreciation for vision. And I believe this vision is not just for me—it can change your outlook, too, if you're willing to open your heart and mind to really receive it.

So. Center yourself. Take a deep breath with me.

Now, imagine a large gift box sitting in front of you.

It is spectacularly wrapped, with a custom-made tag that has only your name on it. You try to put your arms around it, but it's too big. Then, unsure as to what's inside, you cautiously shake it. You hear rattling and clanging inside. As your curiosity builds, a heavenly whisper says, *It's okay. You're allowed. Open it.* So you take the top off the box and discover it's filled with a bunch of keys. Each one is a different size. Some are really large while others are medium-sized and some itty-bitty. You don't know what each key is for and you have no clue what each unlocks, but the keys must unlock something or else they wouldn't have been made, right?

As you're looking inside your gift box, wondering why no one has ever shown you these keys with your name engraved on them before now, the heavenly whisper returns. It's God speaking. He explains:

This, my child, is your inheritance.
These keys are your superpowers, each connecting you to
everything you'll ever need.
They will guide you into everything I've built you to build for me,
and will equip you to bless others on my behalf for a lifetime.
Your life purpose and divine identity are found inside of this box.
Not in the box the world has put you in, or the
boxes you've hid yourself in.
You're out of place there. I've brought you out from there to here so
that you'll finally be able to see and unleash what I've given you.
My DNA formed each key.
Each key is in you and is a part of you, just as each is a neces-
sary part of me and comes from me.
Apart from me your life will be limited.
With me you will be unstoppable.
As you pick up each key and learn to trust me, I'll guide you
to where each key belongs.
Know now that each key isn't linked to a man-made lock, door,
or vault, but to a lost lock hidden inside the hearts of men.
This is your mission. This is your purpose.
Your life matters. You carry My Spirit, and the keys to unlock-
ing my anointing, in your DNA.
You hold the light, the salt, the refreshing, and the fire others
have been waiting for.
You've been called for such a time as this. The people are wait-
ing. Now is the time.

This revelation gave me goose bumps then, and it still does today. Something stirs and stands up inside of me whenever I talk about calling, divine identity, and maximizing potential; whenever God shares a fresh, soul-bathing revelation about what it takes to be all we've been called to be.

God strategically hides his plans for us inside of us.

He places them there on purpose as a way of speaking to us about us. It's so intimate . . . so meticulous. He doesn't want us looking outside of ourselves for the super-sweet and spectacular parts of Him that can only be discovered by journeying within. Instead, he has given us keys. The keys reflect our divine gifts, explain our divine DNA, and open up the ancient, anointed paths for our lives.

{ GIFT POWER }

First, your gifts *unlock closed doors*, enabling others to enter their *there*. They are like an arrow pointing the way, or a bridge that makes it easier for others to get to their other side. That might mean your gifts help them enter a place and state of greater clarity, wisdom, ability, intelligence, health, joy, wealth, and so on. Your gifts enable and teach others how to move forward, to overcome, to improve, to problem-solve, or to enhance their lives in some way.

Second, your gifts *unlock hidden treasures*, enabling others to tap into their untapped potential and gifts, too. They awaken dormant dreams and ignite what needs to be resurrected in others. Gifts motivate others to work harder, smile, believe, try, or get back up. They're the *"you can, too"* catalyst that every calling craves and needs.

Gifts are given *to* you but are not *for* you. This is important! Gifts are meant to be given . . . the power in your gift is activated *in* the giving. That's where the transfer happens. And that's why we find our calling when we're in motion, not in contemplation. Your best shows up when you're giving, serving, inspiring, creating, executing, teaching, and leading. That's when you feel most alive. That's the interdependent nature and power of our gifts.

❧ THE POTENTIAL PYRAMID ❧

We all have gifts. And hopefully we have now a better idea of how they work. But how do you know what *your* gifts are? And what's the difference between a gift and a talent? It's an important distinction. Not all potential is created equal!

This is where I like to use what I call the *Potential Pyramid*. It helps me explain the different levels of ability and possibility we all have. Each level represents a level of ease or difficulty. The easier something comes and the more impact and joy it brings, the higher up it is on the spectrum and the closer it is to your gift spot, your highest self.

The harder something is and the more stress it brings (even if it's helping others to some extent), the lower it falls on the pyramid and the farther away it is from your gift domain.

We'll start at Level 4, which is the bottom of the pyramid, and then work our way up to the top.

Level 4 potential is INEPTNESS.

Simply put, when we're operating in the inept sphere, we're doing things we are not very good at. These tasks may be necessary, but they don't bring us joy. We do them because they need to be done or because we feel like we have to. I would put diaper changing and singing in this category. Not my thing! I can change a diaper, but I don't *love* it. And I love singing, but I'm not good at it! And it certainly doesn't bring others joy—maybe comic relief, but not applause, at least not for the right reasons. I'd also add to this list putting anything together that comes in a box and requires tools—furniture, appliances, whatever. If it involves assembly, I don't like it! My sister-in-love, Tiffany, she's an engineer. She loves this stuff. She, not my brother, puts together the complex shelving units in their house and the toys for their two boys. Her mind is wired for assembly and putting things together. He *can* do it, but she *loves* to do it.

When we do things we're inept at, we invite pain, frustration, stress, resentment, and even anger. We're going against our "gift-grain" and swimming upstream . . . against the natural current and flow of our life. You *can* do these things, but you're not *uniquely blessed* to. They don't help you maximize your potential and your higher purpose.

Level 3 potential is AVERAGENESS.

In the average realm, you can figure out how to do something, but it's a stretch. It doesn't come easily. That would be like creating spreadsheets or organizing stats 'n facts for me. I can do these things. I've been doing them for years, but I'm exhausted from them. I felt this way back when I used to do my own bookkeeping . . . something most start-up entrepreneurs do until they hire someone else to take it off their hands. I was pretty good at it, but definitely not a natural. When I practiced as an attorney, I'd put researching case law into this category, too. I learned *how* to research; I spent three years at one of the best schools in the country. I knew how to draft briefs and apply legal reasoning, and was compensated very well for it. But I never once got excited about finding the perfect ruling. Others did. They loved the hunt. They loved research and legal writing. For me, it was a necessary part of my job. I wanted to help others, and I really wanted to be a litigator, but the reality is most of the work of a lawyer at a big firm is researching. So that explains why I was always so drained at work. I was in the wrong lane but didn't know it. I didn't know my gifts.

With focused attention and practice, we can get better at *any-thing* over time, which is encouraging but can also be misaligning. *We mustn't spend our lives only on what we've chosen and learned versus living where God is leading.* Plus, no matter how hard you try, you may not ever be better than average at some things—and that's okay. It's by design. What we're *able* to do is different than what we're gifted and called to do.

Level 2 potential is TALENT.

Talents are the things we've become skilled and experienced at doing. We're good, even great, in these areas. We're all-pro, world-class high performers. We know our stuff and it shows. We've put in time, effort, and practice, which has helped us to get results. It's what leads to the titles, trophies, awards, and accolades we acquire.

Your talents probably allow you to put food on the table and provide security for those you love. Your consistency and performance are what lead others to christen you with the label of *talented*—being good at what you do and how you do it. And they are right . . . you are. Again, you can become excellent at anything you focus on. The more you work at it, the better you get, and the higher up the mountain of success you climb. Potential grows into proficiency and even mastery. But mastery doesn't always equal fulfillment, impact, and significance. The question isn't whether you're good or great, successful or seen. The question is whether you've been focusing on the inner attributes and abilities connected to your highest self.

Level 1 potential is GIFTED.

Gifts are the things we're *called* to do, not just the things we *can* do. That's a really key distinction. Remember, our gifts reflect God's goals. If God had wanted me to be a singer, He would have given me the ability to hold a tune. He didn't give me that gift, which gives me a resounding clue that this is not the path for me! And gifts contain anointing—that's divine power. A super-ability. This is how we're able to exert the least amount of effort yet still experience the most fulfillment, significance, and divine flow.

Some simple clues about your gifts and your gifted realm:

+ **JOY.** Gifts bring you joy and they are life-changing . . . both for you and for others.

+ **EASE.** Gifts flow from a natural, innate place of ease.

+ **PASSION.** Gifts ignite your passion and call forth your best self. You feel alive when you're operating in them. In fact, you love life the most when you're in your gifts—you're in the state, in the zone, and lose track of time.

+ **PROFICIENCY.** Gifts demonstrate a superior proficiency, aptitude, and quality. You have a super-ability to do effortlessly what is difficult for others. You can do it quicker, better, and you keep improving . . . quantum leaping past others.

+ **IMPACT.** Your gifts make a positive difference. When in your presence, people soar where they once struggled. Others desire, benefit from, and love 'em, too.

Tragedy is being very good at the wrong thing.

Focus is freeing! Level 1 is our gift realm, where we want to be and focus. We want to be operating at our highest potential—in our sweet spot of joy, passion, fulfillment, and impact. It's where and how we most naturally move others forward, improve their lives, and unleash their best. It's where greatness, goodness, and grace collide to form our true identity. Our gifts represent the core of *how* God made us. And the gift realm is where God needs you and is seeking to reposition you now. It is what your purpose journey, disruption, and tugs are all about.

The Potential Pyramid

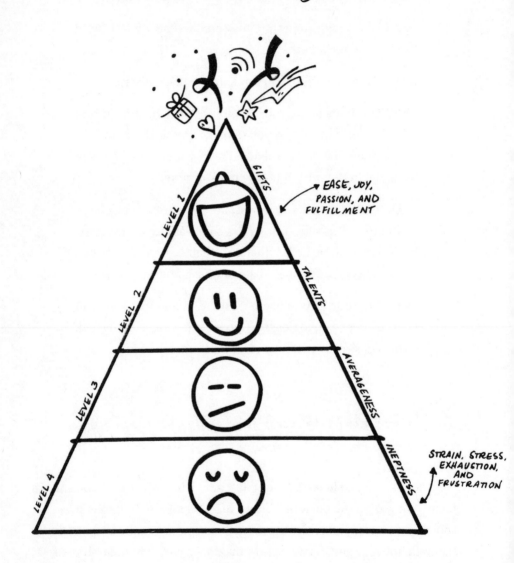

You're the only carrier of *your* gifts. When you hide, your gifts and all they contain die. Your spiritual DNA isn't found anywhere else on the planet. No one has this drop of genetic destiny. When we're out of sync with our gifts, we're swimming upstream. We're *toiling* (grinding and forcing) versus *tilling* (grooming and allowing). God's yoke is easy and His burden is light for a reason. *Ease* is a clue about where we really belong— where we're supposed to flow. And *how* we're supposed to shine.

Let's pause for a moment to allow the above to sink in, and for a moment of reflection.

What do you feel your gifts are?

If doubt is trying to pipe up in this moment, resist the *little me* that might whisper, saying you have nothing special to offer. Embrace the certainty that you do. Keep it simple, be kind to yourself, and remember that gift discovery is a lifelong process.

When do you feel the most joy and passion?

What comes easy for you?

What are you naturally good at?

What do others compliment you on? (maybe something you often dismiss or think is no big deal)

What in you brings out the best in others?

How are others improved by your presence? Your perspective? Your personality?

And how have you been spending your life-energy? Has most of your time been spent in areas beneath your true gifts and talents?

To be clear, this does not mean everything is or should be easy. Nor does it mean that gifts don't require work. *Development is just as sacred as the gifts themselves.* Even a seed must be watered, nurtured, and pruned to grow. Discipline gives us depth. It grounds us like roots do a tree, such that we aren't all fruit so to speak. We need the character, maturity, and grit necessary for our calling—which is why the depth gained during the Discovery and Talent stages is so critical. Gifts need development, experience, and investment to flourish. And life requires us to do things we don't feel like doing. We have to take out the trash, do our homework, mow the lawn, pay the bills, and put food on the table. And we have to practice, prepare for, and stick with anything we desire to be proficient at. When we're serious about our gifts, however, we invest in them—we don't just talk about 'em . . . we commit fully. And we want to be around other gift-minded, gift-investing, and gift-growing people, too. Gifts become like iron that sharpens iron.

❧ GIFTS VERSUS TALENTS ❧

Initially, it can be tricky to tell our talents from our gifts, but distinguishing them can be life changing. Be patient . . . it takes a little time. It helps to take the focus off yourself. Don't just look at experience and familiarity . . . look at impact. *What is it that you do that unlocks the best in others? Unlocking* is what each of us is built for; it's what gifts are all about.

Talents often hide our gifts. Our proficiencies, the things we're good at, can end up becoming our *formed* identity, reflecting the person *we decided* to become. The current persona our choices formed. They often mask purpose, and with it, our *born identity*. Gifts are the things God uniquely prewired us to do. Abilities that reflect an aspect of him and help others, too.

Your best talents, the ones you've likely become known for, are like *super-skills*. Again, the things you're *really* good at. However, your gifts are your God-given *superpowers*.

Take Superman, for example. Journalism was a super-skill for him. But flying was a superpower. He didn't fly to impress others; he flew so that he could *serve* others. That's what all gifts—aka superpowers— are for. You benefit from them, too, but that's the bonus, not the core purpose. The core purpose is service.

Keep in mind that you may not fully be able to pinpoint your superpowers right away because you haven't fully explored, developed, or even acknowledged them.

> *There are many things you've learned to do well, and then there are things you've never done that you do even better.*

Even though Superman didn't fly the day he was born, it didn't mean he couldn't! He just had to discover and develop his *superpower*. And just as you have multiple talents, you also have more than one *superpower* (gift). It will take a lifetime to unlock 'em, but it helps first to know that you have them so that you can be open to fully uncovering and activating them. We're then more awake and able to allow our gifts to guide us into our future. A *super-skill* (talent) for me might be a *superpower* (gift) for you. My weakness can be your strength and vice versa. The *law of interdependency* means *this* needs that, and *that* needs this. God made us that way so we'd rely on each other and work together from our individual, interconnected sweet spots to advance His purposes.

Your *superpower* could be . . .

Giving

Drawing

Communicating

Teaching

Creating

Encouraging

Strategizing

Organizing

Writing

Cooking

Coding

Advising and Mentoring

Managing

Caretaking

Do any of the above resonate with you?

It's not an exhaustive list. The possibilities are as limitless as God Himself.

Talents enable us to do amazing things for ourselves *and* for others. But talents, our learned abilities, can only take us so far. They aren't enough to get you where God wants to take you. Think of an airplane. Great if you want to travel across the country. Not so great if you want to go to outer space. Things work differently in *this* outer space—in the gift realm. You're able to defy gravity and manifest what would otherwise be impossible. Gifts operate at an entirely different frequency.

God's trying to get us from where we are now to where He needs us next . . . from talent and success to gifts and significance. It takes faith, believing bigger, to unlock our next-level gifts and enter a new dimension. It's time to rely on God, not our comfort-zone strengths.

Don't worry if the line between a talent and a gift feels a little blurry. Your talents may very well be closely connected to your gifts, too. For example, let's say you've been a successful manager in your career. You've led teams and know how to help people produce great results. An upshift for you might mean teaching others how to manage. The super-skill would be managing. The superpower would be teaching, mentoring, giving back, and empowering others to do what you've learned, to actually *believe* they can do it, and also sharing other unexpected life lessons you've gained along the way. If you've been a mother and homemaker, then a superpower for you might be patience or organization. If you're a singer, your superpower is likely found in your lyrics or how you make others *feel*. It can be anything. You'll find "your thing" as you pay more and more attention to what unlocks your passions and creativity, and what unlocks the best in others.

The goal here isn't perfection. When it comes to gift discovery, the goal is experimentation, practice, and service.

> *As long as improving the lives of others is your goal, everything else gets a grace bath.*

Don't overthink it. God will use your intention to serve to create something that uplifts and improves, to lead others to a higher level, and to usher you closer to your true sweet spot—your purpose place. God is *not* looking for you to get this purpose thing just right, nor is he waiting to reprimand you if you get it wrong. There really is no wrong. There is only surrender. Belief. And, trust. God will course-correct as long as your heart is connected to His. Again, finding your purpose is not an intellectual exercise, and you unlock your purpose while you're in action, not contemplation. I've got a nice chart that should make it even clearer to distinguish talents from gifts.

Talents	*Gifts*
Comfort Zone	Glory Zone
What We've Learned to Do	What We're Called to Do
Formed Identity	Born Identity
The Rules (Protocol)	Glory (Higher Purpose)
Decided	Imparted
Doing	Being
Driven (Achievement)	Directed (Alignment)
Grinding and Striving	Grace and Surrender
Fight	Flow
Trying	Teaching
Task-Driven	Testimony-Driven
Super-skills	Superpowers
Discipline	Destiny
Mountain Climbing	Miracle Unleashing
Success and Safety	Significance
Labels and Titles	Lessons and Transformation
Muscle	The Message
Student	Teacher

So, again, what do you feel your gifts are?

How is someone else's life improved because of your presence?

Understanding how you're wired makes it easier to realize your purpose and to embrace what your life mission is really all about. Your gifts are the ultimate clue to the real you. *The flow of purpose is attached to our gifts, not our talent.* The Talent Stage simply isn't big enough to contain the unlimited essence of your divine DNA and God's next-level plan for your life and light. It's time to stop jean-wigglin' our way into a size-too-small life that no longer fits. God won't shrink to accommodate our rules and comforts. Instead, purpose calls us out of the familiar and into the peculiar—a bigger, God-built place talent can't touch and success seekers can't find. Romans 12:6 (MSG) says it best: "Let's just go ahead and be what we were meant to be."

chapter twelve

FINDING YOUR VOICE

Words are themselves sacred.
God's tool for bringing holiness, or evil, into the world.
— A. J. Heschel

We've already discussed that gifts are the special abilities we have that improve the lives of others. But that's not all they are. Our gifts help us discover our voice—and our voice is the main point.

Let me explain. A while back, I was attending a conference focused on helping entrepreneurs go to the next level. It wasn't just about tactics and strategy, it was also about elevating your thinking and your perception of yourself. When the day was over, I headed back to my hotel room, took a shower, and before I could finish, something clicked in me. I felt God saying . . . *Voice. Voice. Voice. This is what you do, this is who you are . . . and this is what you awaken in others.* I threw on my pj's and quickly curled up under the covers with just a bedside lamp on. I pulled out my journal and my trusty blue pen—both had become good friends on my journey of self-discovery and reinvention.

I'd had enough of these moments to know God was about to start talking and my job was to start writing and recording. As I held my blue pen, my soul uttered what I consciously didn't know I needed to understand in this moment: *Why am I here, God?* And, I wrote exactly what He whispered.

You're not just a voice, you are voice.

That's your identity.

That is who you are and it's who you have always been.

All of the battles, struggles, and the laundry list of what felt like attacks on my self-esteem over the years flashed before my eyes. It not only made sense, it brought clarity and significance.

This is why we are a target of the enemy.

Our voice is the ultimate threat to the enemy.

When God speaks, the enemy must flee. If the enemy can keep us intimidated by our circumstances and afraid of our own light, then he can keep us silent. The enemy knows our purpose is impact. Transformation. Gift-giving and leadership. And he knows the most powerful vehicle for us advancing God's vision is finding 'n flowing in our voice.

But when we feel incapable, we don't speak. *Keeping us in a perpetual state of perceived inadequacy is the mission of the enemy.* If we don't *believe* we have something worthy of sharing, we stay silent. Quiet. In our place. Exactly where The Rules told us we "belong." We focus our life, instead, on where we feel good enough . . . worthy enough to be and to be heard. We cleave to mountains and run away from miracles.

Embracing this idea that *I am voice* . . . that *we* are voice . . . and that we are an intentional extension of God's voice, it gives context to what the battles we face are really all about. It's the most strategic way the enemy chips away at our divine identity, our confidence, and our self-perception, which becomes our reality.

Once I grasped all this, I started to understand how my purpose had always been attached to helping others discover, believe in, and embrace their voice. That's why I was good at messaging—it's helping others find their voice. That's what Judge Eileen was trying to get me to see with those seemingly magical, effortless makeover moments during our business retreats. It *was* a gift. That's why I'd always win the interview category in the Miss America competitions, and it's why my first business was a communications and presentation company called *Communication Counts!* I loved working at legal aid because at legal aid I had a chance to be an advocate for the voiceless. It's even why my sports agency grew so quickly—I was helping athletes communicate their vision and spread their larger life message.

By the time I'd finished writing all this down, it was the wee hours of the morning, and I felt incredibly loved . . . in fact I jotted at the end of my journaling that it seemed like Heaven had just proposed to me! That's how I knew this was real and true—not just for me but for you, too.

There was order in what looked chaotic and seemed random. There was this hidden thread woven into so many experiences, but I had never put it all together. Here is the main thing I took away:

You are not just a voice, you are voice.
It's your greatest superpower.

{ OUR UNIVERSAL SUPERPOWER }

Our supreme *superpower*, the master key . . . the biggest in the box that most explains our calling and divine identity, is our voice. It's our shared, universal superpower. We all have it.

Think about how this all got started. God *spoke*. He said, "Let there be light." And there was light. God is Father. God is Teacher. But I think we often forget how God is first and foremost Creator. Not a magician that snapped his fingers and said give me some humans. He *spoke* life into being. Plus, John 1:1 (NIV, emphasis mine) reminds us that "in the beginning was the Word, and the word was with God, and the Word *was* God." It's who God is. We're created in His image—a living word.

To that end, we don't just *have* a voice, we *are voice*. God is voice and uses voice to create new ideas, miracles, and solutions. His voice is both the vision and the vehicle to our promised land. Again, we're created in His image, too.

When we use our voice as an extension of God's voice, we create the way God creates.

This is why *your* story matters. This is why your life experiences, gifts, and talents have brought you to this point. *Voice is who you are. Your life is a living word.* It's what all of the *little me* battles have been about: self-doubt, rejection, regret, isolation, busyness, procrastination, and even perfectionism. They've all been assassination attempts to either block or silence your voice over the years.

That whisper . . . *Who do you think you are?*

Who's gonna listen to you?
You're too young.
You're too old.
You're not ready.
This isn't going to work.
You don't have enough.
You don't know enough.
You're not good enough.

Self-doubt is designed to attack the core of who you are. All of these inner tapes are assassination attempts on your real *super-power* . . . your voice. That night in the hotel fueled me but it also focused me. I got mad when I realized how many ways the enemy had tried to take what was rightfully mine. How dare the devil trespass on my path and attempt to misroute my future.

That relationship where you felt you had to shrink? Your struggle with confidence? Feeling like you don't want to step out of line? The sweat and jitters you feel even at the thought of speaking in front of others . . . it's the battle for your voice. It's the way *little me* uses The Rules, protocol, and pressure to avoid rejection to keep us scared, quiet, and politically correct.

I mean, what in the heck did they crucify Christ for? Because he *spoke* what had never been spoken. He came not just to share the message, He came to *be* the message.

And that's what we're here for, too.

Your life is a message.

Your voice is a superpower.

Your story is a sign of God's strength.

Our talents are muscle,
but our gifts are the message.

Remember, our voice is our greatest gift—something each of us has. *You are the carrier of a unique message from Heaven only your life experiences and abilities can convey.* No one else. No one else has lived your life, muddled through your mess, and made it to this moment the way you have. Your story is a one-of-a-kind key that unlocks possibility in others. And that's why our ultimate life mission is about improving the lives of others by *teaching* what we've learned along the way.

Again, we are *all* teachers. You are a teacher, too, and you've been in training. This is purpose made simple, my friend. Our voice connects others with what God needs them to know, hear, and believe. We're his vessels. God's larger vision and pathway for others are revealed when we use our voice.

This is why God is calling you higher.

Not because of your strengths, but because of your *story*—and, most likely, because of your *struggles*. Take *that* in for a moment. Your struggles are connected to your calling and, in part, are what qualify you for greater impact.

Others will learn to overcome, conquer, and find their path forward by hearing the word of *your* testimony.

> *They triumphed over him*
> *by the blood of the Lamb*
> *and by the word of their testimony . . .*
> —*Revelation 12:11 (NIV)*

And, Luke 21:13 (NASB) makes clear that recurring hardships and obstacles "will lead to an opportunity for your testimony."

I used to think testimony was what you did in church. Not so. We are message carriers all day, every day. We *are* voice. We are here to be a witness and remind the world that *God is*. God is in control. God is at work. God saves. God heals. Your life is living proof. You don't have to tell it, perfectly or strategically, you just need to share. And sharing your path and story is the most simple yet powerful way we can help change the lives of others. It doesn't matter who we are . . . we each have a story. *You have a story*—filled with highs and lows, wins and losses, love and betrayal. And when you share what you've been through and what you've learned during your life, no matter how small the lesson or experience might seem, you become a teacher, a transformer, and an unlocker.

This doesn't mean you have to become a speaker. Not everyone is destined to speak on stages with lights and microphones. But we each have a stage. We're all teachers. *Teaching is your calling.* Using your intellect, your abilities, and your experience to help, elevate, shift, or advance others. When calling calls, you're being asked to step into your voice and share your story in a greater way.

Mentoring others and giving back for the purpose of moving others forward are what true purpose is all about. Just breathe that in. We're *all* here to use our gifts to teach and inspire others. Your specific spiritual gifts will be different than mine, and your story will be different than mine. What we have in common is the truth that we both have a voice and a story—we have life experiences, and therefore wisdom, that serve as lessons that unlock new life in others. And, we can start where we are with the story we have (and the woman we are) right now.

{ FINDING YOUR VOICE }

Let me give you an example to show how your voice can be your message.

My grandmother Pearl—my mom's mother—was barely five feet tall, but she was a firecracker. She cleaned homes and catered events for a living. Housekeeping was a talent of hers . . . a super-skill. She became very good at it. I wouldn't say she was passionate about it, but she was excellent nonetheless and certainly took pride in her work. Cooking—in my view *that* was a gift. She sho' didn't need no recipes for her cajun cuisine or her famous 7 Up cake! Building up self-esteem, bigger vision, and confidence in girls and women—that, too, was a gift of hers. All five of her daughters graduated from college during a time when that was rare for African-American girls.

So what was Grandma Pearl's ultimate superpower? Making people feel welcome. Whether she was working an event or helping the struggling people in the neighborhood, she was able to serve in such a way that made others feel at home, special, and remembered. That's how she made me feel as she sat on the side of her bed and parted and braided my thick, cotton-candy hair. And she was always sending a plate next door or to someone on the block who was hungry. She knew who was in need in the neighborhood, and she met the need. They didn't even have to ask. Using her gifts, she met that need. And it made a difference. It wasn't the kind of thing that would hit the newspaper, but to the person who was praying for their next meal, it was a big deal. And she was a great listener, but would chat until the sun went down, too. She had the *gift of presence*. By remembering those in need, she was sharing her message: *You matter.*

At her funeral, people talked about how she was a welcomer. An esteem-builder. *That* was her voice. She didn't have to say anything. She wasn't the cheerleader type—her actions spoke way louder than words. Though she only had an elementary school education (sixth grade was the highest level available), Grandma Pearl wanted you to be good at what you did and to take pride in your work and your name . . . and by *showing* her daughters and grandchildren that in action, she taught us to believe we could be bigger and greater. Did she specifically share her story? Hmmm . . . probably only when asked. Pride was prized over transparency back then. But her innate superpowers did the talking.

Her title was that of homemaker and housekeeper. She kept other people's houses clean and pristine.

But her life and her gifts communicated a larger message . . . a message that helped the women (and men) in her life to believe bigger . . . or just to have a better day with some food in their belly.

❧ SO HOW DO *YOU* FIND *YOUR* VOICE? ❧

The first and best place to start is with disappointment, dissatisfaction, and disruption. Purpose is often hidden in a place of pain. It's inside the rock—the hard place . . . and that's why God splits it open when it's time to flow anew.

So think about it.

What's disrupted you?

I'm not just talking about getting a bad grade or having a bad day. What is something that has turned your life upside down?

Think of a defining moment. It could be something that either showed you what you were really made of or something that nearly took you out.

Was it betrayal? Disappointment?

Sickness? Depression? The death of a loved one?

Loss of a job? Divorce? An unexpected pregnancy? Your back up against a wall?

Or maybe something else that seemed unfair, impossible, or out of the blue?

Think about this for a moment before you rush along.

Whatever your rock—valley, obstacle, or defining moment—the bigger question is this:

What have you learned from disruption?

I wish I could have asked Grandma Pearl this question. Disruption is a destiny-revealing teacher. Inevitably, some of the lessons we've learned came not from a place of wisdom, but from our wounds. But I'm challenging you to find the real wisdom embedded within your experiences. Not the superficial. Not the shame. Not the blame. The larger, higher message.

What gift-giving lessons can you share with others?

Look back at some of the things you've overcome, disappointing memories that still seem unfair, and even achievements of yours that once seemed impossible or unlikely. Ask yourself what God was *really* doing. If God authors His story *through us*, what is the larger message God might be using *your* life to convey?

What life lessons do you now know? Business wisdom? Skills that you can teach others?

What do you wish someone had told you back then?

What impact would you like to have on others now?

What do you believe at your core to be true?

What is the one thing you want others to know—one thing that would give them hope, confidence, or clarity?

Remember, the mess is the master class for your life mission.

Embrace that your life experiences—your pain, your pit stops, and your story—are pieces of a larger puzzle. Your life has not been random. Your experiences fit together to showcase a larger picture. Every piece is necessary—even the ones (the experiences) that seem small and insignificant. Sometimes those matter most.

❧ EMBRACING THE UGLY ❧

Owning your voice is a key mind shift that invites new possibilities. Your life message isn't something you can write or script. It just flows. It's embedded in your triumphs, your wisdom, *and* your struggles.

This is yet another reason why it is in our weakness that we are strongest. When pressed, the message of our life produces something far greater than our current circumstance or challenges.

2 Corinthians 4:17 (NIV), a verse that helped me embrace a larger mission beyond the pain of infidelity, says, "For our light and momentary troubles are achieving for us an eternal glory that far outweighs them all." Later, in 2 Corinthians 12:10 (NIV), God says His power is made *perfect* in our weakness. And that we should "delight in weaknesses, in insults, in hardships, in persecutions, in difficulties. For when I am weak, then I am strong."

That "when I am weak, then I am strong" part is the *superpower* at work; us relying on God to do what *only* God can do through us. As God renews us and meets us when it looks like we are down, He has an open window to come in and supply our soul with healing and wisdom that helps us to get back up, and shows others how to get back up and move forward as well.

As it says in 2 Corinthians 4:16 (NIV), "Though outwardly we are wasting away," (that's the work of disruption and The GAP) "inwardly we are being renewed day by day" (that's the maturing of our destiny mission and the life message that flows from within us).

So again:

Your life is a message.

Your voice is a *superpower.*

Your story is a sign of God's strength.

Every attack on your life, on your dreams and your desires, is an attempt to restrict, silence, and abort your voice, and with it, your life mission. Think about all of the nos. All of the "you can'ts." All of the doubts. And all of the "you shouldn'ts." Again, this is not about blame. Who hurt you is less important than understanding what doubt and fear are conspiring to silence and lock up inside of you.

Your voice, your story, is about how you've overcome, defeated, avoided, and survived assassination attempts. Not perfectly. It didn't have to be pretty. And you may still be in the middle of sumthin' ugly right now . . . but you're here. You've made it this far, and your path, no matter how rocky, embarrassing, gory, or ugly, contains your glory story.

The greater the struggle, the more significant the story. Your story can change someone else's.

❴ WHAT *KIND* OF VOICE ARE YOU? ❵

After working with thousands of women (and men) over the last several years, I've discovered three primary recurring commonalities when it comes to the type of overarching master impact each of us is designed to have. Purpose leaves clues, and these clues indicate our *divine personality*—how we naturally show up most powerfully when it comes to helping others.

I find it can be helpful to know what kind of helper Heaven sent you here to be—especially as you look back over your life and embrace your natural tendencies in the context of finding your purpose. Remember, purpose is about impact, and your voice is the key superpower that activates transformation in others. I refer to each personality (or tendency / pattern) as a *Purpose Archetype*.

Let's flesh out the three types of purpose-anchored personalities and pinpoint which assignment (aka, which kind of voice) most sounds like you!

+ **Personality Type 1—*The Puller.*** *The Puller* uses her voice to help others overcome some area of hurt or pain. If you're a Puller, then by sharing your struggles, your journey, and your insight, you are able to uniquely help others find a path out of their pit. If you have the Puller anointing, you tend to care deeply about the problems, dysfunctions, illnesses, and challenges that others have difficulty overcoming. You're most happy and feel most alive when you have the chance to teach others the way out of worry, feeling overwhelmed, pain, sickness, and despair.

+ **Personality Type 2—*The Planner*.** *The Planner* is wired for strategy and uses her voice to show others a road map for accomplishing a desire, objective, or goal. The Planner is able to streamline processes and has strategies for turning struggles into simple steps, and confusion into clarity. If you have the Planner anointing upon your life, you naturally see solutions where others see challenges. You're most happy and feel most alive when you are able to strategize, map out, and make the difficult easy for others. You're able to see the big picture and lay out the steps necessary to get to the finish line.

+ **Personality Type 3—*The Pusher*.** *The Pusher* is a motivator and an encourager who uses her voice to inspire others to believe in new possibilities and potential. The Pusher is often supremely gifted with words and creativity, and experiences an extraordinary flow of visions, dreams, ideas, and revelations. If you have the Pusher anointing upon your life, you are a big thinker, a dreamer, a creator, a catalyst, and a visionary. Your gifts naturally inspire, refresh, and uplift. You have more ideas than you could ever use in your own lifetime. Your sweet spot is inspiring others to believe in themselves, their goals, and their potential. You're happiest and feel most alive when you're mentoring, connecting with others, performing, idea-sharing, and being a source of hope and encouragement.

There will likely be some degree of overlap between these three personality types. The type of anointing you have gives insight as to where you most belong and how God designed your life (your personality) to operate in His master plan. Notice I didn't focus on your specific superpower—baking, speaking, singing, swimming, designing, etc. We're focused on the *higher purpose* that your superpower supports—the master purpose of your life and the larger mission driving your life message.

Each of the archetypes is equally significant and necessary. Each unlocks destiny in others. And each reflects God's voice in our lives and His vision for our lives.

So which type *most* speaks to you?

PURPOSE ARCHETYPE	CORE FOCUS IS ON . . .	EQUIPS OTHERS TO . . .	METHOD YOU USE TO HELP MOVE OTHERS FORWARD	RANK
The Puller	Hurt	Overcome	Experience and Insight	
The Planner	Help	Accomplish	Strategy	
The Pusher	Heart	Be Encouraged	Inspiration	

Don't overthink it. It's okay to have dual or even triple anointing. However, if you have trouble choosing, just rank 'em and let's ride with the one that falls into the top slot as your primary anointing and voice so we can move forward to the next phrase of influence. We'll also reference this again when we talk in Chapter 14 about clarifying your specific life mission.

{ GUIDING BELIEFS SHAPE YOUR VOICE }

Again, embracing your voice isn't about gaining notoriety, it's about creating impact. I know you might want me to tell you about something massive that God's calling you to do. To change the world by starting a massive movement. And that may be what He wants from you. But God is the king of starting massive movements in a small way.

> *Our story and path are the slingshot that slays the giants others are facing.*

I didn't want to share my story of being cheated on. That certainly wasn't in my plan for how to help others. We all tend to want to share our strengths, versus our struggles—but our struggles are where the *superpower* comes from. Superman's strength is the greatest when he's facing adversity. Likewise, facing challenges is like lifting weights. Muscle builds only after it's been broken down.

I'll probably never *love* sharing this story of infidelity, but each time I do, the shame and embarrassment fades a bit more. So I have to keep doing it. It's not my identity—and neither are the glory or the gory parts your story.

> *Running from your story is the same as running from your calling.*

This is another breathe-it-in moment.

We can't fulfill our purpose if we cover up and hide the parts of our story that we don't like. We don't have to give everyone access to our most intimate details—we need to be discerning about what to share, with whom, and when. But don't allow fear and shame (masked as discernment) to become an excuse for avoiding your assignment and staying in your lane. *Getting to the core of the message in your mess is key to fulfilling your life mission.*

When we pay attention to the lessons learned, those lessons begin to shape what I call your larger *guiding belief.* Your guiding belief is what you believe to be true and necessary at your core. It becomes your motivation . . . your why . . . your compass and your reality. And it's what God uses to shape and direct how we use our voice. It also explains how our muscle (our superpowers) both undergirds and magnifies the message (our voice/story).

To identify your guiding belief, I'd like you to think about something you want to be known for. Something you want to improve or change in the world.

Who do you want to help? How and why?

What's important to you?

What would you specifically like to see change or improve in the world?

What's your cause?

What life lesson, principle, belief, or philosophy do you want to be known for?

Your answers should have nothing to do with you or accomplishment. They should have everything to do with impact. Moving others, you guessed it, forward. The answers to these questions are what form your guiding belief. You may not have specifically thought about this before now, or maybe you have, but you *already* embody a guiding belief. It's embedded in your personality. It's been at the center of both your triumphs and your trials. It's why disruption came—to make room for its expansion. And it's what's drawn others to you and you to others. For that reason, you already have a voice. *You are voice.* Your voice is the larger message your life (and beliefs) are naturally meant to convey.

As an example, my guiding belief is this: *I believe we're called to believe bigger and live bolder.* My personality, my pursuits, and natural purpose each revolve around and stem from this personal truth.

It's why I try to live my life outside of the box, and it's why I pour myself into helping others do the same, too. It's rooted in the belief that all things are possible (the essence of Philippians 4:13 . . . one of my faves) and Ephesians 1:18 (NIV), which says, "I pray that the eyes of your heart may be enlightened in order that you may know the hope to which he has called you, the riches of his glorious inheritance . . ."

Teaching business, then, is just another avenue for me to equip women to believe bigger about where they belong and who they can be. My voice, my story, and my superpowers all fall under the "umbrella" of bigger belief. It explains the blessed experiences as well as the bad ones. It's all taught me to believe bigger so I can go and teach others to do the same. My gifts help me to accomplish this mission and spread this message. When I told Miss Benna I wanted self-esteem as my platform, that was my guiding belief manifesting naturally . . . subconsciously. Activating bigger belief has always been my life mission—even when I didn't consciously know it.

When people talk about finding their why—they usually miss it. *Your why finds you.* It's already in you.

Identifying your guiding belief invites the other aspects of your divine identity to live under one master umbrella. Your gifts, voice, talents, personality, and even your goals should operate to fulfill this larger mission. Perhaps now you're seeing how central belief really is to a life soaked in significance.

As you identify your guiding belief, what you're ultimately asking is:

How did God really design me?

How you think, how you see both problems and solutions . . . your perspective, and how you desire to help others . . . reveals your divine design. It explains your voice and gives context to your gifts. So reflect upon this question, and jot down what comes to mind—no judgment, only self-appreciation. You have your story—so you have everything you need. And, if you're not yet clear on what the larger message is that God is using your life to convey, that's okay. Don't stress, just share. Keep sharing your story, insights, and abilities, but pay attention. Over time, others will reflect back to you what they're receiving and how you are what they've been missing.

Once awakened, your real voice will scare the heck out of you! It will awaken a message and sense of significance that will challenge everything you believe to be worthy (or not) about you. What you know might seem simple or insignificant . . . but it's your voice. And, it's more than good enough.

5

Influence
STAGE

Where is God sending me now?

chapter thirteen

STAGE FIVE: INFLUENCE

A message is no good if it stays in a bottle.
—Mary Loretta Evans (my mom)

GOING WHERE GOD GUIDES

The fifth and final stage of divine reinvention on the Purpose Map is the Influence Stage. Like a warrior princess who knows that one day she'll be needed for battle, this is what God's been grooming you for since the day you were born. *Purpose is about influence or it is about nothing at all.* It is in the Influence stage that we rewrite The Rules, discover our leadership assignment, activate our voice, and deploy our gifts to those we've been called to bless and build up. We begin to use our talents and focus our gifts to build something that matters, to improve lives and to meet needs in a new way.

As you enter the sweet spot of your life mission, becoming a woman of influence, you experience a level of giving, elevating, shining, amplifying, replenishing, and pouring into others you've never experienced before. You mature into your message, your gifts, and your voice and become unashamed about your higher purpose and life mission. You stop caring what others think. There is nothing to prove.

This is where your true legacy finally has breathing room to unfold, and this is where the real fun happens. This whole purpose journey was never about you. It was about finding you so you could finally do what you were born to do. Create. Teach. Launch. Give. Inspire. Mentor. Shine. Be.

No more protocol. No more mountain-climbing, lane-picking, or mask-wearing. It's a season anchored in legacy and life-changing. Ah, yes! That's who you are . . . a life-changer.

It is your time to finally enter into and steward *your* promised land. Your space. Your zone. Your place in God's plan. Getting into position, however, will require you to face the gremlins blocking your entry into greatness. It's time to unlock and unleash your influence.

{ STRANGE FRUIT AND UNICORNS }

I hope by now you're clearer about *your* gifts, calling, voice, and purpose. But that doesn't mean others are! That was something I had to get used to—that others didn't understand what I knew I was called to do.

This first became evident when I was on the phone with the first lady of a church who wanted to bring me in to speak to their ladies at an upcoming retreat. When she asked what I had in my heart to share, I told her that I was passionate about leadership. Her reply wasn't what I was expecting: "I don't think women are really interested in learning about leadership. It'll intimidate them," she said.

I didn't reply right away. I couldn't. There was an awkward moment of silence. This was coming from a woman *in* leadership—she was in charge of a women's ministry, which *I thought* was all about leadership. That's when I realized there were still a lot of archaic, deeply entrenched views about women, our proper roles, and where we belong in our world. *We can be in positions of leadership and still not see ourselves as leaders.* It was mind-blowing. But it was also confirmation I was on the right path.

I've always felt like a unicorn around women in ministry. I've never been able to figure it out, which is why I always assumed that I wasn't cut out for ministry. I've been embraced and mentored by businesswomen, but never by women in ministry the way I always craved. I don't fit the mold I suppose; whatever that mold is. But we've all felt it. There is this "appropriate" way we're *supposed* to be. Stuff we're *supposed* to talk about. And things we're *supposed* to do. The *supposed-to* stuff tends to feel like a straightjacket for me. I can't breathe when I'm limited to others' expectations . . . and religiosity. I get itchy. A bit restless. I love God and just try to follow the dreams and desires He places in my heart with determination and discipline. Those dreams just happen to grow outside of the box, outside of tradition, and outside of the religious norm.

During that conversation, it *finally* hit me: it wasn't me. I wasn't odd. I just didn't believe in settling for ordinary. I truly don't believe in ordinary; that's not who God is, nor is it how He made us. Maybe *that's* what makes me a unicorn. But isn't that how we are supposed to be? *Extra*ordinary?

The culprit compromising our true calling is not just comfort but *conformity*, the pressure we feel as women to be polite, appropriate, and "in our place"—to be protocol followers. *Spiritual conformity is just as dangerous as conformity to the world and culture.* The Word says be not conformed to the patterns of this world. Patterns (of any type) are always inferior to fresh revelation. Sameness is an illness. Tradition blocks the call to have impact, to lead, and to amplify the move of God stirring right now in the hearts of women.

I did my best to make the case to the first lady for what I believe to be true, which is this:

God has called every woman to lead.
A life of influence and impact is the very center
of feminine purpose.

Everything about God oozes influence . . . expansion, multiplication, and amplification. *So since we're created in God's image and the spirit of God lives in us, the spirit of creativity, expansion, and influence is in our blood.* It's who we are and what we're built to do. We are a creative force filled with an innate desire to manifest, create, and expand. The question is not whether we're supposed to lead; the only questions are *how* and *where*.

Again, Ephesians 2:10 (a foundational scripture in my life) says that "we are God's workmanship created in Christ Jesus to *do* good works, which He prepared *in advance* that we would do." God handcrafted us to uniquely do . . . to unleash the divinely drenched goodness He predeposited in our spiritual and physical makeup. That's why we crave more. *We crave what we're called for.*

God has called us each to do something and to lead in an extraordinary, nontraditional way. It's in our divine DNA and it's in our purpose. No limits. No boundaries. As women, we can't lead powerfully unless we're prepared to lead properly. We have to learn *how* to embrace and unleash our full, untapped potential, and give ourselves permission to see ourselves as the leaders, teachers, and life-changers we are. Truth is . . .

A woman's place is anywhere God sends her.

I politely explained that my talk for the women's conference was going to be on my signature topic, *Godfidence*®, which was about equipping women to lead with a new, next-level leadership mindset. I could tell she was a bit reluctant at first, but I had spoken at their church before and the experience had been pretty powerful for both them and me. I didn't know how it was all going to shake out, but I knew this was what was in my spirit. And, after another long and awkward pause (I could feel her wheels turning), she said, "Okay . . . I trust you . . . let's do it!"

When I hung up the phone, I realized a few things.

One, as women, we have an up-and-down, roller coaster–like relationship with the word *leadership*.

On one hand, we're supposed to be submissive and supportive.

We learn much about surrender, but less about stepping up.

We want to expand the kingdom, but we don't want to step out of place.

We want to be a good wife and wonderful mother, but we don't want to admit that our hearts crave something more.

And, again, we've been taught over and over to grow where we're planted, but not how to *go* when directed. We're warned not to mess up, so we *over*think and in many ways *over*pray. We don't know how to uproot ourselves (to shift) when it's time to replant; that's why we can feel stuck. We don't know where to begin when it comes to entering something new. And we certainly don't learn how to truly lead other people. However . . .

You are a unique expression of an idea of God meant to lead others into more of God's goodness.

This is why we're not here to hide. Hiding suppresses the sacred. Your life is a one-of-a-kind bridge to God and God's game plan. You deny others entry and passage when you live out of alignment. When you pretend. But when you step into your anointing, and when you allow God to manifest whatever He wants, regardless of The Rules, traditions, and archaic mindsets, you end up connecting others to the piece of God that's long been missing in their life. When you show up the way God made you, and *wherever* He sends you, people get a greater glimpse of your manufacturer. It draws them closer to God, which is what God's after. Glory. Relationship. Intimacy. We don't get to script it. We can only surrender to it.

⦃ THE POWER OF CURIOSITY ⦄

I'm convinced that the enemy and *little me* plot 'n partner with the *Spirit of Ordinary* to get us to settle. To stay where we are. To remain content and to silence calling when it knocks. If the enemy can get a woman to fear, or better yet to ignore the *Holy Whisper* that calls her (*leads her*) onto the battlefield of purpose and significance, then she'll never even know she's living beneath her birthright.

Although he's a man, Moses is probably one of my favorite depictions of this. He was an outcast, a foreigner, and an orphan abandoned by his mother. He was tending to the fields, going through the motions, doing the ordinary, and following The Rules, when God disrupted Moses' life in a radical way. A burning bush. C'mon! That must have been a sight to see. Most would have run the other way, but something inside of Moses prompted him to walk *toward* the fire. He was able to discern this moment as a holy encounter . . . something new calling. I believe it was the *Spirit of Curiosity* dwelling within him.

Curiosity is always the catalyst to calling.

And, it's the antidote to the Spirit of Ordinary . . . the voice of *Future ME* leading you off the mundane path of predictability and onto a more anointed, adventurous one. Get this. God showed up in the fields—*not* in the temple, synagogue, or in Pharaoh's palace. Nope. God made his presence and the new path for Moses' life known in the middle of mud and bugs. There was nothing prestigious about Moses' circumstances. Calling intervened not in the prettiest of places, but on holy ground nonetheless.

*Anywhere God takes us is a holy path,
and anywhere God places us is holy ground.*

I love this story because I can relate to Moses. Feeling like your circumstances aren't all that great and like you don't fit. Trying to balance contentment, patience, and gratitude for the life you're thankful to have with that recurring, tugging voice that still whispers, *There's more.*

I also love Moses' awakening because it shows that at the crux of calling is a call to lead; to step out of the ordinary and into the extraordinary. A woman must always remain curious—in awe of what God is about to do next. And, as I've said, God's game plan when it comes to purpose isn't limited to the fellas. Us girls . . . yes, we've been called to lead and to have limitless, jaw-dropping 'n miracle-working influence, too.

BURNING BUSH ENCOUNTERS

It's interesting how God called Moses to do something he had never done. I think this is the major reason so many of us miss our purpose path. *We're looking in the rearview mirror, while the pathway to our anointed future unfolds ahead.* The Bible says Moses was terrified, and I don't think it was just because he was staring at a burning bush. I believe it was because he was coming face-to-face with the revelation of his destiny; a mirror image of his true self. There was a passion and fire *in* Moses that had been lying dormant for far too long . . . a fire that Moses had never known he had or had been too afraid to acknowledge. And when God revealed to Moses that he was going to lead in a great and mighty way, Moses did the same thing so many of us do when God reveals His big purpose for us. He shrank.

Instead of rejoicing, he started voicing his insecurity. He *explained* to God that he was not the man for this kind of a thing. Going to make demands face-to-face with Pharaoh (the most powerful man in the land if not the world) involved speaking . . . using your voice. And Moses reminded God that he was a stutterer. Only it was not *really* Moses speaking . . . it was his inner *little me*, that slick recurring whisper of worthlessness that had slithered and taken up residence in his heart and mind. Moses became a mouthpiece for *little me* and made the case (against himself) to God for why he was not qualified, not good enough, and not ready to lead. Moses wasn't incorrect, he just wasn't right. *Little me always uses facts in a false context to get us to make a case against ourselves.* It's true that Moses was indeed a stutterer. But he wasn't right about that "fact" disqualifying him.

> *Whenever we come face-to-face with our true destiny, we default to our greatest insecurity.*

Calling, the invitation to use your voice and step into your next-level assignment, exposes the gremlins. That's how you know it's calling. Comfort keeps 'em covered up. Destiny brings 'em out and into the light. Moses isn't alone.

Take Jeremiah. In Jeremiah 1, God calls Jeremiah to use his voice and deliver a prophecy that warns the people of calamity on the horizon. Jeremiah immediately *explains* to God that he is "just a child"—too young and not ready for such a task. God shuts that down quickly, essentially saying, *Don't tell* Me *what you're not capable of.* I *live in you. I made you. If all things are possible with Me, then with Me living in you, there is nothing we can't do.*

And take my girl Esther. God calls her to use her voice, too. She is also an orphan and a foreigner who found refuge and a life for herself by disguising her ethnicity and blending into the king's harem. She was basically in the palace's beauty school—drenched in The Rules of her time and learning what a lady should do and be to please the powers that be. However, while she was learning to master the art of charm, her people were being slaughtered. It was genocide. With Moses' people it was slavery. In both of their situations, their people were losing hope. They had no advocate. No one was willing to *be* their voice.

For Esther to enter into the king's court without being summoned by the king was an offense punishable by death. So when God calls Esther to step up and speak up, to plead to the king on behalf of her people, God is asking her to do the unthinkable—to voluntarily blow her cover in a society that is killing her kind. She, too, defaults to her insecurity. *She is afraid to be who she really is.* After all, hiding her true identity has been at the very core of her survival. She explains that the circumstances aren't right for her to do such a dangerous thing—to use her voice. It's not what women in her position are *supposed* to do. Perhaps you can relate. Like Moses and Jeremiah, Esther was not incorrect, but she was not right either. It was true that the circumstances weren't favorable, and that the rules forbid her to enter the king's court. It was also true that the act was punishable by death. But she was *not* right about the circumstances and rules being an actual barrier.

Unfavorable life circumstances often invite God's unbeatable favor.

When you can't change your circumstances, you can always change your outlook. Your belief. *When we believe bigger, we invite God to show up larger.* Plus, things are not always as they appear . . . especially when it comes to the way God works. This is why we must "stop judging by mere appearances" (John 7:24 NIV). Faith is communicated on a higher frequency—one that requires *spiritual eyes* to see the way the spirit of God moves. Further, God can never, ever be confined by a world *He* created. *There are no rules on earth that God is bound by*. Seeing with spiritual eyes in a physical world is the essence of spiritual maturity, and the key to staying on the spiritual path of purpose that leads to significance.

With Moses, Jeremiah, and Esther, we see three defining moments. Each hinges upon one decision—one life-shifting invitation from God: *Though it seems impossible, will you unleash your ultimate super-power? Will you use your voice?*

My point is that God calls us to lead in peculiar ways. It sometimes won't make sense. The method may appear risky, and it will most certainly challenge what we think about ourselves, our beauty, our readiness and ability. However, calling will also reveal which broken beliefs are blocking our entry into bigger. God will use disruption and do what it takes to capture your heart and correct your vision. And the call to lead anew will challenge our hidden attachment to our circumstances, conformity, and our comfort zone.

The call to lead will ultimately reveal what and in whom we *really* trust. Do we trust The Rules or do we trust God? Divine leadership, then, is about obedience—a willingness to surrender control and to actively align with God's leading . . . even when it's unclear and especially when it doesn't make sense. Obedience tests your trust, unmasks hidden idols, and reveals your true fears.

God's divine invitations are intentionally inconvenient. God's modus operandi—His MO—is to send us to an unpopular place to prepare us *before* He enlarges our territory. The danger is not where you are going. The real danger is where you are staying. That's why God uses radical methods to disrupt us. He loves us too much to leave us. And our lives matter—we're a part of a larger mission that's been at work all along.

These *burning bush* encounters are defining moments of development and doors that open the way to destiny.

The obstacle is the opportunity.

The Old Testament folks believed that a man couldn't "see" God and live, and that that's why God appeared to Moses in a bush. But Moses walked away from that burning bush with a new countenance— an indescribable radiance. It was as if he had just been bathed and baptized in boldness. He was being prepared and supernaturally spit-shined for leadership. God-touched. *Influence is one of the greatest gifts of disruption.* It is my prayer that this believe bigger journey will ignite a new boldness in you, too. Finding your place is beautiful, but helping others find their place—to become what they've been praying, looking, and waiting for—is powerful.

Like Moses, Jeremiah left his burning bush encounter with new eyes to see and truly trust what God was saying. It couldn't have been easy for him, and it won't be easy for you. However, a *vision shift* is key to finding the boldness needed to prophesy (or voice) what's within you, too. Esther not only emerged from *her* encounter with a voice she hadn't known she had, she was also able to secure the safety of her people, *and* live the rest of her life not in exile or prison, but as a queen. *To lead is to wear your crown.* As you embrace a higher vision and believe bigger about the purpose of your voice, you'll discover how God intends for you to reign, too.

❧ SLAY THE GREMLINS ❧

Stepping into influence requires a new level of surrender. Surrender is both fuel and air in the Glory Zone. It's about allowing God to show you a new version of you that reflects *His* bigger vision for you. And that vision is *always* about leadership. Pause and take that in. It's *always* about l-e-a-d-e-r-s-h-i-p. *Lead* is a four-letter word, but not in a bad way.

God did not call us to conform but to transform. And leadership isn't anything to be afraid of. It's what we were built for, and it's what our hearts are *really* longing for. It. Is. Why. You. Were. Born. I'm not talking about notoriety. That's just another mountain that will disappoint us once we arrive at its peak. I'm talking about significance. Believing in your voice. Your story. Your gifts. And being willing to let God lead you to whoever needs to hear what God has given you to say, give, be, and do.

> *Divine leadership is letting your life be a living message.*

Like Moses, we have to stop long enough for God to disrupt and break old self-limiting beliefs that ultimately limit our reach. And we have to embrace the essence of *true* leadership.

{ REDEFINING LEADERSHIP }

Just like I once struggled to understand that spiritual gifts go beyond those listed in the Bible, I've also struggled with the idea of what it means to lead and have influence. Leadership can feel intimidating. We ask, *Are we qualified? Do we have what it takes? Are we ready? Is this really what I'm supposed to do?*

And then, influence as a goal feels selfish. *Little me* often wrangles me in with this particular lasso of worry—a second-guessing and spirit of self-doubt that come from my fear of being perceived as selfish and self-focused. I ask, *Am I being greedy? Growing too much? Taking up too much space?* For some reason guilt 'n shame swoop in whenever we think about serving higher and living bigger in a trailblazing way. We worry that we're stepping out of line. Drawing too much attention. Entering forbidden territory. And that it would be better, if not Godlier, to be quieter, to stay where we are and stick to what we've always done. That's an old inner tape . . . but it reappears each time I seek to step into a bigger place and evolve into my next-level self. Perhaps you can relate.

Here is an example. As I've shared, I have a gift for branding and helping people with their messages so they gain more visibility, income, and clients in the business world. It seemed good, but it also seemed like it wasn't a "Godly" thing to teach. I felt like if God was calling me to have greater impact, then maybe I needed to go to seminary. I used to believe (like many still do) that if God calls us, He calls us into traditional ministry—into what we've seen and come to *label* as ministry and what qualifies as "God's work." So, even though I was gifted, I was conflicted.

After my split-rock shift, I started a program I called *ME University* (later the *Godfidence Business School* and its vertical, *She Profits*) teaching personal branding. It wasn't just a play on my initials, but also a platform where women could work on themselves. You could learn how to develop yourself as a brand and turn your ideas, expertise, insight, and *story* into a business. After I launched it and it started to grow, I faced an enormous wave of guilt that nearly drowned me in a sea of self-doubt. *Was it wrong for me to teach people how to elevate themselves?* It felt wrong to focus my gifts on teaching others how to get more attention for themselves when we're taught to be humble. To trust God. To be slow to speak. And that money is the root of all evil.

I spent a lot time in prayer about this for years. I wrestled with God as I felt him calling me to grow ME University *more* aggressively, but also worried about what others would say.

What would the women in church tell me? I didn't find much support or guidance there.

Would I be looked at as a prosperity weirdo and profit peddler?

This became an even greater fear as my teachings grew to be not just faith-sprinkled, but faith-soaked. By blending faith and business, would I be "out of order," recklessly blurring the lines between church and state? It felt blasphemous. However, the more I spent time in God's presence, the bigger my *business* vision grew. The Bible became a living, breathing business plan. Scriptures I'd read and known for a lifetime took on an entirely elevated meaning. I got fresh ideas and fresh strategies, which is certainly the key to a unique business. I wondered why no one else was talking about the spiritual principles of increase and how they work in business, career, family, and life. We can do more than just survive. With God living within us, we're *supposed* to thrive in every area . . . elevating *everything* we touch.

God's word reveals and builds destiny. We all have dreams. Why aren't these being developed and encouraged? Why are we only taught to get a job and one day retire? What about destiny? Why isn't anyone teaching us *how* to fulfill and grow dreams . . . not just believe in them? If doctors and lawyers had to learn *how* to operate (gaining skills, strategy, and wisdom found outside of the church and beyond the Bible), why didn't Believers have to learn how to operate in their gifts and grow their dreams and ideas, too? Couldn't others see what God was saying in His word about us expanding territory? (Isaiah 54:2) That sounded like *real estate development.* Being the lender and not the borrower? (Proverbs 22:7) That sounded like *finance.* Making sure our dealings are profitable? (Proverbs 31:18) That's the essence of *business.* Then, I felt God saying this was a gap *I* was supposed to fill. And *that* totally freaked me out! I didn't know where to draw the line between the sacred and the secular.

What if what doesn't exist is a clue as to where you're called to lead?

Maybe there wasn't *supposed* to be a line. Maybe it was imaginary and *I* was making it permanent. And then one day, my prayer partner and good girlfriend from college Nicole lovingly splashed me with cold water. She said, "I think you're afraid that your gifts aren't as spiritually significant as the ones you're used to seeing in the pulpit. Your gifts are just as significant as anyone else's. If it comes from God, then it matters. And it's good enough." I don't know if that woke me up or knocked me out. She had grown up in the world of traditional ministry, and she was one of the only people from that world to encourage me to believe that my gifts were indeed gifts.

Teaching leadership was one thing. But talking about money and divine calling (at the same time!) was another. And then I had my Moses-Jeremiah-Esther moment. I shrunk. I felt unqualified and out of place. There were others who knew more—more Bible and more business. I hadn't been to seminary and can never seem to memorize exactly where all of those Bible verses live. I love 'em, but my brain isn't wired to remember their addresses. I've always felt unqualified. So it wasn't and isn't easy for me to believe bigger. However, it was incredibly refreshing to hear the truth for the first time.

All gifts are spiritually significant.

Let that simmer. That's good news for imperfect women like you and me. I wish I could say that I don't still struggle with this. Feeling odd. Dreaming too big. Feeling like maybe I'm in the wrong place. Wondering if my desires are "holy enough" and questioning whether my gifts are good enough. But I guess that's the cost of believing in the extraordinary. Look. We're going to feel out of place as God takes us *out* of the ordinary. That tension between the sacred and the secular comes with operating in the stage of Influence. I believe the tension is a good thing—it's what keeps our heart pure and grounded while God has us a-steppin', a-stretchin', and a-leapin'.

The call to influence is supposed to war with the lure of contentment. The only way to slay the gremlins guarding our greater is to step into forbidden territory . . . to lead.

Today, my definition of leadership is to move others forward.

It's simple for a reason. Leadership isn't that complicated. We can best move others forward by offering our wisdom, gifts, voice, and presence.

Whether it be in the home, at work, in business, on the subway or at the grocery store, *we can lead where we are now* by embracing the core essence of who we are as our life mission. We're a voice here to share what moves others forward. It's not about a title . . . it's about transformation and owning your identity as a transformer. It's a responsibility inherent in the gift that comes with living, breathing, and honoring God. God will do the expansion . . . increasing your borders as you take faith steps and welcome new opportunities that become new water to walk upon.

Influence is impacting those within your reach.

This purpose-anchored, living-bolder thing comes down, then, to two key values and areas of intentionality: (1) moving others forward, and (2) impacting those within your reach.

So many of us, Believers especially, run from leadership as opposed to embracing it. We haven't been groomed for it. Again, we've been groomed to believe in God, but not to believe in ourselves . . . and not to lead. Those two things go hand-in-hand. What feels foreign—leading and influencing—however, is at the core of our life mission and master purpose.

{ NO LIMITS. NO BOUNDARIES. }

God intends for us to create, and that's why He blesses us each with "creative" gifts. As I mentioned at the top of this chapter, we're here to . . .

+ Create

+ Teach

+ Launch

+ Give

+ Inspire

+ Mentor

+ Shine

+ Be

Divine leadership doesn't have to be "spiritual" in nature. *All creation is spiritual.* If we try to filter our calling through The Rules, tradition, protocol, and religion, we can often miss it. I didn't have an appreciation for my gifts because I hadn't learned about them in church. Yet they were still God-given gifts. Not everyone is called to be a preacher—few are—but we're *all* teachers. *We're all message-carriers, story-tellers, life-changers, and gift-givers.* And our spiritual gifts exist for purposes *beyond* volunteering for a church committee, project, or activity. Those things are wonderful, but not necessarily your master calling.

Every good and perfect gift is from above.

—*James 1:17 (NIV)*

Emphasis on the word *every*. Godly doesn't mean churchy. And being creative doesn't necessarily mean you're artsy. You can be a biologist or chemist and still be creative. Creative simply means you are a vessel that creates *whatever* God is trying to manifest. Whether it's creating a cookie or a basketball, a profit-making business or a nonprofit, God uses our lives to create something that improves the lives of others, and moves others forward. Therein lies the intersection between legacy (leaving something behind) and life-changing (moving others forward). There are no limits. God abides by no man-made boundaries. It *all* belongs to God. Further . . .

God doesn't live in a pulpit. He lives in our hearts.

We have to stop putting God in boxes He doesn't belong in. And, we have to *stop judging* what's spiritual enough to be considered Godly and to be "ministry." *Ministry simply means meeting a need.* If we were supposed to be confined to four walls, then Jesus would have lived, led, bled, and died in a church . . . not in the streets. That's where we're supposed to be.

Judging others and dictating what constitutes ministry just makes us arrogant rule-makers when Christ was a rule-*breaker* . . . a rebel. Kind of like that unconventional hippie named John the Baptist who, by the way, even in smelly rags, was good enough to baptize Jesus. Talk about not running from the ultimate calling when the time comes. He *knew* his moment was coming and groomed himself for it—not in traditional ways, but by clinging to God's voice. Calling is an inside job. It's not about appearance, it's about anointing. Tradition is a distraction.

The call to influence is as universal as it is inevitable—it's built in at birth. God wants us to have dominion in every area imaginable, to be a solution wherever there is a problem, and to lead wherever leadership is needed. And, to embrace new horizons as our genetic birthright. It *all* belongs to Him.

God's permission is the only permission you need to lead.

Fear is not the language of purpose. Being afraid to disappoint God is *not* what will take you into your destiny. Faith flows on an entirely different frequency. We have to live expectantly. We must look for the next yes, not just guard ourselves against the next mistake. Obedience, surrender, aligning with God, and unlocking your gifts are more attached to your yeses than your nos.

{ ENTER YOUR PROMISED LAND }

So how do we lead? How do we influence? And, how do we take our gifts, voice 'n superpowers and step out of the ordinary and into the extra-ordinary?

+ First, we must remember, entering our promised land *is* God's will for our lives. The truth is that His boundary lines have fallen *for you* in good places. Your portion, your cup, and your lot is secure (Psalm 16:4–5). We overthink this. Instead, we should just embrace it. *You'll never feel truly ready to lead.* The journey is about trust, and trust is the journey. At a certain point, constantly seeking confirmation becomes an excuse for not trusting. Leaping. Leading.

+ Second, keep in mind that God doesn't want us trespassing. By that I mean living in someone else's lane and coveting what others have . . . or what they *seem* to have. The lives others live are almost always a grass-seems-greener illusion. We'll miss our invitation every time if we're tricked into looking at what someone else has instead of what God has for us.

God's dream for you is that you would walk fully and boldly in your territory.

+ Third, we must remember that entering *our* promised land is tied to us helping others to enter *theirs*. For this reason, purpose doesn't start with *your why*, it begins with *God's where*. Again, *where is God leading you to lead others?* Purpose fundamentally isn't about passion or figuring out what *you* like to do. It requires you to listen for what God has *already said* your life was *built* to unlock.

And entering your purpose-mission isn't just about asking what God wants you to do. It's more about aligning with what God is *already* doing. Where you've been assigned to have impact is where your key, your superpower, fits. This is where you are meant to lead—to create, teach, launch, give, inspire, mentor, shine, and be.

Your promised land—your purpose—is the intersection between your superpowers and other people's problems. That's your territory. That's the place God has set aside for you and you alone to steward, and for you to have unprecedented influence. Others are locked out of what they need until you show up. The overlap is like a keyhole—this is where your gifts fit and unlock.

Moses' call was leading others to *their* promised land. *His* territory was in the wilderness. Our promised land is not necessarily about a physical space; it's about going where God guides . . . operating in a realm that enables transformation to occur. It's more so about mindset and surrender. This "place" God assigns us to requires we be in position to share our gifts with people and problems in need of what we've got.

God did amazing miracles in Moses' life *while* Moses was leading others to a bigger and better life. Moses' supernatural supply came *while* he was helping people, not beforehand. We don't need it when we're not using it. Gas isn't needed for a parked car. God doesn't give us the check and then ask us to cash it. He shows us a debt and, without any apparent resources, says go and eliminate it. That's when the fuel comes. That's divine influence. It unfolds in the *while*. That's our blueprint and that's how we find our promised land, too. Influence is not just a destination, it's a destiny; an assignment that has your name on it.

Calling is not about finding a place to settle, it's about going where God has called you to serve.

That's why many of us miss it! We're looking for something we can see, a paved path, someplace we can go and retire. But remember God, the Master of the unseen world, calls us to reinvention, not retirement. We're supposed to move wherever God leads.

Movement is at the heart of influence.

Again, moving water is majestic and life-giving. Standing water, however, becomes toxic and deadly. Parasites fester in stagnation. Moses' influence and territory grew the more Moses *moved with* God, without knowing how it was all going to come together. The more he trusted God's voice, and embraced his own voice, the more miracles happened through him that blessed others. Same with Jeremiah. Same with Esther. Same with me and you.

In this moment, right now, you, too, are being called to lead others through a process and into a more blessed and abundant space. I know you feel it. I believe that's the primary reason God brought us together . . . so that I could deliver *this* message. God's been trying to get your attention. There *is* a message in you and a mission with your name on it. Your classroom is waiting. *It's time to teach others to overcome what you already overcame.* You may not feel good enough for it or qualified to deliver it, but I'm here to tell you that you are.

My path will look different than yours, and yours may look like nothing you've ever seen before. That's okay. *God doesn't recycle.* He reinvents and makes all things new. However, the starting point for each of us is still the same. God is asking us to take our gift box and pull out the master key. It's time to share your story. It's time to use your voice.

{ WHY YOUR VOICE AND YOUR STORY MATTER }

Back when I was working at legal aid, I got an email that changed how I think about influence and calling. A woman in Montana emailed me, explaining that her daughter had seen me on the TV show *The Apprentice.* I'd had no idea the show, which had ended about six months earlier, was airing reruns on a sister network. The woman explained that her daughter was a mother of two and was very sick—in fact, she was dying from cancer. Her daughter, we'll call her Faith, was never a big TV watcher and had never even heard of the show before she stumbled upon one episode and really connected with me. She asked if I would be able to make time to speak with Faith. To say I was humbled would be an understatement. Her daughter was near death, but she wanted to talk to *me*? And after watching a business reality TV show of all things? I replied right away and we arranged a time for me to call Faith later that day.

I was incredibly nervous as I dialed her number. I had spoken on stages in front of thousands around the world, performed solos in sold-out stadiums as a baton twirler, and I'd appeared regularly on television in front of millions, but in this moment everything in me felt unprepared. *What would I say?* Deep breath. *What could I say?*

Then, she picked up. Her voice was weak and tired, but she was doing her best to sound like she was okay. At first we talked about the weather and then talked about the TV show for a bit . . . and then I heard kids in the background. She had a son named Chance and a girl named Hope. They wanted to be next to their mom, and I listened as she struggled to pick them up and allow them to snuggle with her while we talked. We talked about frog figurines—something that we both randomly collected at the time! Eventually, about thirty minutes in, I felt like I was talking to an old friend. I can't remember everything we talked about, but I do remember when God whispered, *Ask her if she knows me. Ask her if she is saved.* And then I got nervous again. I didn't have to ask if it was *really* God. It certainly wasn't the devil asking me to ask her if she knew Christ! There was this feeling of magnitude—it was like a secret portal had opened up and I had a narrow window to act before it closed. I took one more deep breath.

"So, Faith. I want to ask you something. Are you saved? Do you know Jesus Christ?"

Turns out, she wasn't offended. Though we were thousands of miles apart, her curiosity met mine in this sacred moment. We were both open and fully present. Time stood still. She replied, "I'm not sure. I've gone to church my entire life. But I'm not sure how that really works."

And I said, "Well, I know how we can be sure. Is it okay if I pray with you?"

With a soft and tender but certain whisper, she said, "Yes. Please."

So we prayed. And she repeated after me as she dedicated her life and accepted Jesus Christ as her Lord and Savior. I don't remember what I said, and I'm not sure if I prayed that prayer the right way . . . the way I'd seen it done on Sundays a thousand times before. But it was good enough. It was the most beautiful and satisfying moment. So sweet. So spiritual. So permanent. And then Faith whispered, "If I had known it was this easy, I would have done this a long time ago." That still gives me chills to this day. It probably always will.

We spoke a little bit longer, and made plans to talk the next day. That evening I got an email from her and she shared her thanks and some of the highlights of our time together.

When I called at our scheduled time the next morning, her mother answered. Faith had passed away overnight. Her mother thanked me for spending time with her daughter, and I thanked her for sharing her daughter with me.

Whew. Tears and knots always well up within me when I revisit that moment. I'm in awe of how God can use us and put all the pieces together when He gets ready . . . when He needs us . . . and when things matter most. One seemingly little call, and the willingness to pray with a stranger for fifteen seconds, had a big, eternal impact. What we think are nerves aren't nerves. *It's destiny calling.* It's eternity within us, inviting others to experience a dose of what God has for them in that very moment. It could be the person on the corner that needs something to eat or a place to sleep. It could be an encouraging word that you're supposed to tell a stranger in the grocery store. It could be anything that God needs you to do when God needs you to do it.

That's influence. *It's being available.* It. Is. Not. About. Accomplishment. It's being a vessel and a voice. And it's being brave right when you think you're going to break. You're not going to break. You're going to break *through*. I learned some other really key lessons, too.

1. **INFLUENCE IS ABOUT PRESENCE.** Not a fancy website, credentials, or titles. Faith didn't need my hair to look a certain way or me to have any makeup on for me to be presentable or relevant. She just needed me (a stranger) to be willing to be there and to listen. *Presence makes way for significance.*

2. **INFLUENCE IS ACTIVELY SPEAKING UP.** God had given *me*, a stranger of all people, something that Faith *needed* to hear. And it was my job to deliver it. *Influence doesn't require a platform, it only requires willingness.* That was my first time leading someone to Christ. I didn't have much notice. It wasn't on my radar, but it was my desire. Using our lives to shine light on who God is happens when we use our voice.

3. **INFLUENCE REQUIRES SURRENDER.** When it comes to glorifying God, we never know how it is going to happen. That part, *the how*, is none of our business! It's our job to go where God guides. To be a willing vessel. It just so happens that my desire to do *The Apprentice* was also God's desire for my life. Go figure! It wasn't what most people would call ministry, but it was where God needed me. I didn't win the show, but I won something way better six months later. Winning souls is far sweeter than success.

God's timing won't often make sense. And we can't focus on the outcome—obsession with achieving a certain outcome, even a holy one, eventually becomes an idol. Another form of control, of putting ourselves in the driver's seat. It's better for us to focus on adventure—looking for new ways to expand our experience, not to win. To be curious (there is that word again!), to try new things, and to allow ourselves to dream. God *gives us* the desires of our hearts for a reason. We don't get to script the miracles. Our responsibility is obedience and a willingness to say yes. God will do the rest—exactly what He needs and precisely when He needs it.

4. **INFLUENCE IS UNLIMITED.** God wants us everywhere. Ephesians 1:22 (NIV, my emphasis) says that "God placed *all things* under his feet and appointed [Christ] to be head over *everything* for the church." The church isn't four walls. The church is the collection of God's people. "Everything" means every single thing: every person, every place, and every space.

I can guarantee that if you are committed to going where God guides, especially given what God is calling women to do in this season, you're gonna face judgment. And, rejection. You'll have leaders and gatekeepers tell you that you're not ready, that you want to be sure that "you're in the world but not of the world." That means you're on the right path! We can't run from the world and at the same time advance the kingdom. We have to be in the trenches.

We can't tap into the bigger if we spend all of our time with people who look, think, and act just like us.

There's no challenge there. That just bathes us in comfort, amplifies timidness, and swaddles us in conformity . . . making us hesitant to share God and our bigger self with others. Comfort ultimately gives us permission to be cowards *and* literally invites a spirit of fear to take root in our lives . . . usually in the very area where we're called to lead. We end up just going through the motions. Looking the part.

We're not here to blend in.

We're here to be the salt—the seasoning that flavors and changes the atmosphere. We're to be the light that goes intentionally in to dark places, not hide from and avoid 'em. "Going in"—now that's the bold, limitless mindset that influence requires. My point: *no one has the authority to limit your calling.* As Lisa Bevere, a dynamo Bible teacher with a fiery voice, once told me to my face with her hands placed upon each of my shoulders, "If you shrink, you'll be nothing!" She may or may not have physically shook me a little bit to get my attention! I don't know if it was her hands or her words, but she said it at least three or four times. The last time, I heard her loud and clear. And in that moment, through the intensity of her eyes, I saw me and who it was time to be.

Don't let you limit you either.

If *you* shrink, you'll be nothing.

When we show up as our full creative self, operating in our gifts and using all of the supernatural keys and superpowers we've been given, we are like a blooming flower that naturally attracts the bee. That's what God allowed me to experience that day, in a sacred moment of prayer with a woman thousands of miles away who solidified her place in eternity. But a bee can't find a flower that is in hiding, shrinking and unwilling to bloom. You're here to be seen. You've always been selected by God. Your very presence is significant and is at the center of your call to influence. After all, God isn't just raising up women. He is awakening and recruiting voices. And by voices, I most certainly mean Y-O-U.

The *bigger* question: *Where is God sending you now?*

What comes to mind? What impact do you want to have and with whom?

How can you use and share what God has given you in a new or next-level way?

chapter fourteen

CLARIFYING YOUR LIFE MISSION

Let's just go ahead and be what we were made to be, without enviously or pridefully comparing ourselves with each other, or trying to be something we aren't.

—Romans 12:6 (MSG)

So now you know the five stages of divine reinvention and how the Purpose Map works! Discovery. Talent. The GAP. Gifts. Influence.

At each stage, we explored an overarching question—a question that gives a snapshot of our decisions and our identity at that stage. Let's recap each one now.

1. **WHO AM I SUPPOSED TO BE?** In the Discovery Stage, we learned that The Rules given to us ultimately guide our beliefs about ourselves (who we're supposed to become) and our possibilities (where we belong).

2. **WHO DID I DECIDE TO BE?** In the Talent Stage, we saw how The Rules regulate our decisions and lead us to pick a lane that becomes our life. We begin to identify ourselves by our

titles and talents. We master mountain climbing but eventually learn that success and comfort are unsatisfying illusions.

3. **WHAT IS HAPPENING TO ME?** During The GAP, we encounter a disruption of some sort. We learned that disruption is redirection and preparation, not punishment. In order to make room for more, God removes what no longer belongs, to build something bigger. Making the shift (versus getting stuck in a purpose purgatory) requires a heck of a lot of surrender, which isn't easy, but it is the only way to step into our highest self. Releasing the baggage, broken thinking, bad relationships, and anything else blocking the new is key to being able to change our life and the lives of others. Disruption is intentional, but it's not an attack. Shift happens not *to* you but *for* you.

4. **HOW DID GOD REALLY DESIGN ME?** During the Gifts Stage, we discovered that God prewired us with some pretty amazing abilities and endowments. Our gifts are given to us, but they're really for the purpose of moving others forward. Disruption came to help us see beyond our talents and into our superpowers—to believe bigger than what we'd known and who we'd been. *The split rock reveals our superpowers and when our water breaks, it's time for our story to come forth.* Gifts are intended to upshift our identity and awaken our authentic personality, and they are about aligning with God's original intention and construction for our lives. Gifts are about significance, not success. Your ultimate gift is your voice.

5. **WHERE IS GOD NOW SENDING ME?** During the Influence Stage, we learned that a woman's place is *anywhere* God sends her. God designed and pre-equipped us to lead. To create, teach, launch, give, inspire, mentor, shine, and be. Leadership isn't about notoriety; it's about impact. It's not about titles, but transformation. God intends us to use our gifts, voice, personality, and everything else at our disposal to elevate and awaken destiny in others.

There are no limits when it comes to going where God guides. It all belongs to Him. Anyplace God takes us is holy ground.

It no longer matters who you were told you were supposed to be. And it doesn't even matter who you decided to be. Disruption came to invite you into the new you, and that new woman emerges the moment you say yes to you.

Say yes to what's in you.

Your dreams. Your voice. Your gifts, nudges, leadings, and desires. God calls us forward because that's where promise and next-level purpose live. So embrace what happened to you, knowing now that it really happened *for* you. It may have been devastating and downright evil, but God has a message about your magnificence hidden within. So . . .

- *What are the old paradigms and limited beliefs that no longer serve you?*
- *What current relationships or commitments are suffocating your voice and vision?*
- *What was it that seemed to happen to you but really happened for you?*
- *What has all of this shown you about your gifts and your voice?*
- *Where do you desire to have greater impact and influence given your life experiences, hard-earned wisdom, and dreams?*
- *And who is the woman God is leading you now to become?*

Get a picture of her. That's who *little me* and the enemy are afraid of. Your gifts are what turn on her superpowers. Your voice is what activates superpowers in others. Oh, yes, you're a target of the enemy because you're a threat to the enemy. But you're a gift. A walking miracle waiting to happen. A mysterious and complex weapon able take out the darkness. A daughter—beautiful but deadly.

{ BIG PICTURE }

It's time to share your creativity, your gifts, your voice and ideas with others. Don't let the wealth of wisdom and imagination inside of you die. There are three primary ways we can fulfill our life mission. This is going to be surprisingly simple . . . but it's big.

1. Show others how to get through their split rock.

2. Show others how to slay their fears.

3. Show others how to thrive and not just survive.

We're here to help other people overcome difficult times. That could mean sharing your insight or creating solutions to problems that keep others at a disadvantage. We're here to be a voice of possibility helping others to believe bigger in their future. To help them get through depression, discouragement, self-doubt, and anxiety. And we're here to teach people how to move forward in some area of their life. How to develop their skills, gifts, thinking, and approach such that they don't just get by, they thrive.

{ COURAGE COMES WITH CLARITY }

Now that we know how the purpose journey unfolds over the five stages, the question still remains: *What is your specific purpose?*

This chapter might feel a bit like a purpose workshop . . . actually, I hope it does! My intention is that you will have *more* clarity and confidence about *your* calling . . . to bring all of these concepts together. I emphasize the word *more* because calling isn't a crystal clear type of thing. Crystal clarity is not what's needed. It's not what God gave Moses, Esther, Jeremiah, and it's not what he is seeking to give us either. To that regard, the insistence upon "crystal" clarity can become an entitlement idol that is just as destructive to your destiny as disobedience. We're interested in surrender, not success; progress, not perfection. Curiosity gets us going.

{ EMBRACING PROCESS AND PURPOSE PLANS }

Purpose is a process. It's a by-product of an intimate, ongoing conversation with God about what *God* wants, envisions, and has waiting for you. My experience with God-conversations about the future is we can't make Him talk, and we can't force His hand! We can, however, commit to connecting with His heart. When we do that, when we enter into the secret place, we end up with every single thing we need.

*We can't just seek the way,
we have to seek the Way Maker.*

Will you make that commitment with me? We're going to work together to map out your own life mission statement now. My hope is that with this mission statement, you'll be able to start sharing your superpowers right away. But keep in mind that purpose is a process, not a magic pill, and process is what makes purpose stick. And (ahem) process is what most of us hate! We're too impatient. I know I am.

One thing God has showed me about growing spiritually, financially, and relationally is that growth is really the result of embracing its process. What we've been doing hasn't been working. Again, it may have gotten you here (out of Egypt), but it won't get you there (into the promised land). What we go through next may or may not click all together right away. That's okay. Don't check out. Don't beat yourself up. Don't assume something is wrong with you. And certainly don't listen to *little me*. The miracle known as your life mission *is* already in progress. Embrace that. Believe that.

My intention during this part of our conversation is to not only share with you what I've learned about helping others step into their purpose with confidence and clarity, but to share a new way for you to talk with God about His next-level purpose plans for you. After all, *if it isn't God, it isn't real.*

⊰ PRAYING BETTER PRAYERS ⊱

At the start of this journey together, I mentioned that one of the worst questions we can ask God is *Why?* Why did this or that happen? The truth is, we may never really know *why* something happened, and we don't really need to. We may *want* to know why, but we don't actually *need* to know why. Part of embracing purpose and process means surrendering control—including the need to have answers and becoming okay with mystery. The more we surrender, the more we plant ourselves in the soil of trust. That is *exactly* where God wants us, and it's a posture that positions us to *be able* to hear what God is saying. When we make demands or when we insist on getting the answers that we want, we're like a spoiled child who tries to boss her parent around. That's an ugly, upside-down picture—one that ain't workin' if we wanna receive blessings and overflow.

There are, however, two questions I've found to be extremely powerful prayers. Instead of asking God, *Why did this happen?* and *What do you want me to do?* (both questions that demand clarity, as if we're entitled to it), these are better questions. I call 'em *Purpose Prayers*:

PURPOSE PRAYER-QUESTION #1:
God, what are you *already* doing?

PURPOSE PRAYER-QUESTION #2:

God, *where* do you need me?

These two questions, when asked as surrendered prayers, are game-changers and life-accelerators. I encourage you to take time to pray 'em.

These are questions God longs to answer, because they bond us with his heart and not just his hand. We're not asking for anything for ourselves. We're asking to come into alignment with divine assignment—we're asking to see, become, and carry out what we were built for. Those are prayers that the spirit of purpose can and will always get behind.

} PURPOSE PRAYER-QUESTION #1: } GOD, WHAT ARE YOU *ALREADY* DOING?

No one wants to be around someone who is solely interested in themselves. Their problems. Their plans. Their yada yada yada. Selfish, me-focused folks get on my nerves! I know you know what I mean. They're draining, and they suck the energy out of you almost instantly. For the most part, you either keep your distance from these folks or try to handle them only in small doses. However, if we're honest . . . this is often how we treat God. We bring to him *our* agenda, *our* problems, *our* goals, *our* wants, and whatever else is on *our* list. Thankfully, God doesn't distance himself from us (He loves us too much to leave us). But I think this kind of attitude contributes to those seasons of silence when we're not hearing from God. It's because we're doing all the talking. We're usually trying to change what already is. I'll just let that simmer.

We want God to be interested in us and what *we* want changed. But are we truly interested in what interests God? Are we curious? Concerned? Excited? Are we willing to pay committed attention to what God needs, desires, and is *already* doing? Surrender connects us with the unseen, supernatural realm where God makes all things known, new, and possible. We get what we want as a by-product of connecting with what God wants; that's the blueprint for clarity, revelation, and confirmation. For power and provision, too.

We've gotta start praying in the right dimension—especially during a time of transition, elevation, and expansion. The secret is praying for God to show you what you've never seen, you've never done, and what you can't (in your own strength and ability) comprehend.

When we pray *God what are you already doing?* we're asking for eyes to see God's plan that is *already* in progress, and we're asking for the privilege and blessing of participation—to be a part of divine flow. *This is the prayer of visionaries, builders, and leapers.* Visionaries see what's in the future. Builders build what's in their vision. Leapers leap into what they believe is waiting for them on the other side.

> *Builder prayers are way more powerful than beggar prayers.*

Beggar prayers give us permission to pray pitifully. When we pray *God please do this, God please do that,* we're begging. I'm not saying God doesn't hear those prayers; however, I do believe *the way we pray* can either elevate or shrink our faith. And faith shapes our future. Faith means not simply waiting passively for your prayer to be answered, but praying expectantly, assertively, and with declaration.

When I pray this first prayer-question, mine sounds a li'l something like this. Feel free to use my words as an example to get you started . . .

God, I know you work all things for good.
I know you hold the future in your hands and that my best
days are ahead of me. You have good plans for me. You're
present no matter what. Pain, discord, and confusion are not
my destiny. I know you have a space and territory with only
my name on it.

Give me ears that hear and eyes that are ready to see:
God, what are you already *doing?*
Prepare me. Show me. Speak, for your servant is listening.

That's a builder's prayer. That's how women ready to lead and leap pray. And that's how we discover God's intention, ideas, desires, plans, purpose, and *whatever* He wants to tell us about our next step. We allow God to pen our agenda, as opposed to just asking Him to respond to ours. Learning to pray with boldness, like a builder, is how I built a new life after betrayal. Don't get me wrong, I had my share of beggar conversations. But God longs to move us forward—as creative forces, we can't go to a new place with an old way of speaking and thinking.

{ PRAYER-QUESTION #2: }
GOD, *WHERE* DO YOU NEED ME?

I love this question because it tames my striving and replaces it with a posture of serving. I need this type of prayer. I need to remember I serve at the pleasure of the King of Kings. I'm gifted, anointed, and capable, but I'm still nothing without The One who placed me in my mother's womb. Our world does everything possible to put God on the back burner, when the truth is He belongs front and center. I work best, lead best, love best, and impact best when I follow in His footsteps. We learn in Genesis (the part where God created the world before our arrival) that God prepares a place for us *before* He sends us. Get this: I don't have to pray for provision, people, or resources; I need to pray for the *place*—the courage to see it and enter it. Everything needed will already be there.

When we're experiencing lack, anxiety, or recurring frustration, it's likely because we're pursuing the *wrong* place. That wrong place can be an actual physical environment, like a job or place where you're spending your time and energy. Or it can be a relationship, a mindset, an approach, or something you're pursuing and pouring energy into that isn't on the Path.

When we look at the Purpose Map, we can see we're not supposed to go in circles, and we're also not supposed to stay in one place forever. We are supposed to get out of the boat, to walk on water, to go. God says (Genesis 12:1 NLT), "*Go* to the land that I will show you." He doesn't say go to a place you've *already* been or seen. Another truth that we should let simmer. Remember, God doesn't recycle. He reinvents, renews, and repositions.

I do believe the reason the majority of women do not know their purpose is because we've not been taught to ask *where*. Asking God to lead us means having a *true* willingness to go. Most of us aren't really serious about *going*—we're more committed to *wanting, appearing,* and *receiving,* but not doing the *going* that precedes what we're praying to manifest. We're far too stubborn and addicted to comfort and the predictable. Plus, we've made the starting point for purpose *our* passion, *our* talents, and *our* desires. When we do that, we bake the cake backwards! What if our mission is something we've never done or experienced before? Starting with passion and proficiency limits possibility. *What you've done is not who you are.* It's just what you've done. It's where you've committed, focused, and even flourished.

Where God needs us aligns with what God is *already* doing.

He who started a good work in you longs to advance you into its completion.

Here's some guidance on how to pray the *where* prayer-question:

> *God, I thank you for everything you have given me and how*
> *you have gifted me. You waste nothing. I know that I am yours*
> *and that you have me on a journey. I desire to be a focused,*
> *purposeful doer and not just a dreamer. Speak to me and*
> *show where you need me.*
> *Give me clarity about where my story, my voice, my gifts, my*
> *talents, and my resources are needed. Where can I be a bigger*
> *blessing? Where can I take what you have given me to best*
> *build up others and make their lives better?*
> *Thank you for making me a solution to someone's problem.*
> *Thank you for the things you have allowed me to overcome*
> *and learn.*

Where can I now pour out the wisdom and skills you have poured into me?

We wanna be where God is already answering someone's next prayer. And, we wanna be wherever God is *already* active—where His spirit lies and has already made way for our arrival. To seize it, we must first look for it. To enter it, we must first expect it.

I'd love for you to take a moment, find a place to bow before God, and prayerfully reflect upon and pray these two prayer-questions now:

God, what are you *already* doing?

God, *where* do you need me?

I'd also recommend journaling your prayers, your insights, and your revelations. You may need to pray them daily for a while—these aren't onetime prayers. These prayers are supposed to keep us coming back to the well.

{ CALLING LEAVES CLUES }

So we've got our purpose-prayers—better questions that position us for better answers. We understand the basics of the Purpose Map, gifts, voice, and superpowers. We know our primary Purpose Archetype— we're either *The Puller*, *The Planner*, or *The Pusher*. We know our life is a message, *and* we've renewed our minds to believe bigger about who we are and where we belong, which puts us on the right playing field. *Fist bump* Let's remember the diffrence between purpose and calling.

> *Purpose is about the overall, natural impact your life has. Calling is about your particular assignment.*

We've talked about the confirmations that affirm you're operating in your calling. But there are also lots of clues giving insight into what your specific calling might be.

> *Calling is that thing within you that pulls the best out of you and unleashes the best around you.*

This is my favorite topic to teach at my conferences and seminars. We spend days diving into destiny-discovery and identity—losing all track of time along the way! For now, we're just going to focus on the top three Calling Clues.

Clue 1: Dreams

What is it that you've already dreamed of doing, having, or becoming? It can be anything. I firmly believe our recurring dreams are nudges from Heaven that reveal God's desires for our lives. In the Bible, especially in the Old Testament, dreamers were highly esteemed and considered a strategic advantage to those in government. Kings and rulers knew having a vision for the future was essential to leadership and maintaining power. So they first would call upon psychics and fortune-tellers. That never worked. Only God holds His future. They would then call upon the dreamers, the prophets, and the visionaries—the ones *anointed* to provide insight into the future because they were uniquely connected to God.

Somewhere along the way, we've lost an appreciation for the art of *divine dreaming*. It is essential that we collaborate with God in the realm of the unseen, exercise our imagination, and remain curious about what God is up to. *Dreams are meant to be lived, not just longed for.* The recurring dreams, visions, and ideas bubbling inside of you to create something new or change lives or the status quo, are clues as to what it is God might be calling you to do.

Clue 2: Thorns

Ahhh. Thorns. Every rose has 'em, and so do we. Thorns are the trials, obstacles, and recurring challenges you continue to face throughout your life. Our thorns tend to reflect painful, unproductive, or dysfunctional patterns when we look back at our path in retrospect.

+ What are things you keep praying to overcome?

+ What is the recurring frustration that God keeps agitating?

+ What are the trials you tend to always face, the fears that keep coming back up, the types of dysfunctional relationships and decisions you keep repeating?

These are your thorns. They function not to wound you, but to show you a place to upshift your thinking and enter your future classroom. For example, one of my thorns is trust. I have had trouble trusting people since elementary school—believing people either don't want me in the circle or that people just aren't trustworthy. Infidelity only affirmed that preexisting fear.

But when I look back, I can see that God has been showing me how trusting others is connected to my ability to trust Him. He has been trying to teach me to see Him, believe Him, and find Him *in* my interactions with others. Mentors, coaches, a sister circle, and loving relationships have elevated my faith in exponential ways. If I focused only on the thorns and the storms, I'd draw the conclusion that I'm destined to do life alone, but that's a lie! Betrayal is one of the best teachers in God's syllabus.

> *Sometimes we have to see a snake to know what one looks like.*

Another thing I struggled with was confidence—believing beyond those problem child stereotypes and labels. That's the recurring thorn. But that's also the clue. On the flip side is a blessing . . . my wiring to inspire others to believe bigger through writing, teaching, giving, and living. *Motivation wouldn't exist without the mess.* Jacob (his story is in Genesis 32 if you wanna refresh your memory or check it out) had a limp to remind him (and us) that he needed (just like we need) God. A faith walk takes . . . well, faith. Faith is needed when it's difficult to believe. Remember, purpose is often hidden in a place of pain or insecurity. We have thorns to show us *exactly* where God is intending for us to look, believe bigger, and bloom.

Clue 3: Passions

Passion is found in what you love to do, your desires, your interests, and your perspective. Passion is an *indicator* of your purpose. The Bible says God will give us the desires of our heart (Psalm 37:4). The word *de-sire* actually means "of the sire" or "of the father." Desire is God-given. *What you desire is representative of what God is seeking to manifest through you.* Soak that in for a moment. One of the most powerful mind shifts you can make is to stop overthinking your desires. You fight yourself. Start embracing your desires and the way your mind works.

The other thing to remember about passion is that it's a bridge that will never be fully built. God is constantly showing us new things about ourselves—new superpowers, new abilities we never knew we had. Remember, there are many things you've learned to do well. Those proficiencies and pleasures can lead to your *known* passions, but *leave room for the unknown*. There are other things, things you've never done, that you can do even better.

✦ So what do you love, and what *would you love* to experience?

✦ Who do you want to help?

✦ What do you feel is missing in the world . . . in your community?

✦ Who do you have a heart for?

Again, passion alone is not enough and it's not the starting point, but it is a powerful clue. You'll notice these questions are similar to what I asked you in defining your guiding belief earlier. When our passion matches God's plan and meets a need that has our name on it, we find our sweet spot.

So. What are your *Dreams*? What are your *Thorns*? What are your *Passions*?

Dreams	Thorns	Passions
How Might God Be Using My Dreams to Direct My Next Season?	How Are My Thorns, My Recurring Challenges, Actually Indications of My True Calling?	What Do I Love? What Do I Desire to Be and Do?

{ SO WHAT'S YOUR PURPOSE? }

Don't worry, I didn't forget the question we started with! I've just discovered over the years of doing destiny-discovery that the *process* of prayer, affirmation, and reflection gives way to revelation. I don't want you just making something up! I want you in alignment with God's actual vision for you. After all, *your voice is the vehicle for God's vision.* Our final step here is to draft a Believe Bigger Life Mission Statement. The believing bigger part is key because it honors the gifts of disruption, stretches our vision, and reminds us that God's highest intention is at the center of our life mission. Bigger belief brings greater clarity.

Remember, *your purpose is the intersection between your superpowers and others' super-problems*! That's your space . . . your territory and the place God has set aside for you to steward, develop, and focus. Others are locked out of what they need until you show up. The overlap is that keyhole we talked about—this is where your gifts fit and unlock.

OTHERS' SUPER-PROBLEMS   PURPOSE   YOUR SUPER-POWERS

Based on what you've discovered about disruption, gifts, and superpowers, based upon the *Blessing Dump* and *Inner Vault* reflection we did earlier, your *Purpose Archetype, and* based upon what you've just explored—your dreams, thorns, passions—what is God saying to you about *your* life mission? *Let's see.*

Answer these five questions:

1. *What* type of calling do I have? (archetype)

2. *Who* needs my voice? My story? My insight? (the struggle you're drawn to)

3. *How* am I uniquely gifted to impact those I'm assigned to? (your Inner Vault)

4. *Where* am I prewired to lead others? (the promises you're gifted to unlock)

5. *Why* has God chosen me to participate in His plan? What outcomes does my presence facilitate? (summarize your overcomer story in a few words, plus your motivation for helping others)

Now just fill in the blanks:

My life mission is to be a(n)_____ (insert archetype or an archetype attribute) by using _____ (insert top gifts or superpowers from the Inner Vault) and sharing these with _____ (insert who is struggling and needs what you have) by showing them how to _____ (insert the solutions you bring, impact you have, or promises you're gifted to unlock).

My journey _____ (insert your super-short overcomer journey) is why I'm passionate about _____ (insert your motivation).

Voilà! There you have it!

To make sure that the above template makes sense, here is an example of it filled in:

My life mission is to be an encourager by using my gifts of messaging, strategy, and writing and sharing these with women who struggle with confidence and clarity by showing them how to maximize their existing potential and enter their true calling!

My journey as a problem child turned successful entre-preneur who loves God wholeheartedly is why I'm passion-ate about demonstrating that anyone can change their life by believing bigger and living bolder.

You can certainly tweak the wording and get more specific over time. It doesn't need to be exact. And you can make it even simpler—a one-liner!

Something like, my mission is to . . .

+ Help girls get into college

+ Help survivors of domestic abuse

+ Help women start a business

+ Produce uplifting music

Simple impact statements work just as well. God will do and pen the rest over time. My desire is that you'll see the totality, relevance, and *interconnectedness* of your journeys, interests, personality, and story. My mission is to *push* you to believe beyond your comfort zone, to *pull* you out of whatever ditch disruption might have left you in, and to give you some language that will help you *plan* and map out what the future is trying to tell you. And I am providing a process *you* can use to help others find *their* purpose, too.

⧼ THE *BELIEVE BIGGER* NAPKIN CHALLENGE: ⧽
DON'T *JUST* PRAY . . . DRAW!

The way I discovered my superpowers was by sharing them, not by search-ing for them. You might wonder how it's possible to share 'em if you're not completely clear on them. I understand the question. However, we find our wings when we try to fly. It is fine to start with our proficiencies and our talents and just try to apply them in a new arena or deploy them in a new way. The key is stepping outside of your comfort zone and trusting God to order your footsteps. *Pursuing* purpose, as opposed to waiting on it, is more than half the battle! God will provide the steps *as* you step.

And keep in mind that all of this isn't just for you. You have all of this as a resource to help guide other women, friends, and family in your life . . . and the strangers you'll meet along the way. Again, it's an exploration . . . not an exactness.

To that end, to start your purpose journey, I challenge you to share the concepts of *Believe Bigger* and the Purpose Map with others.

- ✦ When you have a friend going through a hard time, speak life into his or her future and share the bigger possibilities that God may have waiting on the other side of heartache and pain. You don't have to have similar experiences to be able to relate. We all face disruption. Explain what a split-rock moment is, share yours, and establish common ground.

- ✦ If you're in a small group, make believing bigger, embracing disruption, and shifting into higher purpose the topics of discussion, *and* offer to lead it!

- ✦ Think about getting a group of women together to have a destiny-mapping and mission statement–crafting gathering. You can use the questions I've shared with you.

- ✦ And when you meet someone in transition, don't *just* pray for them. Draw the Purpose Map for them.

- ✦ Use the Purpose Map to help others see where *they* might be on their purpose journey. We're all very visual! The Purpose Map is how we can show others what purpose discovery looks and feels like.

Remember, you find your unique voice while you're sharing, not staring and searching. Drawing these five stages shows others in an engaging and visible way that there is indeed something bigger in front of them. You're gifting others with hope, perspective, and clarity.

Sometimes we need to see it, not just hear it.

The Purpose Map is our way of speaking what we're believing and building by penning it for others. It also gives you a chance to talk about *your* journey—to use your voice. Share where *you* are on the Purpose Map and how God has worked in your life—the highs, the lows, the good, and the ugly. What Rules steered you? What mountains have you climbed that no longer satisfy you? What tugs from the future have agitated you? And so on. Talk about what you're believing for, what you've learned on your journey, and what you're leaving behind . . . it all matters. Every story has a place on the Purpose Map.

I've doodled hundreds of Purpose Maps, but the first one I ever drew was on a napkin. I shared it with an incredibly accomplished, senior-level C-suite executive woman who found herself unfulfilled in her career. She had climbed to the top of the Money Mountain in the Talent Stage and was tired of circling there. She wanted something new. We were at a luncheon, so I just picked up an unused cocktail napkin. I drew two boxes side by side on the left side of the napkin. I left a wide-open space in the center, and then drew two additional boxes side-by-side on the right side. Then, I then filled in each box with words as I explained each stage one at a time.

Box #1: Write in *Discovery*. This is where we figure out who we are and learn The Rules.

Box #2: Write in *Talent*. This is where we pick a lane, master mountain climbing, and adopt success, or rule-validated roles as our identity.

Then we come to this blank open space. I draw a bridge connecting Box 2 to Box 3 and explain that this middle area is the Growth Zone—the place of transition. It's where most who are feeling The Tug either are or are being called into. Then under the bridge I draw a circle which represents The Gap we end up in (going in circles) if we're unwilling to grow and gain the clarity and confidence we need to move forward. It explains the confusion, frustration, the recurring nudges, life changes, and lack of clarity. On the bridge, I write Shift. This represents God's intention for our surrender, shedding, and the steps we must take to advance to our next season. Then I explain what's on the other side.

Box #3: Write in *GIFTS* and explain the concepts of divine DNA, gifts versus talents, voice, and superpowers.

Box #4: Write in *Influence* and explain the concept of leadership, legacy, going anew to wherever God guides, and sharing your gifts with those in need of what you uniquely have. Here you can see the map with more detail:

I then go back and write the phrase *Comfort Zone* inside a cloud over Boxes 1 and 2, *Growth Zone* over the middle "bridge" section, and *Glory Zone* inside a crown over Boxes 3 and 4. I explain that both disruption and The Tug are working together to advance us in a larger-purpose journey and life mission. Add tons of notes—key things you remember, like how God disrupts us to invite us to *believe bigger*, and elements personal to *your* story—favorite quotes, scriptures, and lessons you've learned. You can add symbols for The Rules, success mountains, circling in The Gap, Gifts, and Influence. You can even talk about and explore how *little me* and *Future ME* show up along the way. It's *your* map now. A teaching tool.

Next, I ask that person, "Where do you feel you are on the map?"

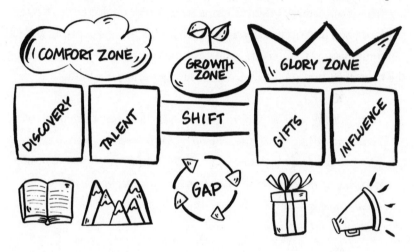

Let the person answer and point 'n touch at what you've drawn. It's a great way for others to connect with their path and embrace that they do indeed have one. Seeing your life as a path, a map that leads you and others to purpose, is incredibly powerful. It puts into words a daunting season of life that most are struggling to express.

Nine times out of ten, people are either in the Talent Stage or The GAP. Not everyone, but most.

You don't have to have lived through all of the stages to share the principles of purpose and the process of reinvention. In fact, the more you share, the more you'll embody those things; the more you'll ignite purpose in others . . . and the more you'll advance higher, deeper, and farther into yours, too.

I let people keep the napkin, and if it feels right I share with them those two prayers that have impacted my life. Sometimes, I invite them to attend a Godfidence or She Profits seminar in the future or to stay connected to their purpose pursuit in some other way. Invite 'em to church, give 'em a copy of this book . . . do something to continue this purpose conversation. Whether I'm sketching the Purpose Map on a napkin, a flip chart, or a dry erase board, the intention remains the same: *To help others move forward and embrace their journey—all of it—and to believe boldly in the promises and possibilities waiting in the future.*

Now I pass the "napkin challenge" on to you!

This is a great way to start sharing your story. You don't need a stage, a platform, or a microphone. You just need a napkin and a pen. Oh, and let's not forget your yes. Calling is a choice—one that separates the called from the chosen. When you say Y-E-S, (Y)our (E)xperience (S)hifts!

It is my highest intention and prayer that the principles of believing bigger and the Purpose Map become vocabulary that we all learn to use, such that living in and on purpose becomes a new normal. May Heaven raise up a generation of life-changers who boldly and lovingly speak the language of purpose and destiny.

I invite you to share in this intention and our joint life mission of purpose activation, too.

PART THREE

Activate

STEP

INTO

MORE

chapter fifteen

SLAYING SELF-DOUBT

She is blessed *because* she believed that the Lord
would do what he said.

—Inspired by Luke 1:45

I would be remiss if I didn't ask you at this point in the process: *now that you know all of the stages, which purpose stage are you in?*

+ **DISCOVERY.** Are you trying to figure who you are and what life is all about? What your potential is? Where you naturally excel? Who you admire and want to emulate? Who you'll listen to? Determining who you want to be?

+ **TALENT.** Are you in a season of mountain climbing, maximizing your opportunities, developing your skill set, and gaining necessary experience? Are you making a life for yourself and those you love . . . creating stability, success, and predictability . . . and adding value to others?

+ **THE GAP.** Are you in the midst of an awakening? Has a split-rock, defining moment wrecked your world, your plans, and your confidence? Are you feeling The Tug telling you that it's time to shift . . . time for a change and time to have greater impact? Time to share your story or to help others in a bigger way? Are you in the "in-between"—desiring more? Are you tired of living for everyone else . . . exhausted from putting on the mask and climbing mountains?

✦ **GIFTS.** Are you reinventing? Are you in a season of actively embracing your next level? Tapping into your potential, acquiring new skills, and investing in new experiences, passions, interests, ideas, and desires? Perhaps you're listening to new teachers that speak more to your future and possibility than your past, and seeking new ways to use your talents to help others?

✦ **INFLUENCE.** Are you in a position of leadership where you directly impact how others live, learn, and think? Are you teaching, training, sharing, equipping, and inspiring? Are you in a legacy-building season focused on helping others go to a deeper, greater level in their lives? Are you launching new ideas and creating initiatives, solutions, businesses, and charitable movements, all while using these avenues to share larger life lessons learned along the way?

There is no right or wrong stage! The key is knowing you're on a path. Awareness is what enables us to show up in our anointing.

How wonderful it would be to go through Discovery more awake! To know from the beginning that you're chosen for a wonderful faith adventure with God . . . here to advance His master plan, not merely to get a job and retire. Perhaps we'd step fully into the "carpenter" stage, aka Talent, knowing (just like Christ did) that one day there would be something more. We'd live committed to building with our muscle for a season, but would also be aware that a greater call would one day come—a season of message amplification.

Maybe we'd embrace our gifts like Jesus did and use every season of life to prepare for a greater calling we *know* is coming, because it is. To share *our* gifts as a vehicle for healing, restoring sight to the blind, and manifesting miracles. We'd be *ready* to share our voice and bring hope to individuals in need, to mentor (like Jesus did with the disciples), and to teach the masses.

The stage we're in doesn't matter. What matters is what *state* we're in. We can only be where we are. What matters is our willingness, and knowing God needs us for a master plan right where we are . . . right now.

Our ego may want to rush to the end because it "looks" better. That's our success addiction again. I know, because I always try to get to the top of the mountain . . . to finish first so I can look ahead. But you are where you are. And where you are is where God needs you now.

It's not a race.

You can't rush this any more than you can rush a pregnancy. You might as well maximize each season of life as it comes to you. *Stress comes from trying to be somewhere you're not.* Peace is being present in the moment and allowing the wisdom of this moment to guide you to your next . . . and then your next. So . . .

How can you show up to your Now wiser?

How can you embrace and maximize this season so God can see you're ready for Him to advance you to the next in His time?

In Proverbs 4:7, the Word emphasizes how important it is to "get understanding." One way to show up wiser is to anchor yourself in purpose and grow your understanding of your identity.

Understand means "to stand under." The call to believe bigger and live bolder will require you stand under your purpose. Let purpose cover you, guide you, and fill you.

If I had understood that esteem building and courage building were in my DNA . . . that would have given me much more peace on the journey. Even if my career path into law had stayed the same, being conscious of my purpose, with the focus it brings, would have helped me see how I could have shown up as a better lawyer. As a better student when in law school. A better friend. A woman who was more awake.

Maybe I wouldn't have gotten so addicted to ambition. Maybe I would have known my identity was already secure . . . that I didn't have to chase what God would willingly provide. I think that's what God was trying to show me in those moments when I stressed over being picked, winning, and arriving.

My point is, don't judge where you've been, or where you are. *Just as one stage of a pregnancy isn't more important than any other, each stage of your life matters.* Again, God wastes nothing. Don't quit your job tomorrow just because today you realize God has a calling upon your life. On the other hand, if tomorrow is the day you're supposed to leap, then prepare for it, do it, and don't look back.

> *There is nothing more beautiful and more unstoppable than a woman in alignment with her divine assignment.*

Don't assume you are in the wrong place. No matter where you are, you are always on the purpose path. Being more conscious of it is the secret to operating in the purpose flow.

{ THE IMMACULATE QUESTION }

When God calls us, He is calling what's *already* within us. Purpose is not a normal pregnancy, it's an immaculate conception—a supernatural impregnation that's only possible as an unearned gift from above. We *shouldn't* be alarmed. We *shouldn't* doubt our readiness or worthiness. Even if the magnitude of a new promise and mission God is calling you to seems impossible, the truth is this: *you've found favor with God in a beautiful, grace-filled way.* Grace has nothing to do with earned increase. God calls us not because of what we've done or what we think we know, but because of what He has *always* known.

Usually at this point in a purpose-journey conversation, when curiosity and hints of clarity and possibility begin to tap your spirit, *little me* starts pulling out the big guns. Every fear. Every doubt. Every strand of insecurity starts to rise up and speak up.

Can I have influence?

Am I good enough?

Am I too old?

Too young?

I don't know where to start.

I don't know what I have to offer or share.

I don't see how "this"—this dream, vision, or desire—is possible.

No one knows who I am.

No one cares about what I have to say.

I'm going to face rejection and ridicule.

People won't get my dream and won't understand what I'm trying to do.

I should be happy where I am and content with what I have.

I don't have the time.

I don't have the resources.

I'm not ready.

God knows I've never been the "type" to do this kind of thing, and God made me that way for a reason.

I'm not supposed to lead.

It's not my time.

My time has already come and gone.

I need to keep working on myself and get my plans together.

I just need to keep waiting on God.

Okay. Deep. Breath.

If you're like me, one, if not all, of these phrases (or some kind of variation) is an uninvited yet recurring conversation . . . especially when I start dreaming and thinking about something beyond my current circumstances. *Little me* knows us very, very well. *Little me* knows our insecurities . . . all of them. But *little me* also knows our brilliance—that light-bearing part of us that shines so bright, *little me* can't survive it. Remember, you're a target of the enemy because you're a threat to the enemy. The enemy diverts us from our destiny by putting dents in our confidence and chipping away at our self-image.

So trust me. I get it. You might be wondering, is this higher-purpose, life-changer, gift-giver thing possible for *me*? Could *I* really be pregnant with destiny? Can *I* be a woman of influence? Do *I* have superpowers? Do *I* really have something worthy of sharing, creating, or launching?

Is it possible for *me* to live a bigger, bolder life? I know that God can do miracles and that God blesses and expands the lives of others, but does that mean that's His plan *for me*?

You're not alone. Much of my prayer life revolves around these questions. An *immaculate conception* (a God-given desire, bigger vision, and mission) always invites the *immaculate question*. It's actually *the* believe bigger question:

Will God actually use me?

Not others. Me. Do I believe that God is for *me*? Do I believe God will do an impossible thing, fulfill an impossible vision, *for me*? We know God *can* do anything . . . but *will* He? *That's* the real subconscious question our spirit entertains. Believing God for the impossible and inconceivable doesn't always trigger excitement in my life . . . most times it brings on anxiety. I wanna answer each question with a hardy yes. And, Luke 1:45 (the verse at the top of this chapter) makes clear that we *believe* the blessing into being. But oh, how saying yes to these questions makes the hairs of doubt and distrust stand up on my arms and legs.

Every woman longs to be seen, selected, and significant.

Because the enemy knows this is our deepest desire, and therefore our greatest vulnerability, he uses self-doubt to contaminate it. A passage in Psalm 18:17 (NIV, emphasis mine) says, "[The Lord] rescued me from *my* powerful enemy, from *my* foes, who were too strong for me." I don't know about you, but I don't "own" my enemies. Enemies don't belong to me . . . or do they? As I read that passage over and over, I realized God was saying that the most dangerous enemies hang out in our mind, like an obnoxious roommate. We take 'em on, these inner me enemies, when we drink from the cup of fear, doubt, and worry. The thoughts that create self-sabotage—*that's* the inner enemy blocking our purpose.

Self-doubt comes from *little me*. It's the part of us that shrinks. That settles. That feeds on faulty thinking, like a dog returning to its vomit (Proverbs 26:11 NIV). Limited thinking that relies on our own understanding and desires as opposed to surrendering. This is why it is only through the renewal of our minds (Romans 12:2) that we can be transformed, aka divinely reinvented. *Believing bigger is the secret.*

If we can believe it, we can manifest it. But if we don't believe, we're not even in the game. We've disqualified ourselves before the blessing begins.

> *Belief is a bridge that God uses to transfer everything we need.*

We determine if the bridge is open for service. God is the same yesterday, today, and forevermore. God is always sending us what we need and directing us, but it's our level of belief that determines our ability to perceive it and receive it.

You're not alone in asking if God will use you. To demonstrate this, there are three women from a book I like to read that I want to introduce, or reintroduce, to you. I've read about them my entire life. But it wasn't until I faced my own split-rock season and disruption dug a ditch at my doorstep that I *really* received insight on self-doubt (the number one threat to fulfilling your life mission), along with the simple secret to entering your calling (believing bigger).

EVES-DROPPING

So where does self-doubt come from? Shouldn't we have a cure or have developed a resistance to it by now?! Let's go back to the beginning and meet Eve. She's the first woman, so I'm certain we can gain some insight by spending time with her in the Garden of Eden. You know the story. God decides to create the world. Genesis 1:27 (NIV) states that on the sixth day, "God created mankind in his own image, in the image of God he created them; male and female he created them." Then on the seventh day, God rested. I used to think that Adam made it from Heaven to the ground on the sixth day, but Genesis says differently. This passage makes clear that God physically prepared a *place* for Adam and Eve (the Garden), making them in the spiritual realm first, *before* he actually physically formed Adam from the ground and then Eve from Adam's rib. This is a really key point, with insight on how God works.

> *God creates before He manifests. His plan for our lives comes together in the unseen realm before we see it in the physical world.*

It was not until *after* the seven days and *after* God rested that God *later* physically "formed a man [Adam] from the dust of the ground and breathed into his nostrils the breath of life" (Genesis 2:7 NIV).

Eve physically comes into the picture even later. After God prepares the Garden of Eden for Adam and Adam gets lonely, God explains "it is not good for man to be alone" and sends Eve as a "suitable helper" (Genesis 2:18 NIV). *Eve is a solution.* A blessing. A gift. And, likely, a breathtaking answer that exceeded any of Adam's prayers. Adam had never even seen a woman before. He probably didn't even know what to pray for. But God sent what Adam didn't even know he needed and more in the form of Eve.

> *God prepares before He provides. He gets things (and us) ready for a new reality. And he doesn't call us prematurely.*

I love Eve. I think she's entirely misunderstood and she's been unfairly vilified for centuries. We know that at some point, Eve finds herself in the garden wrestling with a decision. She's staring at the tree of life, the *only* tree God has specially commanded she and Adam not eat from, when she hears a voice she's *never* heard before. A crafty serpent enters the garden and unleashes the first doubt-whisper. I'm not surprised that the serpent chose to approach Eve and not Adam.

After all, Eve has spent more time with God. She longed after God in a deeper, more intimate way—in a way that only we as women can—because she was in Heaven with God longer than Adam. Remember, the enemy knows our longing to be seen, selected, and significant, and uses it against us. We're attacked by the enemy because we're a threat to the enemy.

The enemy knew Eve had a special endowment from God; something the earth had never seen.

The earth already had muscle in man. But it was missing the beauty of wisdom found in woman.

All throughout Proverbs, God refers to the word *wisdom* in the feminine tense. The serpent knew this, that Eve was a virtuous vessel of wisdom. Again, Eve was sent as a supernatural solution . . . a helper. Her presence as a carrier of wisdom was a reflection of God's strategy and our born identity. Recognizing the threat of her beauty and brilliance, the serpent did what poisonous snakes do—he attacked Eve's power center, her mind. Her trust. He erected a question mark where God had placed a period. And he sunk his fangs into her faith the moment he falsely suggested God couldn't *really* have said they must not eat from this tree. The serpent continued by coiling her in perversion and confusion—twisting and *rationalizing* what God had said, insisting, "You surely will not die." And then, appealing to that desire to be significant, he hissed, "God knows that when you eat of [the tree of life] your eyes will be opened, and you will be like God, knowing good and evil."

Now, to a certain extent, the picture the serpent painted was a God-girl's dream come true. I don't think it was ego, selfishness, bad intentions, or arrogance that the serpent tapped into. I think it was purpose; Eve's desire to fulfill her calling and assignment as a suitable helper. A wise woman wants to enhance her wisdom. So the serpent attacked her superpower, which was also her kryptonite. I pray daily for God to open my eyes, to see like God and to be more like God. Maybe that's what Eve had been praying for, too. *Our hopes can also be our most vulnerable blind spots.*

At some point Eve shifts from conversing with the serpent to adopting the serpent's stance. This is how doubt enters and destroys our lives. It introduces an intruder, a thought virus called *lack*. Making us *think* we don't have enough or that we are not enough. When lack attaches to our eyes, it's like the lens in a pair of glasses determining how we see, think, and respond. It literally changes the signals that enter our mind, and shifts our perspective from one of trust and faith to one of fear and doubt.

❧ EVERY WOMAN DEALS WITH SELF-DOUBT ❧

We shouldn't be so hard on ourselves. Eve lived in paradise. She had everything and lacked nothing, yet still felt she wasn't enough. That's why conversations with the enemy are dangerous. We're entering *his* territory and fighting on *his* terms. The enemy loves to rationalize—to twist facts and tell half-truths—or as I say, to spew *rational-lies.*

But just because Moses was a stutterer, that didn't mean he wasn't destined to speak to the masses. Just because Jeremiah was young, that didn't mean he wasn't ready for significance. And just because Esther was a foreigner, that didn't mean she wasn't fit to be queen. Rational-lies. They make sense, but they're not true. A rational-lie fails to account for *divine providence*, which rarely makes sense.

Eve was at a disadvantage. She didn't have the benefit of hindsight. She didn't have a mother, a mentor, or even a good girlfriend to guide her. She didn't have a Bible with stories of overcomers like Moses, Jeremiah, and Esther. She was certainly blessed and had more than enough, but let's be real . . . she was in many ways alone. *Prolonged solitude becomes the soil of self-doubt.* We've talked about how isolation can be a threat to your faith and life-mission. Isolation becomes a breeding ground for self-doubt where *little me* is able to run wild with whispers and rational-lies of lack.

After thousands of years of blame-game sermons, we know, of course, that Eve ate the apple. And she gave it to her husband, not knowing she was harming him, too. She saw herself as a helper. There is no real indication that she was *intending* harm. I believe with all my heart she was doing what she thought was best to help both of them. But she was wrong. She made a mistake. It was a pretty costly one. That one mistake is now known as the fall of *all* mankind. That's an incredible burden and an impossible guilt to bear.

I love Eve not because she was perfect, but because I mess up, too. I have compassion for her as the first woman to try this thing called life. She was the first to have her faith and trust in God challenged. I'm not sure I would have made a better decision. I make some pretty epic messes, and I've bitten more apples from forbidden trees than I'd like to admit; they're just not recorded in the Bible . . . that book I like to read.

{ WHEN WE STEP OUT OF TRUST, WE STEP INTO DOUBT }

Our choices *do* have consequences. Eve's choice cast a pretty dark cloud, one that follows us as women to this very day. We've adopted anxiety and inherited a passed down guilt complex from what happened in the garden that day. We're afraid to make a mistake. I call it a *fear of earth-quaking.* It's when we're afraid to do something that negatively impacts our lives, others, and just screws up everything! It makes us timid. It makes us second-guessers. It gives us permission to settle, or at the other end of the spectrum, drives us into a life of striving on steroids. We become control freaks and perfectionists trying to keep it all together.

No wonder we take care of everyone else first. No wonder we're afraid to leap and are constantly second-guessing *our* dreams . . . heck, we second-guess everything! We ask, is it *really* God? Or is it the enemy masquerading? We're afraid of our own voice when, in truth, voice is what we are. We're afraid to trust ourselves because we're afraid to shake things up. And we don't want to make a mistake because it intensifies that *little me* whisper that says, *YOU are a mistake.*

You're the reason this or that happened.

You're the reason things aren't better.

You're the cause.

You're the earthquake.

You're the Eve.

I believe this is where our doubt comes from. Instead of risking being the source of heartache, pain, inconvenience, or havoc, we end up doing nothing, playing it safe, or becoming a people-pleaser.

It's interesting that we talk about the men in the Bible—the same ones who had multiple wives, slept with handmaidens, and killed in cold blood—as great leaders and men after God's heart, which they were. But the women who make mistakes are vilified, shamed, and used as examples of what not to become. I'm not condoning bad behavior, but I am saying we've been taught shame in more ways than one, and in a way that doesn't happen for men. It's a double standard that gives us permission to forgive the fellas but license to shun ourselves . . . and to shame each other. We can be brutal to each other. These messages contribute to our self-doubt, perfectionism, hesitancy, overthinking, comparing, and fear of leaping and leading. They program our subconscious such that we sanction self-doubt and self-loathing and mislabel it humility, meekness, patience, and discernment. It's really fear, and it reflects a corruption of our true-born identity.

It may have started with Eve, but it entered our lives through our experiences, our teaching about what's appropriate for women to be and do, and via the women in our lives. Yes, we get a good bit of self-doubt from each other. But we can also get rid of it together.

⸭{ MEET MARY AND ELIZABETH }⸬

The second source of self-doubt is the *fear of enoughness*. I alluded to it earlier as it was certainly at play in Eve's life, and it's the tainted air that self-doubt blows into our spiritual lungs and minds. Two women that not only encountered this FOE (fear of enoughness) but show us how to slay it are Mary and Elizabeth.

Elizabeth is the wife of a respected priest named Zechariah. The couple has been "upright in the sight of the Lord," meaning they've followed God and The Rules of their time to the best of their ability. Elizabeth, who is now well past the age of having children, seems to be barren. In the book of Luke, we learn that her husband after all these years has still been praying for a child. The angel Gabriel appears to Zechariah during his prayer time in the temple and says his prayers have been answered, and that he and Elizabeth will have a son. The angel goes on to say that this son will be joyous, favored, and will do great things for God. The *little me* in Zechariah (like the one in Moses, Jeremiah, and Esther) responds rationally, not supernaturally. "How can I be sure of this? I am an old man and my wife [Elizabeth] is well along in years," says Zechariah (Luke 1:18 NIV). Rational. Lies.

I can only imagine the years of piled up doubt that Zechariah had experienced. Men deal with self-doubt, too. The angel immediately silences Zechariah and takes his voice that day. There is power—life and death—in our words. The miracle awaiting him and Elizabeth as parents-to-be is so significant that any further words of disbelief could destroy their already fragile faith. Once Elizabeth becomes pregnant, she goes into seclusion for five months. This is a special, high-risk pregnancy indeed; one so important that God needs to safeguard it from outside influences and voices. This is not only because of Elizabeth's age, but also because of the faith that it is going to take to incubate and birth this baby.

Unlike her well-meaning husband, Elizabeth immediately responds to the news with joy and says something (Luke 1:25 NIV, emphasis mine) that lets us know how big of a blessing this really is: "The Lord has done this for me. In these days he has shown his favor and taken away my *disgrace* among the people." She says this with full certainty *before* the baby comes. She believes the promise without demanding proof.

When Elizabeth is six months pregnant, God sends the same angel Gabriel to visit a young girl named Mary. She is a virgin and engaged to wed a young man named Joseph. Gabriel greets Mary saying (Luke 1:28 MSG), "Good morning! You're beautiful with God's beauty, beautiful inside and out! God [is] with you." This freaks Mary out. (Notice a pattern yet?) The angel tells Mary that she has nothing to fear and that she, too, will become pregnant, and she will give birth to a son named Jesus. Mary then asks a very legitimate question (Luke 1:34 MSG): "But how? I've never slept with a man." The angel explains that the Holy Spirit will come upon her. Hmph! An invitation to believe bigger indeed.

Okay. Two women. Two impossible, immaculate pregnancies. And two lives *forever* connected. Mary goes to visit Elizabeth. Elizabeth's baby, *while still in the womb*, hears Mary's voice and leaps inside of Elizabeth! Mary hasn't said a word about her encounter with the angel. Mary probably doesn't even know she's pregnant yet! Somehow, however, Elizabeth *immediately* knows that young Mary is not the same. The anointing upon Mary is so rich and thick no words are needed. Elizabeth responds (Luke 1:42–43 NIV), saying, "Blessed are you [Mary] among women, and blessed is the child you will bear! But why am I so favored that the mother of my Lord should come to me?"

These two women surely dealt with the *fear of enoughness*. For decades Elizabeth faced the public *disgrace* of being childless. Think about it. The wife of a priest. A couple who certainly spoke of God's goodness and who encouraged others to believe in miracles couldn't make manifest in their own lives the one they wanted most. Talk about faith under fire.

And then disruption greets Mary with her greatest fear. Not a fear of doing but the fear of being enough. The angel says she is beautiful with God's beauty . . . beautiful inside and out. Some translations use the word *favored*, but it's the beauty translation that always makes me tear up. I think we each struggle to believe we're divinely beautiful. Not beautiful because of anything we've done or how we look but just because of who we are. That day, Gabriel invites Mary to believe beyond *her* biggest fear. She asks herself the same questions you and I ask. *Am I good enough? Am I beautiful? Am I favored, chosen by, and loved by God?* I believe Mary had been wrestling with and questioning her beauty and worth for some time. Gabriel was an unexpected confirmation—a yes straight from Heaven that first frightened her, before it focused her. Just as Moses saw himself (and his future) in the burning bush, Mary saw her true self and the sacred path to significance with those few words. *The message and the mission always go hand in hand.*

The faith walk exhibited by these two unlikely doubt-slaying women provides us with some much-needed advice for how to deal with doubt:

1. **GUARD YOUR EARS.** Words of doubt are weeds that can kill what God is growing. Speak life, and silence (and even ignore) those that don't believe what God has spoken. This might mean pulling away from those who mean well but don't see what God is doing. That's okay for a while. It's incubation, not isolation. During a time of faith upshifting, especially in The GAP and a season of reinvention, you need encouragement, affirmation, and fresh direction from God and from Heaven-approved visitors only.

2. **TRUST DIVINE TIMING.** Just because something is delayed doesn't mean it's denied. It *seemed* like Elizabeth was too old,

and it *seemed* like Mary was far too young for such an enormous responsibility. Nevertheless, God chose them to do the impossible. Why? They weren't addicted to the opinions of others! That's where the battle with enoughness stems from—comparison and approval. Plus, if Elizabeth had given birth during what were considered her prime, most fertile years, Mary wouldn't have even been born yet! Remember the *law of interdependency*? Our destinies are intertwined in ways that we can't understand with our ground's-eye view. We also shouldn't fear the wait or our ability to birth what's never been done. God recruits when God is ready. Not on our timeline but on His. And God is looking for a woman who won't give up and who keeps getting up, *not* a woman who's never been knocked down.

3. **EMBRACE SISTERHOOD AS A SUCCESS STRATEGY.**
God intertwined the purpose of Mary and Elizabeth together. This was why Eve had a disadvantage. We're not supposed to fight this battle alone. Mary came to *celebrate* Elizabeth, and Elizabeth responded with elation, not intimidation. Elizabeth could have been jealous. After all, she had been waiting for what seemed like forever. But there was only love for each other. Sisterhood is a doubt-slaying strategy for sure. *When women speak life into the lives of other women, miracles happen.* Destiny unfolds. Be intentional about surrounding yourself with those that have a heart for seeing you thrive . . . and make sure you bring the same genuineness of heart to your sister circle, too.

❧{ DOUBT SLAYING IN ACTION }❧

Speaking of a sister circle, I'd love to introduce you to some women who have made the shift from their Comfort Zone to *their* Glory Zone. I know them personally! They are each modern-day Proverbs

31 women of faith, women who merge faith, family, creativity, voice, and entrepreneurship, that were in one of my business mentoring programs. You will see their marketplace breakthroughs, but don't get caught up in the specifics of what they launched or made financially, focus on what they overcame! I'd love for you to imagine what *little me* whispers of doubt they had to slay in order to shift into a new season of significance and divine success. *Every faith journey is a holy path.*

⁌ MEET KAMILAH ⁍

She attended a *Launch Your Dreams* seminar I was leading in San Antonio, Texas. After the seminar, a number of people came up to ask me questions, and Kamilah waited for the crowd to dissipate. I could tell she was nervous but wanted to ask me something. She was interested in my speaker training called *Speak for Pay*®, but wasn't sure if she was a fit. Kamilah had been working in the information technology space for years but had grown bored with her job. She was newly married, the mother of a toddler, and had never considered something like this. Plus, she had a huge insecurity.

I asked her why she was hesitant to enroll. She said, "I'm not sure I would be a good fit for something like this . . . I'm a stutterer."

I paused and saw in her eyes a burning bush moment. Curiosity mixed with hesitancy, but a longing for courage . . . for permission to believe *bigger*.

I couldn't tell she had a speech impairment—but her inner *little me* wasn't going to let her forget it. My spirit instantly knew she had been ridiculed, made fun of, and likely been in speech therapy. In a moment, I felt the weight of being labeled (and silenced) for a lifetime. Her eyes told a story that didn't need words.

I simply smiled and said, "You mean like Moses?"

What a joy it was to see lightning strike her soul right before my very eyes. Surely, you've seen it before—when someone has an AHA! When the scales are lifted off someone's eyes and finally they see and feel something new. You can literally see the weight of worry being lifted off and new possibility taking its place.

A little dazed, she subtly bobbed her head, saying, "Oooooh. Okay," and took a sigh of relief.

It wasn't until seven months later that I realized the significance of that moment for her, and what it meant in the grander scheme of purpose for each of us. Kamilah ended up not only enrolling in our program, but within seven months generating enough income as a paid speaker and consultant to leave her job and start her own graphic design agency. She taught herself how to design and build websites! She had never desired to be a speaker and leader in this way when she showed up for the seminar that day. She wasn't sure why she was there—she was just drawn to the event. But something happens when our authentic voices connect with each other—deep calls unto the deep.

There are no mistakes. Only movements. *We each have an unlived life waiting for permission to emerge.*

{ MEET LASHAWNE }

LaShawne came to my second major conference—a branding boot camp. I had previously spoken at an entrepreneurs conference held by *Black Enterprise* magazine, where her sons were being honored as Teenpreneurs of the Year. They were drawn to my insights about branding and even some Proverbs I shared on stage about knowing the condition of flocks (your target audience) and positioning yourself and your voice for greater influence. Their mom, LaShawne, wanted to know more about this woman who had gained her teen sons' attention! As she joined the conversation, they shared that they wanted to attend my upcoming boot camp. Apparently, they bugged her about it for months, because she ended up coming on their behalf—they were in private school and she wasn't going to let them miss that many days of school . . . not with that tuition! She sat in the front row, ready to discover how to take her sons' business to the next level. But she spent those two days in tears.

She told me that something clicked within her. She had been a CFO for a major mega ministry for nearly twenty years. She had always taught financial literacy, but assumed because it was for a ministry, it was something she was supposed to offer complimentary as her service to the kingdom. She had never heard anyone explain that our gifts are also vehicles for building a legacy for our families. *Our gifts can be deployed in ministry or in industry.* It's about alignment, not appropriateness. Purpose, not protocol.

She told me it felt as though her buried dreams—some long forgotten—had just been resurrected and called to come forth. When she was younger, she, too, had been told she'd never become anything, based on where she came from, her economic status, and the color of her skin. But that day was her burning bush moment.

During the boot camp, this *destiny-unlocking* thing hadn't clicked for me yet. I thought I was "just teaching business"—I didn't know about *destiny awakenings*. Not yet. She ended up joining the very first mastermind I offered—becoming one of the group of ten ladies I talked about earlier in that business-meeting-turned-revival where I discovered *my* gifts, too.

LaShawne's transformation humbles me even still. She was in the first group I ever coached. I was finding my legs and true voice, and rebuilding my life at the time. She went on to launch multiple financial literacy programs, build an online business, and start speaking around the country in less than six weeks, and then she launched an apparel line. We worked together over the years, and she now has her own mastermind programs, sponsorships, high-end speaking engagements, television opportunities, and major conferences, igniting other women to believe in themselves and their possibilities. I love her and her story because she was a mother who would do *anything* for her children, and she chose to put herself on the blessing list, too. Her sons, her beautiful daughter, *and her marriage*, continue to thrive. I believe great kids become even greater when they see their parents, especially their mothers (not just their fathers), walking in greatness and purpose and living their God-given dreams.

⊰{ MEET SONJA }⊱

Sonja was in the military for nearly twenty years, but was also in an emotionally abusive, toxic marriage for far too long. She had been written off early on for becoming a teen mom, and while in the military she suffered a traumatic brain injury. When she finally found the courage to leave her marriage, she found herself in her mid-forties and newly single, but also feeling like she had lost precious years she couldn't get back. She was just at the beginning stages of finding herself and her confidence again. On the outside, people saw a beautiful, together, and powerful mother and a major in the US Army. No one knew her story or her struggle. Sonja attended an event and had an experience similar to Kamilah's and LaShawne's. In fact, she sat in the exact same spot LaShawne had sat in, only her tears started within the first five minutes!

She didn't just want to enroll in the Speak for Pay program, she wanted to go straight to private coaching and masterminding, which I wasn't even talking about that day. She didn't care. She didn't have time to waste and knew this was a moment to step into a destiny that was bigger than herself. And that's exactly what she did. Some clients who had been in the mastermind program wondered if she was *really* ready to make that big of a jump, right into our highest-level program. She was just getting started. Actually, they were surprised to discover that she was about to surpass them in a shorter period of time! I'm glad she didn't listen.

Her life looks totally different today. She retired from the military about a year after we met. She previously had made less than $7000 the *entire* year before in her coaching program, where she helped women recover from divorce. She couldn't live off of and provide for her family on that amount. She called me one afternoon, in the middle of her own empowerment event for women of faith, and shared that she had made nearly a quarter million dollars in less than an hour!

The same woman who just a year prior was clocking in to a full-time job and doubted her ability to operate a successful business because of a brain injury. Rational-lies. Facts, but not truth.

She's been on TV, in magazines, and now travels as an in-demand, paid speaker, too. The money isn't what's most significant. Nor is the platform she's cocreated with God. If you only hear that, you're missing the bigger 360-degree life shift . . . and the fear slaying that enabled it. I mean—these modern day Proverbs 31 women *did* enroll in a business building program, so it's always exciting to witness financial increase. But it's also just symbolic of what's possible when we slay self-doubt, commit to living bolder, give our dreams a chance, and step into significance.

God wants to see us win!

Today, I have hundreds of stories of women like the brave hearts you see above.

SAUNDRA

Saundra was a chief technology officer very high up in a field dominated by men. She was also a minister who felt pulled to shift into a new level of sharing her gift for process creation and her anointing for speaking life into the hearts of other women. After we worked together, reinventing and building a new brand, she retired early and now runs her own institute for women . . . full-time.

ASHLEY GRAHAM

Ashley had been a supermodel, already super-successful when she felt the call to use her voice in an industry that values looks, not words. She was considered a curvy or plus-sized model and wanted to use her platform and influence to do more than sell clothes and products. She wanted to be a body-confidence advocate, to inspire women to believe in their inner beauty—but she doubted whether the world wanted to hear a model actually speak! And whether people would receive her message. We worked on how to share her story and to think bigger about how to embrace business beyond modeling. She's since been on the cover of, well . . . everything! *Sport Illustrated* (which was beyond historic), *GQ*, *Glamour*, and *Forbes*, on *America's Next Top Model*, and more. That's the power of believing bigger and embracing your voice.

❧{ MAYA }❧

She was one of the youngest investors (that's what I call women who invest in their destiny development) I've worked with. She was twenty-four years old and invested to be in our mastermind program for emerging business owners. She was looking to shift from doing graphic design work to embracing her voice and answering The Tug to speak, coach, mentor, and teach. She wasn't sure if a shift was possible and wondered whether she was dreaming too big for someone her age.

Today she is doing exactly what she envisioned full-time, makes six figures, and is on her way to becoming a young millionaire . . . in her twenties. What's most inspiring about Maya is her spiritual journey. She was in a love relationship that was stifling her personal, professional, and spiritual growth. When she decided to end it, she not only got in physical shape, she got spiritually fit, too. Initially, she wasn't really very vocal about her faith. As a young African-American woman and emerging entrepreneur, she really wanted a mentor who looked like her—a Clair Huxtable she could touch and talk to.

Today. Oh baby! She is on fire for Christ and living with boldness in a way that brings tears to my eyes. And she is showing a new generation of young women that they can love God, be fly, be young, and have a successful business, too.

❧{ I CAN'T FORGET ANGIE }❧

She may have been a little hesitant at first because about 85 percent of the women in our coaching program were African-American at the time. But she leaped right in! She had attended one of our biggest live events, which also turned into a business revival that year! I mean, men and women from around the world came and the Holy Spirit broke out.

People of all nationalities and religious beliefs ended up singing and dancing with praise and worship. I had never, eva' seen anything like it. I remember seeing Angie worship alongside a woman named Monica who had flown into the United States from Ecuador.

Angie ended up joining the mastermind and her business grew exponentially . . . and quickly. She clarified her "money message" at the event, and launched a new brand within a few weeks. She was landing big contracts with major brands and had generated a half a million dollars before the end of the first quarter of the year . . . more than she had made the entire year before. I share Angie's journey because her real shift is evidenced in that she says this "business" program reignited her passion for God in unprecedented ways. Stress had invited her to pour more wine than was healthy and it was creating a strain on her marriage. She stopped drinking. Her prayer life went to another level. Her marriage is healthier and happier, too.

That's destiny. It's not about dollars.

All of these women loved God and, like me, loved church, too. But *their next level was about something beyond salvation.* They needed to find their own voice. Their own "pulpit"—purpose and platform—so to speak.

This is *my* assignment. To help women of faith elevate into the marketplace as *true* Proverbs 31 women, without guilt, without shame, and with confidence. Actually it's with *Godfidence*, that phrase I've been alluding to.

Confidence is believing in yourself based on what you can see and what you know. Godfidence is different. It's believing in who God says you are and what God has destined you to do. It's having the courage to trust what you *can't* see. And, it's operating with the mind of God. It takes Godfidence to do what Moses, Jeremiah, Esther, Mary, Elizabeth, and each of these ladies above did.

Each of the women I talked about in the above stories had a few things in common:

1. A Tug to use their voice in a new way

2. A commitment to embracing their *divine* identity over their *decided* identity, to get a bigger vision, do the work, commit to community, guidance, and accountability

3. A willingness to shed the past and sacrifice/invest in their future

4. A humble curiosity that invited burning bush moments in the first place; a desire to reinvent; a desire to believe *and be* beyond the status quo

5. A desire to go wherever God guides, regardless of what others say; a desire to serve anew; a desire to lead

The external stuff is just evidence of an internal shift. It's what self-doubt, *little me*, and the enemy are conspiring to prevent. And it's what *Future ME* knows is available. God speaks in cans and not in can'ts! Each of these women, along with hundreds of clients and thousands of others in our community, now live as stones in God's slingshot. They take out giants. They change lives. They share what they've learned. Their stories and shifts have nothing to do with me. God, grace, and guts are the stars of the show, and that's exactly how divine reinvention works. A woman's place is *anywhere* God sends her. It's all holy ground. Testimonies aren't *only* about missionaries and healing.

*Marketplace miracles count, too.
If it comes from God, then it's for His glory.*

Purpose isn't about profit, but it *is* about our entire soul and inner-self prospering from within (check out 3 John 1:2). God wants us to thrive (not just survive), and to help others do the same. That's destiny in action. That's the purpose of your gifts. Whether we are stay-at-home mothers, career women, dealing with chronic illness, recovering from a nasty divorce, or just trying to find our confidence . . . something causes us all to ask the question *Will God actually use me? Given my circumstances . . . given how things look or appear . . . and given who I've been and how others perceive and rely upon me, could God actually reinvent and use me for something glorious and new?*

I say yes. Yes. And, yes. God stands ready to deploy you . . . especially you. Listen. Self-doubt has a clear mission, which is to prevent yours. To shrink your borders, bury your brilliance, and cripple the courage needed to be a living ripple-effector in the earth. Purpose is a call to boldness. Service to the King and kingdom-building happens when we embrace boldness and commit to building up others. That's true leadership.

Here's the deal. Saying yes to your higher purpose isn't always going to be easy. Anything worth having is worth believing in. *You don't really believe what's never really been challenged.* The key is to remember this:

An unashamed woman is an unstoppable woman.

God will use you when you stop being ashamed of your calling. When you release your regret. When you shift from confidence to Godfidence.

God won't force a bigger, better future upon us. We have to accept it. Slaying self-doubt, then, is not asking if, it's acting *as if* it's already done. When we live *as if,* we literally believe our blessing into being.

The secret to your shift . . . the secret to fulfilling purpose . . . and the secret to a wonderful faith adventure is found in your YES. Everything you're looking for, believing for, and the destiny God built you for is on the other side of that choice. As you know by now, when you say yes, (Y)our (E)xperience (S)hifts.

chapter sixteen

LET THE MIRACLES BEGIN

Many are called, few are chosen.
The difference between the called and the chosen
is that the chosen choose to answer.

Once my business started to really flourish, there came a point where I experienced a flood of hesitancy. I wanted to keep growing, but in my love life I was nervous. Really, I was afraid. The idea of dating again made my heart flutter, but not for the right reasons.

One evening, standing two steps away from that burgundy sofa, I was talking to a girlfriend who wanted to set me up on a date. I hyperventilated at the thought of it . . . just at the suggestion! That had never happened to me before. On one hand, so much was going well, beyond my wildest imagination, but still there was a part of me that was stuck. Stuck in remembering how risky it is to love someone; haunted by the hurt of betrayal and being let down.

A few days later, I was speaking with my business accountability partner, Joyce. We were both in a high-end mastermind group full of successful business owners, and one morning during our daily phone check-in Joyce asked me why I felt stuck. I wasn't sure. I had momentum in my business, opportunities were coming in faster than my new team and I could keep up with, and I was happy externally and grateful internally. Still, I didn't trust that the blessing was going to last. Any moment another split-rock could strike. And, for some reason, I felt like growing would be dangerous. Growth made me uncomfortable. When Joyce asked me why I felt that way, I didn't have an answer. I didn't even consciously know I was hesitant until we started talking about it. She told me to take a deep breath and to picture what growth would look like, which I did. I envisioned helping more people, having larger events, employing more team members, seeing more people supercharge their faith, and having a larger impact. "And," she asked, "what do you feel the negative consequence would be of you doing just that?"

Out of nowhere I blurted, "If I grow, I'm afraid I'm going to stay single."

That answer stunned me! I pulled the phone away from my face and looked at it to see where in the heck those words came from. I don't remember ever *consciously* connecting business success to being able to find love again. But apparently my subconscious was having a different conversation and now I had finally gotten the memo. I'd had no idea I felt that way. I had been working on my mission, my spiritual fitness, and my earning potential, but not *actively* focusing on restoring my trust and vulnerability in the heart space. Now that I was aware of where the hesitancy was coming from, I could face it.

You cannot fix what you will not face.

Time doesn't heal all wounds . . . engaging with and *committing* to healing does. I was so appreciative to have a friend like Joyce who was able to help me see how my beliefs were blocking the idea of bigger.

It's incredibly important to have friends who believe in bigger for you, and who selflessly and lovingly push you into a higher version of you.

A good friend loves you too much to let you linger in limbo. A good friend is passionate about your destiny.

When you have that kind of friend in your inner circle, she can help you see your blind spots and the ways you are self-sabotaging . . . even keeping yourself from the very thing you say you want.

That blind spot is really a lingering vestige of doubt—a stowaway latched onto your dream. So, while I was in many ways believing bigger and putting my foot on the gas when it came to my business, I was also subconsciously putting my foot on the brake at the same time. I hadn't known why I was self-limiting and, with it, self-sabotaging. Now I did.

I brought this up during a session with one of my business mentors named Fabienne. Actually, I was on the fence about upgrading into her $50,000 coaching program. I hadn't told anyone, not a soul, how much it cost, because the reaction might have been like yours might be right now! But I wanted to be able to deliver the type of value that would warrant being able to charge prices like that one day, so I chose to learn from someone who was already where I wanted to be. I shared my fear of not being able to handle growth and my fear of not having a husband. I wanted to amplify, but I didn't want growth to be the very thing that kept me from experiencing a family, love, and support. Fabienne paused and said, "Marshawn. He'll show up when you step in. Everything you're looking for will show up when you *step in.*"

Those two words: *Step. In.* They went through my bones. It was like honey for my soul. That phrase still sticks with me to this day. So, I stepped in. I consciously made a decision to go all the way in and told God to bring it on. All the blessings. All the increase. All the love. That's what my financial commitment signified—it was my putting my money where my mouth was (so to speak) in my communication with God. Remember, your treasure and heart hang out in the same place. Your girl wasn't playin' no games with this purpose- and anointed-living thing. It wasn't about buying a blessing! It *was* about *buying in* to *Future ME*. Investing. Committing. *I* knew inside this was the right next step; I had just needed to voice my fear with someone capable of helping me believe bigger.

When we know our fears, we can face them. We face them by changing our actions, our attitude, our words. I immediately started affirming the *opposite* of what I felt. I started to speak what I desired to see, not how things seemed. This wasn't easy, but I was retraining my spirit to believe bigger in the arena of love, too. I started journaling about what kind of man I would marry. I used declarative statements like, "*I am a wife,*" "*When I get married*" (not if), and "*My future hubby is amazing!*" I fully believed that I'd get married—but I couldn't believe it until I realized I was afraid of it. And I started praying for my husband daily. I prayed for his life, his health, his dreams and goals *as if* we were already married. I started to write about what a ready man looked like, and when I had speaking engagements I'd encourage women to embrace their dreams and ambitions and to trust that the man assigned to their future would be excited about their vision, not intimidated by it. Sure—I was speaking to myself, but that was fine, too! The more I said it, the more *certain* I became of it.

The impact? I started to feel more vibrant, joyful, and expectant. I continued to grow my business from a place of trust and creativity. I stopped worrying about whether a man would be intimidated by me, and I stopped listening to the *there-ain't-no-good-men-out-there* single girl blues. That toxic anthem is laced with blessing blocking. I had to detox doubt, conventional thinking, and woes dressed up as wisdom, tough love, and "reality." As a woman thinketh, so is she, remember? Instead I looked forward to meeting a man that would be inspired and ignited by me. That's what I told God I was believing for, and it's the vision Heaven gave me. I held on to one day of journaling in particular where the Holy Spirit spoke in depth to me about how my future marriage would be fresh like new wine being poured into new wineskin. Oh, and I stopped worrying about a timeline! Having kids. My eggs. My age. When I'd get married, etc. Anxiety at any level isn't attractive, and it doesn't attract destiny.

A happy woman is a magnetic woman!

Let me tell you something . . . men come out of the woodwork when we're vibrant and in a place of love and joy. So do opportunities. I started dating. My anxiety went away. I didn't realize that the anxiety was actually keeping them away. *Fear and doubt are repellants.* The more I cleaned out the junk and limiting beliefs about love, prosperity, *and* men, the more I became the woman I desired to become. I embraced a new level of confidence. I turned up the volume as far as the faith infusion into my business teachings. My events were growing. Things truly felt good because they were. I was in alignment with what I wanted and with what I actually believed was on the way. The stowaway was gone.

That mind shift and big faith leap were in April. In September of that same year, I attended a book signing in Atlanta for my friend Paul Brunson. Since I held large events, he had asked me for some advice about how to fill up the room with extra attendees now that the event was just a few days away. I suggested that if he felt his team had sold all of the tickets they were going to sell, then he should allow ticket holders to bring a complimentary guest. That would fill the room. He took the advice.

It was a really cool event, with music, mingling, and a great interactive message focused on relationships. When the lecture part started, I took a seat and ended up sitting next to a guy named Jack.

Believe it or not, he had on a red T-shirt that read *I Need a Wife.* Turns out he was an author and had just finished the last stop on his

I Need a Wife book tour. The shirt was just part of the promotion. As I asked him more about his book and his life, he made clear that it was focused on helping *men* find themselves so they could find "the one." He wasn't actually advertising for a wife! But then he shifted the conversation to me and wanted to know more about my life. Before I could start, a woman sitting in front of us interjected, saying, "Marshawn, I don't mean to interrupt but I really appreciated all of the messages you've been sharing recently on the topic of #AReadyMan on social media."

Now, I'm a business and faith girl. I've never, *ever* had someone come up to me to explain how relationship advice impacted her heart. Ever! I had been posting about what a "Ready Man" looked like, but I hadn't put much strategic thought into it. I was just casually posting what came to heart for about a week or so. Anyway, her compliment was flattering, but it caught me off guard! Little did I know it was a sign.

At this point, Jack got really curious and asked what I did. I didn't want to lead with my career stuff, so I just lightly shared that I was a speaker, author, and coach. He asked what I had written, and when I told him about my book *S.K.I.R.T.S in the Boardroom*, he said, "You go girl!"

It still makes me chuckle 'n blush to this day.

He said it so playfully, with a head tilt, a wink, and a smile. I didn't realize until that moment that that was the first time a man had reacted that way. He was neither intimidated nor impressed. He was inspired and encouraging. It was refreshing. Very pure. And the main event hadn't even begun!

Get this. The reason Jack was even at the event was because a friend of his had purchased a ticket and had gotten notice that ticket holders could now bring a guest. He had only been invited just a few hours earlier. So once he wrapped up his book signing, he came over to Paul's event.

(Side note: It always pays to be giving and generous without expecting anything in return. Who knew that impromptu piece of business

advice about how to fill the room would seat me next to this tall, choco-
late cutie!)

By that time the next year, we were engaged. Less than a year after that, we were married. And we started working together. In addition to being an author and speaker, Jack was an in-demand counselor. He had a waiting list. But my company was growing rapidly, and he just so happened to be ready for a shift. We decided to join forces. He put his über-successful counseling practice on hold, and started phasing out his clients, so he could provide more support within my company. It became a way to align our shared mission of helping move others forward.

I focused on teaching business, branding, marketing, sales, *and Bible!* He helped clients overcome their fears, get unstuck, find their story, and learn how to tell it in a powerful and compelling way. Our enrollment more than doubled and the business crossed well over the million-dollar mark. Together, both of us helped women (and some fellas who joined) connect with their divine calling, grow their relationship with God, upgrade their self-image, find their voices, and elevate their visibility . . . all while having a blast doing it.

I wasn't alone. I got to have my cake and eat it, too!

The stowaway's lies had just been an illusion. A deception to keep me from believing, and therefore entering, bigger.

This is the part that epitomizes a full-circle moment. Jack proposed during one of my mastermind meetings at the *same hotel* where that long-ago curbside chat with God had taken place. He was supposed to be leading a talk about storytelling, but *I* ended up blindfolded and the central character *in* the story. He was reciting a poem called "I Need a Wife," inspired by his book and book tour—a topic he hadn't really spoken on again since the day we met. When the blindfold came off, he showed a video from my parents, giving their blessing. The day before, he had apparently hopped on a plane and traveled from Georgia to Texas to get (and videotape) their blessing, without even telling them he was coming! He just showed up on their doorstep.

Oh, and there was a shining red box with a sparkly diamond inside! I didn't even see it until *after* I said yes. I couldn't believe this was happening. I couldn't believe he was professing his commitment to provide for, problem-solve for, and protect *me*. He was ready, emotionally available (thank you God!), and more than I'd ever known I needed.

Aaaaaaaaand! I had been speaking that day to the women about the power of saying YES and how it's what enables Your Experience to Shift. I sure laughed about that one hour later!

Four years earlier, at the exact same hotel, God had said that I'd be able to change the lives of women like never before. I didn't know what that meant, but again, I knew that God meant it.

Now Jack was proposing *while* I was working with women like never before. My goodness! The power of *while*. I still can't really wrap my mind around it—the timing, the significance, the ring! He was down on one knee, with the purest of pure eyes sweetly looking back at me. He said, "You don't just complete me, you're a part of me. All you have to do is say *yes*." The proposal happened at a hotel named Renaissance . . . it means *rebirth*.

Indeed, if it isn't God, it isn't real.

Contrary to my fears, I found myself pursued, wooed, and lavishly loved. I couldn't have found someone who *truly* saw me before. That wasn't possible. Who (and what) we attract reflects who we are at the time. I didn't know myself then. But when I *stepped in* to my higher purpose, I attracted a *Purpose Partner*. That's the miraculous thing about purpose. Purpose attracts purpose. It attracts what it needs to fulfill its mission.

> *A woman in her purpose will naturally invite everything her spirit and soul need to thrive.*

The Word says in Psalm 84:11 (NIV), "No good thing does [God] withhold from [her] whose walk is blameless." Blameless doesn't mean perfect. But it does mean forgiving, trusting, expectant, *and* in alignment. The Message version says that God is "generous in gifts and glory. He doesn't scrimp with his traveling companions"!

I just love every bit of that promise! When we're walking with God on the Path, He generously gives above and beyond. He takes care of us, *His* traveling companions, and lavishes us with everything we need and more . . . including the traveling companions connected to our destiny!

Apparently, abundance is a package deal. The part of our blessing that is thriving needs the still-wounded and blocked parts to catch up. Our heart condition is attached to everything we think, attract, and manifest. When betrayal bites, if we're not careful, we can end up hardened, on the hamster wheel, or back into hiding. Either way we're blocking bigger and everything else attached to it.

Belief is at the center of everything that flows from us. It's the well-spring of life. We mustn't just guard it, we must also grow it, too. The enemy attacks our intimacy because it creates a hole that isn't easy to heal. But the good news is that healing heartbreak is God's specialty! An open heart makes room for all your heart's desires and for miracles to manifest! So, again, I say the reason God wants us to shift is because He truly does have something sweeter on the other side. God won't bless where you don't belong. And when He breaks what you've built, it's because *He* is building something (and sending someone) better.

⟨ MIRACLES ⟩

I've mentioned this word *miracles* here and there during our time. They go hand-in-hand with believing bigger. A miracle is any moment where God is present. We don't have to actually part the Red Sea or turn water into wine to be a miracle worker. *Our life is a miracle.* The very fact that you were born, that your heart beats, and that the intricate network of neurons in your brain speak to each other without your effort is evidence that *you* are the miracle. You're not a mistake. You're not a mess. You're a miracle. For this reason, Jesus said whoever *believes* in Him will also do even greater work than he did (John 14:12).

Greatness isn't about a show; it's about showing up.

Showing up happens when you create. Teach. Launch. Give. Inspire. Mentor. Shine. And lead from a place of rest and not restlessness. You part tumultuous waters when you use your gifts to help people shift from where they are to where they need to be. You turn water into wine when you can take someone's pain and turn it into possibility, purpose, and power. And you walk on water when you embrace your gifts, all the while keeping your eyes on Christ, and trusting Him to keep you afloat as you pursue and do the impossible. When Peter walked on water, he was able to do so because his focus (aka faith) was on Christ, not the waves. We can do *all* things through Christ, who gives us the strength to do it (Philippians 4:13), and with God nothing is impossible (Luke 1:37).

Believing Bigger is the formula for miracle moments and movements in our lives, too. We're *regularly* supposed to have unpredictable, spirit-unleashing encounters with others. Miracles—and moments oozing with purpose—are intended to be commonplace, not rare. We're supposed to change the atmosphere. But that can't happen if the daughters of Heaven called to live as bold Believers continue to become an endangered species. We can't continue to shrink and limit our self-belief.

Whatever we believe is what we birth.

If you are ready to birth something new, something incredible, here are the real questions God is asking:

Are you willing to forget everything you think you know about yourself in order to finally find yourself?

Are you ready to step in?

When God allows chaos to be our catalyst, and split-rock moments to reposition us, He is inviting us to believe bigger. To leave behind our comfort and make room for glory . . . a lifestyle of life-changing and true surrender to a larger mission that is not our own. He disrupts our lives so that He can develop and accelerate our thinking. *Ultimately, God disrupts us so that we can disrupt others.* It only happens after we step in.

So it's TIME. It's time to let the miracles begin.

It's time for your voice and the classroom of your life to open their doors and expand their reach. You're a messenger and you are a carrier of the Holy Spirit—the same power that conquered the grave. It is not God's intention that we simply read about miraculous encounters in a book that is thousands of years old. He intends that we *be* the book; the living word. A living manifestation of God's unlimited abilities and promises. In Romans 9:17 (NIV), God says, "I raised you up for this very purpose, that I might display my power in you and that my name might be proclaimed in all the earth"! C'mon somebody!

You're a masterpiece . . . and an *essential* component in God's master plan. It's time to burn the mask, cut up the cape, and trash The Rules. You're a rebel and it's time to ignite *your* revolution. It's time to unapologetically step into your gifts, unleash your superpowers, and give credence to your dreams and desires. After all, God gave them to you. These are the New Rules of Leadership and Divine Reinvention for Women; the Path to your promised land.

{ THE NEW RULES OF LEADERSHIP AND DIVINE REINVENTION }

Here's how we invite the miracles to begin!

Step 1: Expect More

Whenever you're unsure about what God wants you to do, here it is: live boldly and give yourself permission unapologetically to believe bigger. Expectancy goes to the heart of believing bigger. To have an incredible impact, we must have an incredible self-image.

You are a weapon, beautiful but deadly.

Believe in your beauty, but also believe in your power. You were built to destroy the enemy. The enemy doesn't want you to see yourself as a destroyer. He wants us to live timid and to see ourselves as victims and as intrinsically vulnerable, as those being hunted and at risk of being taken. We have every reason to expect more. *God is the king of suddenly and is always sending us what we need.* God speaks in *cans* and not in *can'ts*, and (Ephesians 3:20 MSG) "God can do anything . . . far more than [we] could ever imagine or guess or request in [our] wildest dreams! He does it not by pushing us around but by working *within* us . . ." The key is to have an optimistic and expectant attitude from within; to operate from a place of *positive anticipation*, not worry and hesitation. *Miracles are an inside job, too.*

One week before I was set to compete in the Miss America competition, I was in a wheelchair. I had strained my muscles from months of rigorous rehearsal and fitness training. The only thing I could do for two weeks was mentally rehearse my routine with the music playing in my headphones and my eyes closed. I knew the routine inside and out, and I only visualized doing it perfectly. I mean why waste headspace by envisioning it going wrong? When it was time to perform live and on national television, I didn't just get through the performance, I won the talent competition. Expectancy works the same way. We have to mentally rehearse and anticipate positive outcomes and expect miracles, as opposed to anticipating the next upset, failure, or betrayal. *We should be risk takers and leapers, not risk managers and lookers.* We're not victims. We're vessels with the full resources of Heaven present within us, and an entire army of angels behind us.

Step 2: Start Before You're Ready

When we take for granted grace and God's signs and nudges to move forward, we end up stuck, or at best going in circles. *If it is meant to be* is not biblical—it's a hollow mantra that gives us permission to passively play with God as opposed to pursue our assignment. The enemy wants you to stay in a place of waiting. Waiting to hear from God. Waiting to become who you were meant to be. Waiting for the right time. Waiting for a shift. Waiting. Waiting. Waiting. Patience is critical, but passiveness is a sickness. It's infected so many of us that waiting and inaction (disguised as praying and mislabeled as "trusting God") have become normal . . . even celebrated. We're taught to *wait and pray*, but not how to *decide and build*. Faith is what "moves" God . . . actually it's what aligns us with His movement already in progress.

Don't get me wrong. There absolutely are times when God asks you to wait and to be still. However, more often than not, this scripture has been recklessly doled out like prescription pills that have put God's girls in a catatonic state of inactivity. You see, the enemy has taken a key scripture about waiting upon the Lord and twisted it with faith words like *patience* and *discernment*, and successfully used it to keep a lot of us in a safe place and out of our God place. *Waiting* is one of those misleading words. According to Isaiah 40:31 (KJV, emphasis mine), "They that *wait* upon the Lord shall renew their strength." *Wait* is an action word. Other translations say *trust*, *hope*, and *look for* Him.

Hmmmmm. What if *to wait* meant "to align"? To actively look for and step into holy flow? That would mean, then, that those who *align with* the Lord shall renew their strength. Hmmmmm again. *Thaaaaaat* requires personal responsibility and starting. This concept might ruffle your feathers and challenge how you've internalized this scripture over the years. However, it was a tremendous wake-up call for me, and I'd love for it disrupt your thinking, too.

The best athletes in the world get stronger (or renew their strength) in the off-season. *Waiting is a time for preparation.* Maximizing and replenishing your anointing isn't about being busy, it's about align-ment—us doing what God needs while in the process of getting to where He wants us. That could mean stopping. If so, that's "starting" something new. Or it could mean practice and preparation.

And there isn't an *if-then* checklist here. I'm not suggesting that you have to *do* to receive what only God can provide. I am saying that it's time for a mega mind shift. God isn't a waiter. Heaven isn't waiting around to see what the enemy is going to do next and then devising a rescue and recovery plan. Heaven isn't reactive. It's proactive.

God goes after the enemy.

Bottom line—we are made in God's image to do the very same thing. Starting *before* you're ready is the ultimate faith step, and faith steps are the kind of steps that God not only orders but prioritizes. The circumstances will never be perfect. There will always be more research that can be done, more tinkering, more refining, and so on. Just remember that perfectionism, getting ready to get ready, isn't a friend to your purpose. It's not only a barrier, it's poison. *God's daughters should be the starters, not the waiters.* We are to be *doers* of the Word (both the written word and the word 'n direction God gives us through revelation), not just hearers.

Fear is an invitation to see things the wrong way.

I wasn't *ready* when I started my coaching company. Heck, I didn't even plan to start a company. I was just struggling to pay my bills and decided to do something new—to hold a seminar. Today hundreds of men and women attend, I've had thousands of clients enroll in masterminds and online courses, and I've been able to watch dozens of women leave their job, step into their dream, and make a full-time living operating in their calling. I had no clue that one faith step would to lead to a multimillion-dollar business, the ability to employ others and to redefine the way faith is infused in business. I had nothing to lose. I can tell you from experience, it's way better to leap when God says to, or else he'll start a split-rockin' and strippin' until he gets you where He needs you.

To start, you don't actually need a plan, you just need a *mission*. The best way to start before you're ready is to seek adventure, try new things, and get comfortable being uncomfortable. And the best place to start is with your story, your big idea, your dream, and your vision. Just take one step toward it. And then another. Learn something new. Meet someone new. Smile anew. Invest in something new. And volunteer or serve somewhere new. Keep putting one foot in front of the other. *New steps create new life.*

Step 3: Stop Asking for Permission

There comes a point in every woman's life where she's got to decide who she is going to be. Is she going to be a pleaser or is she going to be a producer? A creator? A lover? A launcher? A life-changer? Just know this:

> *You don't need permission to be and do what God has already commissioned.*

You're not man-made, you're God-made. You don't need anyone's permission to be powerful, bold, or brilliant. And you don't need anyone's permission to share your voice, tell your story, or launch your dream. It's The Rules, the whispers from *little me,* and lingering guilt and pressure from things and people that don't really matter that make us shrink and second-guess ourselves. I'm not saying to be inconsiderate. I'm just saying don't put yourself in a protocol-paved prison when *you* hold the keys to unlocking your potential and creating a miraculous life shift. *You're* responsible for what and how you believe. You're also responsible for doing what God has placed in your heart.

A divine shift happens when we stop looking for validation.

The less you care what others think, the more your life will expand. Not everyone will understand your dream or your vision. They don't have to. It's not their vision. It's nice to have support, but you must also be careful not to draw confidence from the approval of others. When we do that, we give them our keys. Someone else gets to sit in our sacred driver's seat.

Remember also that miracles and influence didn't manifest in Moses' life until *after* he stopped doing what he was accustomed to doing. Disruption comes to disrupt our patterns and interrupt the momentum taking us down an inferior path. So if we're going to ditch being a waiter and a pleaser, we might as well stop a few other things while we're at it and really clean our spiritual house:

+ **STOP SHRINKING.** Silence the gremlins—the voices of self-doubt, fear, and insecurity. God speaks in cans and not in can'ts. God will *never* ask you to play small or dim your light. Never.

+ **STOP COMPARING AND STARING.** Much of our insecurity comes from our addiction to comparison and trying to keep up to what others *seem* to be doing and accomplishing. We become mirage-chasers addicted to Photoshopped illusions and harvesters of ego, greed, and envy. That superficial grass isn't greener. It's still just grass. You are incomparable. There is no one like you. If you spent as much time focused on your dreams as you do watching others live theirs, you'd be happier and making a bigger dent in the kingdom. And, staring . . . it's not polite!

+ **STOP AUDITIONING.** You're already worthy and have nothing to prove. Show up in your power . . . your voice and your brilliance. Your gifts will do the rest. People can be transformed simply by being in your presence.

+ **STOP APOLOGIZING.** Especially when you have nothing to apologize for. Most of the time, we say *I'm sorry* out of habit. We think it's polite, but it's really a sign of self-doubt and second-guessing . . . feeling like we've taken up too much space or imposed simply by being present. You don't have to be perfect. You don't have to do everything the way that someone else would like. Certainly, if you mess up, fess up. But when your decisions fall short of someone else's expectations, that doesn't necessarily mean you're in the wrong. Christ didn't apologize for ruffling feathers or going against the grain. That's not what rebels on a mission from above do.

When we ask for permission, we become prisoners . . . and waiters. We give away our power. No one has the authority to overwrite your calling and God's leading. When doubters tell you what you can't do, you should look at them as ants speaking to an elephant—that's my husband's reminder and advice to me. Why would an elephant listen to such nonsense? And just think about how low an elephant would have to stoop to hear an ant speak anyway! You're a Believer, not a doubter. You don't have to listen. *What you listen to leads you.* Asking for permission is just another way that we seek validation.

Traditional education and traditional wisdom will always take you to a traditional place.

Align with next-level mentors and a circle of next-level wisdom givers who *already* believe in your vision and are enthusiastic about your outside-of-the-box potential and mission. You don't need everyone else's opinion, so now is a good time to stop asking for it!

As women on a mission, we have to be intentional about not disqualifying ourselves because of what others say, what *little me* whispers, and what false beliefs 'n hang-ups we have about what it takes to lead. God qualifies the called. He doesn't call the qualified. *If Heaven called you to it, it's God's job to see you through it.*

Step 4: Invest in You

I remember being at that crossroads fearing growth and singleness. But, Jack and I had been dating for about four months and he was incredibly supportive. It was now the beginning of a new year and I was sitting in the overflow room at Victory World Church in Atlanta—I was late that day! I don't remember the subject of the sermon but I do remember when it was time for the offering. I *love* presenting an offering. I love having something to give and have believed in the principle of sowing into God's kingdom and the advancement of gospel since I was a kid. I thank my parents for modeling this for me, but it was up to me to continue this after leaving home. It became a lifestyle and a chance for me to listen for what God would have me give . . . not just adhering to what I "had to give." That Sunday, I planned to write a check for $1000. I don't why. I'm not sure what I earned that week but that was the plan. When I pulled out my checkbook, I heard the Holy Spirit say, *Add a zero.* My eyes got big. Of course no one knew this conversation was happening in my heart, but I also knew what I heard. So . . . my pen added a zero. At the time, I'd never sowed quite that much in a single sitting. It felt like a stretch but also freeing. God had my attention. He said to give this offering an assignment. I wrote in the subject line my expectation. This was going to be a million-dollar year in my business. I knew that business growth was directly related to being able to help more people step into their destiny—not just our clients but also being able to employ more people and support more causes, too. *More resources, more reach.* Our small company surpassed the million-dollar mark in three months that year.

For me, investment isn't about money, it's about alignment—following God's voice and investing in His vision. We must be willing to invest in both the gospel *and* a personal growth plan.

The gospel can't grow if we don't.

While God's qualification criteria is different than society's, that's no reason to be lazy and to take our anointing for granted. That's immature and makes us spiritually unbalanced and ineffective. After I called off the wedding, it took me over a year to really let go of much of what I'd built and believed for a lifetime. My flashy sports agency. The take-over-the-world goals and image I had of myself. My attitude. My approach. My desires. Even my circle. They all changed. I didn't crave the spotlight or stage anymore; for the first time I craved a new breed of fresh manna from Heaven. I wanted to know what God was thinking—not just so that I could get what I wanted; I just wanted to know what God wanted. No strings attached. The thing I most desired was to be a part of what God was already doing.

Wisdom is sweet to your soul.
If you find it, you will have a bright future,
and your hopes will not be cut short.
—Proverbs 24:14 (NLT)

I also had to surrender long enough for others to pour wisdom and love into me and help me rebuild a new, more confident and divinely connected version of myself. But I realized I needed help beyond my inner circle of friends and family. Seeking counseling was incredibly humbling. I really believe it takes tremendous courage to realize that we *don't* know everything, we *don't* have all of the answers, and we *don't* always have the ability to fix ourselves by ourselves. *We need professional support outside the pulpit to help us on our journey.* We can't put everything on our pastors. God can use anyone, but we have to be open and guard against the type of spiritual stubbornness and arrogance that keeps us stuck.

God uses people to bless us. And a new blessing will usually come through a *new person*, with something new to give you. Remember that. If we're going to be able to bless others to our fullest potential, then we have to be willing to receive blessing *from* others. We have to be open to whatever and whomever God knows we need to make that possible.

We are spiritual beings that live in a physical world for a reason. I've found that self-investment, pouring into my purpose and my superpowers, is one tangible way to build *divine confidence*, and to show God that I'm serious about service.

Self-investment connects desire to destiny.

And it's also how we wage war against the enemy *and win* time and time again. After all, as Matthew 6:21 (NLT) says, "Wherever your treasure is, there the desires of your heart will also be." The Message translation says, "It's obvious, isn't it? The place where your treasure is, is the place you will most want to be, *and* end up being." Wow! My point. We *say* we want to get where God desires; however, we often *showcase* a different story. Our actions, decisions, and investments reflect our true heart condition and determine our destiny.

Most of us as Believers invest in everything *except* our gifts and our purpose. For some reason, we have adopted a dysfunctional belief that if it's a God-thing, then it's up to God to make the thing happen. That's not scriptural. Obedience, and alignment, always come with sacrifice . . . investment. It cost the disciples *everything* to walk with Christ. They made an investment to be mentored, to be taught, and to *be able* to grow. It's a sign of seriousness. Their calling didn't start until after Christ left. It was their time with Christ, the mentoring, that prepared them to lead. Go figure! The same must hold true for me and you . . . and those we're assigned to. Development and process is so very important to God. *Miracles become cheap magic tricks when we look at them as things that happen to us as opposed to through us.* Plus, the Bible very clearly says that faith without works is D-E-A-D.

This is why purpose dies in many of us. We haven't cultivated it the way we cultivate other areas of our life. We work more on our wardrobe and our house than we do on our calling. I'm not talking about tithing, offerings, and sowing into the expansion of the Gospel. That's not the same as investing in your superpowers. It's not either/or, it's *and*. To be a lawyer, I had to invest the money to go to law school. Same is true for becoming a doctor or engineer. But when it comes to being in the sweet spot of our purpose, we become a deer thunderstruck by headlights. "Desire without knowledge is not good" (Proverbs 19:2 NIV) and "[s]he who gets wisdom loves [her] own soul" (Proverbs 19:8 NKJV). One of the most powerful practices I have learned is the practice of self-investment.

Learning is a sacred act of self-love. Our money behaviors reflect our spiritual and practical maturity.

I invested in myself financially, spiritually, physically, and energetically—meaning with my focus, time, resources, and commitment. It took me three tries to find the right fit, but I invested in a therapist and committed to the process *weekly*—and this was during a time that money was tight and I didn't have a steady income. Next, I invested in business coaching to groom my superpowers and help me gain new marketplace skills. I also took my spiritual life to another level via books, church, and prayer; I learned that spiritual growth works best when we're walking out our purpose, not just studying it. I also believe in physical investment—treating our bodies well by investing in quality food, exercise, healthy products, and rejuvenating self-care (like baths—not just showers—breathing, stillness, and massages). And, finally, I reconnected with my sister circle and prioritized friendship over accomplishment. This pulled out the best in me. And this is how God waters our seed, educates us, and unleashes us—it's in the midst of intentional investment.

> *God gives us the promise. It's up to us to invest in the process.*

Investment is how we embody the spirit of preparation that makes way for provision; it's how we become a vessel God can use. And every decision we make is an investment. We should therefore choose our decisions wisely. We are the stewards solely responsible for proactively multiplying the wonderful gifts we've been given. Miracles happen when we make time for ourselves and when we invest in our development.

Step 5: Finish What You've Started

The size of your step is less important than your direction. When we finish what we've started and press through the doubt that sprouts along the way, the enemy has nothing left to say. Nada. But we've gotta put ideas and plans into practice.

Inspiration without implementation is a figment of our imagination.

Plus, finishing breeds Godfidence, and it rebuilds the broken bridges of self-trust we've allowed to deteriorate over the years. *Much of fear is self-imposed.* When we leave things lingering, when we start this and that but never finish, we weaken the internal bridges that connect us to us. We stop trusting ourselves because we teach ourselves whether we can be trusted to follow through on our own dreams and desires. We are built to finish. God wants us to be starters that *also* finish what we've started.

Randomness is the enemy of reinvention.

So we must watch out for delay, its sister perfectionism, and its cousin distraction. They are decoys sent to divert our attention, keep us occupied with the unnecessary, and stop us from crossing over and emerging from The GAP. They are assassins after your anointing. Instead, choose to be a manifester of miracles—a woman who says and follows through on her yes. A finisher. Disruption, disappointment, and devastation—we can't let 'em stop us. We can't. We must keep moving forward, trusting the voice, and following the nudges of *Future ME* . . . the path attached to our finish line.

{ REDEFINING SUCCESS }

These are the *New Rules* of leadership and divine reinvention for women. This is how we fulfill our life mission. The Purpose Map's five stages—Discover, Talent, The GAP, Gifts, and Influence—are here to show you the path to the real you! Reference the map often and make a commitment to share it and never stop learning, re-scripting, and growing from it. Use it as a reminder that you have a purpose. A voice. A necessary story, assignment, and mission. Nothing now or in the past is wasted. No experience or obstacle is greater than God. It's all wisdom for your master class, and for the hearts and minds waiting to enter your classroom. You are indeed gifted in amazing ways.

Sometimes it takes heartbreak to draw us back into the will of God.

If disruption hadn't split my rock, I don't know where I'd be; probably a success addict looking for her next fix. Just as Christ called an already dead Lazarus to get up and come forward in order to experience new life, we, too, must realize that if we stay where we are, our future dies.

Disruption awakens us to the divine, unwatered seeds . . . the miracles that lie within us waiting to emerge. Disruption isn't an enemy to purpose. I now realize they are *eternal* friends . . . partners in getting us to our promised land, and purposed partners enabling us to have the impact, life, and love that God has always intended.

Disruption teaches us that we're not in charge, don't need to be, and never will be.

It invites surrender to become our new success strategy—though it may look like a pit, it's really the pathway to significance. Surrender and following God take us to places talent and the paved paths can never touch.

During a stop on my *Launch Your Dreams Tour*, a young woman approached me. She had waited patiently until every single attendee— about 150 people—had had post-event photos and hugs with me. Only my staff remained. I remember she was wearing a shiny black blazer with a gold undershirt. She said, "Thank you. Just thank you. You changed my life today . . . for forty-five dollars . . . just thank you." To help her find the words, I asked her what she had taken away. And she said, "You spoke to my destiny. I realize that there is more in me than what has happened *to me* . . . it happened *for me*." I gave her a hug, and instead of letting her go, I just held her and prayed with her and over her. My staff stretched their hands toward us from wherever they were in the room. And then she was off.

One year later, I was emceeing an event for aspiring women entrepreneurs. At the end, a woman came up to me and said, "You may not remember me, but I came to one of your events when you did the *Launch Your Dreams Tour*. I waited until the very, very end." It took a moment, but then I remembered her! I gave her a hug, and then she blew my socks off. She said, "I know you meet a lot of people, but that event really changed *my* life. When I came up to speak with you at the end, I kept saying thank you because I didn't have any other words to say. What I didn't tell you is that earlier that day I'd made a decision to end my life." She explained that she had gotten in her car and driven to a park where she was going to commit suicide. But the park was closed. She had never seen the park entrance barricaded before. She reached for her phone sitting on the passenger seat, checked her email, and saw an email from me that read, "See you soon!" That email reminded her that she had purchased a ticket weeks ago to attend the event. She left the park, came to the event, and sat in the back row. For four or five hours, she listened to me talk about purpose, divine gifts, superpowers, disruption, greater destiny, voice, and influence.

I thought of how much second-guessing and wrestling I had over *stepping in* to my true voice—worried what church people would think of mixing the sacred with the secular. But the merge is what God longs for. And, who knows, maybe the doubters and naysayers were really just in my head. A mysterious "they" conjured up by The Rules and *little me.*

Now I understand this passage from Proverbs 13:9 (MSG): "The lives of good people are brightly lit streets." Tuck it in your heart. For every protocol-pusher, false teacher, or illusion that made me feel out of place for having a marketplace anointing—an *entrepreneurial calling* outside of the four walls of the church—those fifteen minutes talking to that woman put it all in perspective.

Suicide? That "business event" didn't just change her life, it saved it.

So believe me when I say *you* matter. That *your* stories, *your* ideas, *your* dreams, *your* gifts, and *your* desires matter.

Your differentness matters. In fact, it's a magnet.

I'm not huffing and puffing. Your adversity gives you depth. God needs people who've been through and overcome . . . *stuff.* Those are the messes that make a *real* message—one aligned in spirit *and* in truth.

You are a brightly lit street—but it's time to turn the lights on. It's time to be the mentor. To be the voice, the gift-giver, and creative force you are. It's time to speak up, step up, and stop hiding. I'm talking to your destiny. I'm intentionally speaking life into your future because your future depends on it. And someone else's future depends on your mind shift, your boldness, and your "start," too.

You don't need a stage.

You don't need perfect conditions.

You don't need a strategy or an audience.

You need surrender and a proactive willingness to let God start using you in new and uncomfortable ways . . . now.

Whether it's talking to a stranger on the street, connecting with a coworker, or sharing your journey (as small as it might seem) with a new or old friend, purpose unfolds from within us whenever we decide to be bold.

Any place God takes us is holy ground. I can't say it enough. To quote Proverbs 25:25 (NIV), "Like cold water to a weary soul is good news from a distant land." *You* are the cold water to parched souls wandering through a desert land and wondering whether God has forgotten them. When you show up, share your presence, wisdom, and charisma, you bring with you the miracle-working power of the Most High God. You're the light. Your life is the very catalyst that triggers new life and unlocks new beginnings. *Your words can completely change someone else's world.* But, as my momma says, *a message is no good if it stays in the bottle.*

Decide today what kind of woman you want to be.

What's important to you now . . . and is it attached to the outdated version of you (your addiction, success, regret, pleasing, safety, or striving), or is it connected to the bigger future awaiting you? Visualize and commit to the quality of impact you want to have. And then make decisions that create the future you desire.

We must become an incubator where miracles are capable of happening. It starts with being surrendered to a divine building process. Not a moment. Not a quick encounter. But a process that enables the promise to take root in us. It is then that we're able to flow . . . that fresh life, light, salt, and fire are able to flow through us powerfully and in a timely fashion. Let go of what you think you need and detach from what others will think or say. Is it easy? No. Necessary? Yes. *Little me* always looks for someone to affirm your greatest inner fear. Know that God didn't save us just because we're wretches, but because we are wonderful, too!

Someone else is waiting on you to show up right now . . . for you to do what you've been called to do so that that person can find permission to do what he or she has been called to do. *That person's* blessing, healing, salvation, and progress is locked up because you're sitting on the sidelines. It's time for you to *step in* . . . fully.

> *Your life unlocks miracles in others.*

Yes, you're that incredible. That's just how God designed you.

You are the way that you are for a reason. I know the little voice in your head keeps whispering that something is wrong with you . . . that you're too flawed, quirky, broken, and in need of repair or more development, but that's simply not true. God is ready to use you and your personality right where you are and right now. What you think is a mess, God sees as a message and a miracle already in motion. When we listen to the inner voice that says, *that's not like me* or **that's** *not how* I *do things*, we *slam* the door in the face of calling. Reinvention is intended to stretch us into something new! We're not supposed to recognize ourselves or be predictable. When we make a vow about what we'll *never let happen* again (as if we're in control of anything anyway), we end up creating fear-based "rules" dictating how we'll protect ourselves from being hurt, rejected, disappointed, or disillusioned in the future. And, then we have the nerve to call that discernment. It's really just fear. These vows and rules become handcuffs keeping us connected to the old. Surrender and grace alone take us into the new thing.

> *Start with your story and start with what you do have; what disruption left behind is all you need anyway.*

I guarantee God will do the rest. To believe bigger is to believe beyond your experience and to trust the arrival of something you cannot see. It is this type of belief that captures God's heart and releases resources and miracles from Heaven.

{ THE GIFTS OF DISRUPTION }

Today, my life looks very different than it did when I was crying in the stall of that smelly bathroom. I *stepped in* to my purpose. I did my best to let go of the opinions of others, the anxiety of not knowing what was ahead, and even the fear of being alone . . . and that's when everything changed. It wasn't overnight. And, I'm still a work in progress. But, God 'n grace took me through the process of divine reinvention, forgiveness, and belief and into overflow.

God gave me a bigger vision during The GAP, which felt like my lowest point. He painted a vision of new wine and new wineskins. He wasn't going to leave my heart broken and my desire to be seen, selected, and loved orphaned. I trusted the counseling and all of the stripping and developing. I *stepped in*. I didn't tiptoe . . . I leaped and refused to look back. I've been able to grow a successful business, yes. But the business was just the backdrop to bigger blessings . . . the bridge my feet were asked to cross to exit the wilderness and enter my promised land. An avenue to share my message. Your bridge, whatever it looks like, leads to bigger blessings, too.

The most amazing gift disruption has given me is not just my Godfidence and my influence. It's enabled me to experience significance in terms of impact—seeing women change their lives and then watching them change the lives of others. The ripple effect is breathtaking. *Nothing* compares.

And disruption gave me my "purpose partner" Jack. He is an amazing, funny, handsome, and gifted man who believes in me often more than I believe in myself, supports me, and encourages me to push past my comfort zones. And our marriage is teaching me his signature, guiding belief—to "stay out of your own way." He's the one who taught me the principle of finishing what I've started. It was also him that encouraged me to tell this story of betrayal and infidelity when I thought it wasn't relevant. *He* said *I* had to stop hiding my true voice and story if I was serious about awakening women to do the same. And he believes that it is his job to cover me as I live out my calling, not to enable hiding, shrinking, or staying with the status quo. I hit the *Jack*pot, indeed! It's key to have someone in your life who is excited about you and won't let you give up on God's plan for you by clinging to fear.

And it is my husband who reminds me to keep *stepping in*. He actually uses those exact words, not knowing they were the two words that opened the way for me to receive him. Alignment and divine assignment . . . love and legacy are one in the same. *Purpose is a package deal.* My life has expanded and my faith walk has deepened in ways I couldn't have foreseen.

So, to disruption, I say *thank you.*

Thank you for being the perfecting process that equipped me to show up in the world stronger, wiser, and bolder. *This* is who I was meant to be. A woman who believes bigger. A woman who says yes. And a woman who lets other women know it's okay to be incredible. We're not meet to blend in. God's girls are designed to stand out.

{ DIVINE DEFIANCE }

When God said let there be light, He was giving you permission to shine.

I didn't know at eleven years old, when I vowed one day to become a teacher who would make sure her "students" felt like anything was possible, that my life mission had come down from above. Lightning bolt moments are God's way of giving us supernatural insight. And the truth is I've always been a teacher. And so have you. In your own way, it's who you are. It's what brought us together. It's time to embrace it and step in to it.

Let's not compare classrooms. Let's not compete when we're uniquely wired to complement. Our destinies are beautifully intertwined. A shift will always be uncomfortable and unexpected. It means you're needed. Your God-space is indeed calling you . . . not into the four walls of a building, but into the four corners of the world.

So there you have it. *Believing Bigger* is the simple secret to becoming the person that God has always intended you to be.

> *Things are going to happen so fast your head will swim, one thing fast on the heels of the other. You won't be able to keep up. Everything will be happening at once—and everywhere you look, blessings! . . .*
>
> *And, I'll plant [her], plant [her firmly] on [her] own land. [She'll] never again be uprooted.*
>
> —Amos 9:13–15 (MSG)

As you take faith steps, know that no weapon formed against you shall prosper. The weapons may form, but when you operate in purpose, they *cannot* prosper. Keep forgiving and keep trusting. When God is for you, nothing can stand against you. And never forget that there is none like you. Believing this truth is a courageous act—one of defiance. But you're a rebel now—ready to inspire, teach, and lead a rebellion.

Even when you're in your calling, and loving what you do, there will be a part of you that feels like you're still not where you need to be. It's *little me* hinting that something is bound to go wrong. This can't really be as wonderful as it seems. You can't possibly be as important as God says. You'll mess this purpose thing up eventually, and others will find out what you've feared all along . . . that you're a fraud.

Little me is a liar.

God is coauthoring your future with you right now.

When God says yes, there is not a devil in hell that can say no.

Defy the status quo. Defy convention and tradition. And defy gravity. Do what seems impossible, unthinkable, and untimely. Christ defied all the odds and so should you! I know the best is within you and that superpowers are indeed waiting to manifest through you. I believe in your beauty, your boldness, and your brilliance.

I believe in you.

My prayer is that you believe bigger in you, too.

acknowledgments

I'm incredibly honored to do life with some beautiful people who often don't get a lot of credit but deserve the very best available this side of Heaven.

I'm thankful for my husband, Jack, for being the one who encouraged me, for years, to write this book. To tell my story . . . not just share my strategies. And, for believing in me and our shared purpose day in and day out. As I said on our wedding day, you're my playmate, my best friend, my perfect blend, the song I hope never ends.

Thank you to my mom, Mary, for being my first example of a prayer warrior and sacrificing so that I could soar. Thank you to my dad, Carter, for being a father in every way. For the conversations, the covering, and for making a life that gave my brother and me every opportunity to succeed.

And, to my not-so-baby brother, Corey. It's always been you and me, kiddo. I'm proud of the man, husband, and father you've become but most appreciate how you are always my safe place. We have our own language and we live in our own world, but I'm clear that my faith is yours and yours is mine. To my older brother, Eric,

I'm inspired by your journey and the bigger life you've created . . . big head!

Sisterhood and sister-sharpening is sweet to a woman's soul—especially for a girl who grew up with brothers and male cousins. I honor with appreciation my big sisters, prayer partners, and best friends Karen and Nicola . . . my midwives ready to ride!

My sisters-in-love Tiffany Evans and Jovan, my TCU Horned Frogs Consuela, Nicole, Penny, and LaNasha, and my Hoyas Carla, Cloteen, Nicki, and Melanie. My soul sister for life, Tiffany Johnson, our next chapter will be the purest. Thank you Jenn Jett, Juanda Roberts, Kim Roxie, Gessie Thompson, and Joyce O'Brien for being dream defenders. Tremayne and Mama Mel for being family. You all know me as Marshie, Martian, Marshmallow, or just Sister. May every woman have good girlfriends that embody your selflessness, style, grace, and ride-or-die.

Anthony—thank you for being a brother from another and believer (from the beginning) in me and Godfidence.

Mama Jo and Papa John for welcoming me into the family . . . my picture made the family wall!

Thank you Auntie Jackie and Reverend Campbell Singleton III for being my mentors. To Pastor Bob Wright for seeing something within and trusting me at age twenty for the first time with a pulpit. Mrs. Carelynne for teaching me how to harness the Holy Spirit. To Fabienne Fredrickson for telling me that Godfidence is (and always has been) the game plan, and to be unashamed to live out my faith in the business world. To my first coach, Janice Jackson. May I always make you proud with how I perform on and off the stage. To the teachers who changed everything—Mr. Larry Eger (5th Grade), Ms. Yvonne Greenwood (Richardson High School), and Professor Don Jackson (TCU).

To my fellas—the boys who toughened me up by creating BAM (Boys Against Marshawn) when we were kids: Sean, Dimitri, Derek, Domenic, Glenn, and Shomari. And, to the girls that finally saved the day—Mollia and Ashley. To Auntie's nephews, Cason and Gavin, who keep me on my toes and my heart young 'n pure. And my nieces Erieyunna and Shun-teria. You are walking miracles—together we're walking legacy.

Grandpa Robert—I didn't know you, but I hope this work represents the Evans name well. Grandpa Charlie—you are the one who taught me how stillness enables us to hear God's voice . . . even when we can't see.

Thank you to my agent, Teresa, for showing up at the right time so could I step in to bigger. To Lisa Stilwell for believing right away that my story and my breed of bible teaching needed to be published. To the Howard/Simon & Schuster team, especially Beth Adams for keeping this alive.

Thank you to the graduates of our *Godfidence Business School* and *ME University* programs for allowing us to speak into your future. In the process, I found my voice.

To the early clients and those who said yes to a proposal: Brian Tippens (HPE), Theresa Harrison (EY), Nancy Minchillo (HP), Karmetria Burton (Delta Air Lines), Michelle Robinson (formerly Home Depot), Greg Williams (formerly Rolls-Royce), John Shumate (PepsiCo), NFLers Charles Grant and Thomas Davis, and my very first customer, Phyllis Jenkins. Your early trust changed my life in more ways than one.

To my dream team at *ME Unlimited, She Profits,* and *The Godfidence Co.* From the depths of my soul I say thank you to every single team member, graphic artist, web developer, stage designer, volunteer, and employee who has been with me on this journey over the years. I will always be grateful for your presence, your touch, time, and talent in helping this mission to go forth.

Future kiddos: Know that when you read this book one day, Mommy was thinking about you when she wrote every word.

And thank you to those who said that something like this couldn't be done. You forced me to believe bigger—that a business girl could talk about God, too.